GOOD IS POWERFUL BEYOND MEASURE

An Anthology of Hope

FOREWORD BY CREATIVE, CULTURAL ICON, BEN VEREEN

GOOD IS POWERFUL BEYOND MEASURE
An Anthology of Hope

WRITTEN AND COLLECTED BY REV. MELONY McGANT
WITH INSPIRED WRITINGS BY MORE THAN 100 CONTRIBUTORS
EDITED BY ANDREA CHRISTOFFERSON AND SHANNON WONG

Good is Powerful Beyond Measure: An Anthology of Hope
Written and Collected by Rev. Melony McGant
With Inspired Writings by More than 100 Contributors

Foreword by Creative, Cultural, Icon Ben Vereen

Edited by Andrea Christofferson and Shannon Wong,

Published in 2024

Cover design and layout by JeremyJohnParker.com

Print ISBN: 979-8-218-34084-1
eBook ISNB: 979-8-218-34085-8

BETTY J. TILMAN

Illustration by Brandon Jennings

AN INVITATION...

WHEN LOVE COMES UNEXPECTED...

Beautiful People,

Sometimes our lives become like a rhythmic journey. One day we are sad. Then we are joyful. Then sad again. We twist and turn. Sometimes we feel resigned to doubt and despair. Then within ourselves, we meet Love Unexpected.

So we breathe and listen deeply. And we begin to question and wonder.

But before we can move on to embrace the Freedom that comes with Love; we must revisit Doubt and Despair. Boooom. Boooom. Boooom. Aaaaaaaahhh.
And everything we never healed appears so that we can offer and receive Forgiveness. Then we are asked to Let Go; but to take that which is precious and healed on the New Journey.

Sometimes, we hesitate because we fear failing like before; and falling into the water when we think we can no longer swim. But we breathe deeply and with Courage, we try anyway. And Love is there to catch us.

Then we discover what it feels like to be forgiven all the sins of yesteryears gone by. To Love Fully and unconditionally means that We Let Go. We Trust and Allow.

Ancients, ancestors, angels, masters and spirit guides whisper and sing...
"Let Go. Trust. Allow."

Ready to receive us, Grace calls with the Invitation. It is a message from Our Mother Father Creator. We cry joyfully as we learn to allow and embrace the Unknown. And then we are ready to swim the Oceans of Love; and with Freedom soar into the Heavens. Ting va boom boom ting. Ting. Ting ting ting. Swisssh. Booom. boom boom ba da ba. Ting ting Swiisssh. Swiisssh. Ting.

Yes. Sometimes, Love Comes Unexpected!

This Is Your Invitation to Embrace a Tapestry of Goodness and Love through the Sacred ReMemberings of Many in GOOD IS POWERFUL BEYOND MEASURE!

TABLE OF CONTENTS

TABLE OF CONTENTS

TABLE OF CONTENTS

SECTION FOUR

MS. BETTY J. TILMAN LEGACY TRIBUTES

TABLE OF CONTENTS

A BRIGHT LIGHT COMING
by Ben Vereen

THERE IS A SOUND INSIDE THE SILENCE that calls to us in stillness. Somewhere there is a calling to live life to the fullest despite the negativity around us. The DIVINE protection surrounds us with the armor of LOVE. In here, we rest as our being is revived and fortified as it energizes our existence. In here, we fear nothing and no one that comes up against us. With this reinforcement of strength, we are caught up in the wonders of good, the plentiful abundance that life has to offer. Oh, how we shine with unspeakable joy. Come within and KNOW. Breathe Deep and Long!

In the winter of 2017, I stopped in a small shop on West 48th Street called Scent Elate in NYC. This store is known for crystals, incense, Lamp Berger, fine soaps, scented candles and a beautiful assortment of items that can be given as gifts. There is something about the energy of this shop owned by Mohamed Rum that is inviting, warm and nurturing. It is here that I first met Melony McGant. She was browsing and looked up at me and said "Ben Vereen, how wonderful to see you," as if she had known me for years. She loved my hat which said "Spiritual Enforcer" and was familiar with much of my creative work. I felt strangely connected to this special, joyous spirit. We talked about many things going on in the world and the importance of kindness. As I was leaving, she shared a paper titled Miss Mellie Rainbow's Love Alphabet. For some reason I gave her my contact information. After I left, I felt joyful and uplifted.

Melony began sending me daily emails with her uplifting messages that always encouraged me to stop for a moment and breathe. Over the years, I have seen her share joy with others in remarkable ways. She came to see me perform at the Cutting Room and sat right in the front row. I could feel her joyful energy as I sang a variety of songs. Then I sang the "Love Train" and the next thing I knew, Melony had encouraged many others in the audience to dance and form an actual love train. It was a magical evening and I felt grateful to have such an appreciative audience.

Over the years, I have learned more about Melony and her remarkable Mother, Ms. Betty J. Tilman, who had worked at the University of Pittsburgh in international affairs for many years. Ms. Tilman was also one of the founding members of the University of Pittsburgh's African Heritage Classroom/Nationality Rooms in the Cathedral of Learning, a beloved bridge builder, and community activist.

Good is Powerful Beyond Measure is a tribute to the work of Ms. Betty J. Tilman as well as a collection of sacred rememberings where people of all nationalities who know Melony McGant speak from their hearts. They have many titles ranging from actor, ambassador, artist, attorney, business owner, CEO, chef, civil servant, dancer, educator, filmmaker, grandfather, grandmother, healer, mentee, mentor to minister, musician, peace officer, photographer, publisher, psychologist, social worker, student, and writer. Their messages are united in healing, hope and light. No matter the circumstance, more than fifty people share their life lessons and their personal truths.

Good is Powerful Beyond Measure represents that no matter how difficult our lives may be, there is always a bright light coming from within, if we allow it. There is a sweet voice heard in us that wants to guide us to the top of the hill to look out over the possibilities of any day. All we have to do is choose goodness. The good that we choose can and will blossom over time. Most of all, remember that as we wrap ourselves in the light of GOOD, we become the light and shine through and above all the darkness.

I invite you to read the many reflections in this anthology of Goodness.

INTRODUCTION TO GOOD IS POWERFUL BEYOND MEASURE
by Rev. Melony McGant

IN HONOR OF MY MOTHER Ms. Betty J. Tilman, We Celebrate Cultural Icon Ben Vereen, Carol Maillard, Louise Robinson and the Grammy Award Winning group, Sweet Honey In The Rock!

"If we plant the right seeds, tomorrow will be better. If you put out good things, then you'll get good things back. That's part of our responsibility as entertainers." Ben Vereen

Cultural Icon and Tony Award Winner Ben Vereen and the Grammy Award Winning group, Sweet Honey In The Rock have traveled the world as Cultural Ambassadors. These award-winning performers use their voices not just to entertain but to make the world better. Through their presence they share a multitude of creative and healing gifts with diverse audiences and celebrate the potential of humanity.

They are known to treat people around them as equals with respect. They take time to acknowledge the gifts of others.

Over time, around the globe they have been spotted walking through city streets, in cafes, museums, as visitors in remote villages, in theaters as performers, as audience members and in classroom as students and teachers.

They offer care and compassion. They actively support people and organizations that strive to do good, heal and offer hope. They themselves are bright stars of hope even when our hearts are broken and filled with despair.

There is something special about these artists who are beautiful human beings who have learned to journey with humility and have experienced a similar joy and sorrow as many of us. They have given and given. Often their gifts have gone unacknowledged and yet they continue to give.

Ben Vereen, you have been wowing audiences on stage, television and film more than 50 years. Sweet Honey In The Rock, this is your 50th Anniversary Year. Your music is the soundtrack of social justice and lives in our hearts. We thank you All for planting many Seeds of Goodness. Because as

International Cultural Ambassadors, you use your voices to make our hearts sing... **We Honor and Celebrate You!**

To our GOOD IS POWERFUL BEYOND MEASURE readers...

On the following pages of **Section One** we ask that you join us in celebration and read the beautiful selections of those who use their writing to represent the multitudes of us who have been positively impacted by Creative Icon and Tony Award Winner, Ben Vereen and the Grammy Award Winning musical group and artivists, Sweet Honey In The Rock!

In **Section Two**, enjoy the candid photo collage pages assembled by celebrity photographer Andrew Zaeh. Read about a life changing moment for him. Then continue on to **Sacred ReMemberings** and move through the alphabet from A to Z. Many of these stories are very personal. Our authors share their musings and poetry from the depth of their hearts. From thoughts on Asian and Black Lives Matter, life in the time of Covid, to taking wrong turns, embracing faith, discovering and living goodness and honoring those who have left this earth realm, our co-authors share the importance of ancestry, compassion, legacy, nature and Love.

Finally, in the midst of collecting these **Sacred ReMemberings in Section Three**, during Covid, on June 29th, 2022 My Precious Queen Mother, **Ms. Betty J. Timan** who lived in Pittsburgh, PA left this Earth Realm. In an instance, my whole world changed. My Mom, the one person on Earth who loved me unconditionally, supported my dreams, offered the tough truths, laughed and cried with me and taught me to dream of goodness was gone.

In so many ways her life is a blueprint of goodness, integrity and joy. I am comforted by the words " Trust in the Light. Trust in the Spirit. Know that YOU will always be a part of who I AM and a part of Me. **In Section Four** of *GOOD IS POWERFUL BEYOND MEASURE: An Anthology of Hope!*, we honor life and legacy of Ms. Betty J. Tilman!

Thank You for joining editors **Andrea Christofferson, Shannon Wong**, our cover and layout artist **Jeremy John Parker, all of our Co-Authors** and me, **Melony** on this Journey of **Sacred Re-Membering** and Goodness!

Believe. Breathe Deeply. Open Your Hearts. ReMember. Forgive. Laugh. Cry. Live. Love. Believe. Breathe Deeply.

Always,

Rev. Melony McGant

Section One

TO BEN VEREEN
by Jason E. Fernandez Bernard

Dear Mr. Ben Vereen, I hope you are having a wonderful day.

I WANT TO BEGIN BY SAYING YOU ARE A LIVING LEGEND. When I teach my dance students all over the world, I share the importance of your work and creating art with them.

To quote Oscar Wilde: *"I regard the theatre as the greatest of all art forms, the most immediate way in which a human being can share with another the sense of what it is to be a human being."*

With the understanding of these words, my students understand the importance of being earnest and the intimacy of the life-changing work that we do. I owe a large part of my teaching career to you. Without knowing, you have been my teacher simply by being and delivering extraordinary work. I want generations to come to know the work that you have done is how we continue to carry the torch of excellence and honor your legacy; the legacy of Tony Award winner, Mr. Ben Vereen.

My name is Jason E. Bernard and I am a tap dancer. I am a native New Yorker, born and raised in The Bronx. I wanted to write you this letter because I want you to know that you have been a part of my life from the time I put on my first pair of tap shoes. I was 6 years old when I took my very first tap class. My dance studio was in the historic Harlem landmark Hotel Theresa, the Waldorf of Harlem. Coincidentally, the hotel is located a few blocks away from where I currently reside. I love the fact that I am right where it all started.

At the age of 17, I made my Broadway debut in the Tony Award-winning musical *Bring In 'da Noise, Bring In 'da Funk*. I want to say THANK YOU for the contribution that you've made in every medium of the arts. In my opinion, to conquer such a feat is quite remarkable and you deserve great praise and celebration. I realized that the first time I saw you was in a video clip standing downstage in front of that iconic black curtain in the Pippin TV commercial. Your light, magnetism, and spirit shined so brightly through your eyes and your smile radiated like mine does. Your presence and movement were both so strong and specific and rich. Years later, when I learned that you were from New York, I now look back at the moment when I first saw you in that commercial and I said to myself "Well, that's about right! That's how New Yorkers do it. THEY RADIATE!"

I want you to know that I have always been connected to the spirit as I know that you are connected to the spirit. I remember learning about your accident and I thought how triumphant to have that life event happen, and then to have the will to heal your mind and body to a place of balance. A short while after, you returned to Broadway Starring in *Jelly's Last Jam* with one of my mentors, the late great Gregory Hines. I saw that production and the two of you lit up the stage with your New

York talents and charisma. You did three more Broadway shows after that, including a play, which is even more remarkable because now the rhythm of your soul and the dancer was speaking a cappella.

Growing up, whenever I would mention to people that I was an entertainer who danced on Broadway, the first statement that they would say was "Wow, like Ben Vereen," and I would say "Yes, like Ben Vereen." Reading about your life-changing events, I also realize that for me, subconsciously, your courage to live through life always gave me hope to know that I could do it too. About 6 years ago, I donated one of my kidneys to my father. We are both doing great, healthy, and thriving. Sharing my life with the man who gave me life has been an incredible journey, and it's made me more connected with the spirit. You are the true testament of the consummate professional. The number one rule of a Broadway performer is to never miss a show. Be there!

When I think of your admiration of Sammy Davis Jr, I always remember you saying that you understudied him in *Golden Boy*, but never had the opportunity to go on. I remember reading that, and I thought the fact that Ben Vereen never went on meant that Sammy Davis Jr, who was mentoring Mr. Vereen, had taught him what it meant to show up. Many times I believe that performers feel that if they don't get to go on stage, their talent and light have not shined, but that is not true. A star will shine wherever they are. I imagine the lessons you learned from watching Mr. Davis perform every night were invaluable that no institution could ever teach. I admire you for the courage to be a great artist, and to tell stories that others would not be so bold to tell.

Knowing the legacy of Mr. Bert Williams, how he changed the world, and I thank you for keeping his name alive as well. I thank you because, through your courage and strength, you showed all of us that what you believe in you must stand up for. As I've become wiser in life, I realize that we as human beings are all we have. We have to support each other. It is our need and our duty to sing our heart's song. We need to be supportive of each other for the betterment of our society. And you did it, you brought us all together through your art! It is so important that the world knows the gracious contributions that you have made and delivering exquisite work. You made it to the silver screen, the small screen, and the stage! The performances that you delivered on Broadway are still a part of everyone's life. Songs from *Pippin* live in my mind, rent-free, and I sing them all of the time because of you. You set the bar so high that the effects of your work are present in every Broadway performer. We know we have to bring it for it to have worth, and I thank you for that. Your role in *Pippin* as the lead gave us the blueprint, the standard of stage performing that we should strive for! You lead the way and we follow the leader. We learned how to step up because your performance left an indelible emotional signature in our hearts and minds on how to do it.

The stage is such a magical place. With every breath that I take and in every beat of my heart, the stage is at the forefront of my mind. The stories that I tell through dance first initiate on the stage of my imagination. I weave every aspect of my life experiences into everything that I do because my contribution matters.

I am a man of faith who believes in GOD! Being a man of faith, I am confident about who I am, and where I stand in this life. I know that everyone else's journey and everyone else's faith are just as valid as mine. Faith and spirit do not discriminate, they embrace, and enlighten with love, guidance, forgiveness, peace, and understanding! Every time I see you wear your SPIRITUAL ENFORCER cap, I smile. I smile because it introduces your energy and lets others know when they encounter you they are witnessing LIFE. I imagine they proceed with respect and confidence that you will see the good in them. That level of understanding of who you are reinforces to me that you are a man who inhales the rhythm of life, who is aware of the multiple possibilities, and who knows that we have the power to heal. At the same time, we must know how important it is to stop and smell the roses along our journey.

Mr. Ben Vereen, I Thank You and all who came before you and all who will come after me. You have graciously shared the baton with all of us. I look forward to the day when we meet for dinner and we can speak about all of the "Simple Joys" and on that day I will bring you your flowers and say "Thank You, Thank You, Thank You." I honor you and respect all that you do and thank you for the courage to create once-in-a-lifetime experiences through art that will live in our hearts and minds for eternity.

Sincerely,
Jason, E. Bernard

A BEACON OF GOODNESS
by Rev. Dr. Sedrick Gardner

GROWING UP AS A BOY in a household that included my maternal grandmother, mother, and aunt Ben Vereen was an icon. He was an accomplished actor, singer, and dancer. All the women of my household fawned over him anytime he was on TV. Over the years he has become such a staple of excellence for humanity to witness God's energy being expressed through his talents. He has a smile that lights up the world and always seems to be shining the goodness of God. It is quite appropriate for him to be a part of this project "Good is Powerful Beyond Measure." Because he is a beacon of Goodness personified. The entertainment projects he has taken on, his love for humanity, and his dedication to children.

His career started at the age of 18 in the off-broadway play *The Prodigal Son* at Greenwich Mews Theater in New York, performing in Bob Fosse's production of *Sweet Charity* in Las Vegas the following year, then returning to New York in the Broadway production of *Hair* in the late '60s. Ben danced with Sammy Davis Jr. in the film version of *Sweet Charity*, which led to Ben being Sammy Davis Jr.'s understudy in the production of *Golden Boy* which toured throughout England. He was nominated for a Tony Award in 1972 for his role as Judas Iscariot in *Jesus Christ Superstar* and won the Tony for his appearance in *Pippin* in 1973. We all remember his performance of Chicken George in Alex Haley's landmark TV mini-series *Roots* in 1977, which introduced him to every African American who was living and watching TV at the time. Since that time, he has become a staple in TV shows, movies, and humanitarian acts.

Ben Vereen is also a public speaker, and a humanitarian promoting black history, overcoming adversity, and the importance of continuing education. His goodness has touched so many of our lives in the media, so it is only appropriate that he is a part of this project that is continuing his legacy that Goodness is Powerful Beyond Measure. I am honored to be a part of a project that includes his hallmark of goodness in the World.

THE GOODNESS OF SWEET HONEY IN THE ROCK...

by Dyane Harvey-Salaam

IN THE EARLY 60's, the Universalist Unitarian Church, I believe a "revolutionary theology church of its time" in Schenectady, NewYork, hosted the Freedom Singers and provided a platform for fundraising. Berniece Johnson, Cordell Reagon, Chuck Neblett, and Rutha Harris, toured the south singing in churches, homes, schools, and helped raise awareness and inspire courage in the struggle for civil rights...HUMAN RIGHTS.

At 12-13 years old, I was a wannabe ballerina, always listening to classical music. When I heard their sound in our church, my mind was blown! I can still hear and feel the echoes of the lives they lived traveling through the South on dusty roads to support Black communities through the power and strength of their voices. Our church, a Friends of SNCC partner, offered them a private home to rest and recuperate. Their added bonus was that we overhauled their car by "souping up the engine," supplying them with a police car engine. This way they could easily escape when situations warranted a speedy departure. The Freedom Singers also returned south with additional funds donated from our community in support of the movement.

1970s - Thank you to Shirley Rushing for introducing me to the amazing magic of Sweet Honey in the Rock, the ACappella group, during a dance rehearsal in NYC. As a young novice, new to the Black dance world, I danced with many small companies; Shirley Rushing Danz was one. When she played the music for a particular piece, I recognized Berniece's voice immediately conjuring memories of home along with the stories shared during presentations of the original Freedom Singers. These memories had a strong impact on my movement interpretation that day and even now.

In the meantime, Abdel attended the High School of Music and Art at the same time as Louise Robinson. Louise asked him to partner with her for a duet in "The Pajama Game" production presented at the school. Always the gentleman, (but never having even studied dance) Abdel agreed, and they danced together. I was familiar with Carol's name as an actress during the Black Arts Movement, but the Artist bond was forged during a birthday party on Isola Ischia (an island outside of Naples) for LeVert Akwabena Mathis, a dear friend of my mother, Audrey Harvey, Ysaye Barnwell, and Carol Maillard. The gift we gave him was music and dance, except it was also a gift we gave to each other.

Kwanzaa time is very special to Abdel and me. Sweet Honey has appeared as a special guest artist during Kwanzaa at NJPAC as well as in our second film *Nguzo Saba*, created for Kwanzaa at the Apollo during (December, COVID) 2021. Carol and Louise represented the principle of Nia, PURPOSE. They were divine feminine spirits charged with enlightening our young protagonist actor

Javier Gooden, opening his mind and heart to the possibility and responsibility of living a positive joy-filled Black Life. It was exhilarating to observe Louise and Carol as they spontaneously created the Nia chant song.

Most recently this past spring we featured the music of Aisha Kahlil. "Wade in Water" perfectly supported Abdel's Memorial Tribute during Dance Africa in honor of the Ancestors.

Sweet Honey in the Rock, always ready to spread goodness.
We look forward to a productive and inspirational future.

Blessings,
Dy

A ROUND OF APPLAUSE
by Joseph H. James, Jr

"If we plant the right seeds, tomorrow will be better. If you put out good things, then you'll get good things back. That's part of our responsibility as entertainers." – Ben Vereen

I AM THANKFUL TO HAVE had several amazing individuals who are not related to me, as role models and sources of inspiration. One of them was the multi-talented Ben Vereen.

I first learned about the great and legendary Ben Vereen when I was approximately 14 years old. I watched him on television in the role of the Leading Man from the Broadway production of Pippin. He performed brilliantly in the part, earning him a Tony award. In regional theaters around the nation, his Tony Award-winning Broadway performance in Bob Fosse's Pippin is still being imitated. When I learned that he was Sammy Davis Jr.'s understudy on Broadway in Golden Boy I was astounded. I kept up with his work because I admired him as the quintessential Broadway performer, singer, actor, and dancer. He inspired me to want to move to New York and be on Broadway under the bright lights.

On the Broadway stage, he has had a successful and extensive career. He appeared in *Hair, Jesus Christ Superstar, Grind, Jelly's Last Jam, Wicked, Fosse, A Christmas Carol, I'm Not Rappaport*, and *Chicago*. He will go down in history as the song and dance man and be remembered as one of Broadway's most prominent figures and brightest stars.

In addition to Broadway, he has been nominated for three primetime Emmys. One was for his legendary portrayal of Chicken George in the television mini-series Roots. Other notable television guest appearances include *How I Met Your Mother, Grey's Anatomy* for which he won the Prism Award, *House of Payne, Law and Order, Criminal Intent, Oz, Touched By An Angel, Second Noah, New York Undercover, The Nanny, Star Trek: The Next Generation, The Jamie Foxx Show, The Promised Land, Fresh Prince Of Bel-Air, Hot in Cleveland, Making History, Sneaky Pete, Magnum P. I., Bull, The Good Fight, B Positive, The Grey House*, and *The Midas Touch*.

One of Ben Vereen's trademarks is his smile that can light up a Broadway stage. I salute Mr. Ben Broadway Vereen for inspiring and motivating so many aspiring actors, singers, and dancers from around the world. I appreciate your work and the fact that you have had a significant impact on the field of show business.

SWEET HONEY IN THE ROCK: INSPIRATIONS, CELEBRATIONS, AND FIFTY ROTATIONS

by Bonnie Johnson

One of my favorite quotes comes from Dr. Maya Angelou:

"I've learned that people will forget what you said, people will forget what you did, but people will never forget how you made them feel."

IN MY ROLE AS AN NPR JAZZ HOST, I reach people around the world, from all walks of life, sharing the universal language of music. I never imagined I would have a chance to play the music of our ancestors from the heart.

It is often said that music is timeless, and when I sat down to write this tribute to Sweet Honey, that message resonated like a "sweet, sweet spirit." For me, celebrating "The Road To Fifty" is an inspiring full-circle moment worthy of praise.

In 2015, I met and spent quality time with Maestro Quincy Jones. We came together at a tech conference held at MIT in Cambridge, Massachusetts where he served as a panelist. We spent the weekend strategizing on how to bring Black folks into the field of technology. After being one-on-one with Q, I walked away thinking, "Wait a minute, he just interviewed me." When he discovered that I play jazz on the radio, he asked if I played what I wanted. When I replied, "Yes!", Q said, "That's right, play what you want to play…Don't let them keep you in a box!"

That moment with Q served as an awakening for me. I recognized and was humbled by the power of the "freedom" given to me because of the work of so many before me; the men and women of the Civil Rights Movement, the young people of SNCC, music makers like Harry Belafonte, Odetta, and Dr. Bernice Johnson-Regon.

My first recollection of joining Sweet Honey in the Rock's audience community came in the early 2000s. At the time, I was seeking empowerment and exposing my daughter Chandra to the arts. At 12 years old, she had been immersed in creative writing, theater classes, and ballet lessons. For several years in a row, her ballet school rented out the performance hall on the campus of Babson College in Wellesley, Massachusetts for their annual Nutcracker. The Richard W. Sorenson Center for the Arts had opened its doors for use to local organizations. I discovered "Babson Arts" programs and we ultimately experienced Sweet Honey In The Rock "live" for the first time on that stage.

Speaking of Black girl power, I was aware of Sweet Honey and had long fallen in love with the way the group weaved African-American history and culture into their music. When they hit the stage on that memorable day, I was struck by a couple of things. First, not only did they look like us, but I'll never forget the expression on Chandra's face when she saw Sweet Honey's sign interpreter, Shirley Childress Saxton. As it happened, my daughter learned American Sign Language at a very young age through her interactions with our deaf neighbors' children. She was excited to see the performance being relayed to the audience in this way and couldn't wait to tell her CODA friends about the troupe. I have always appreciated Sweet Honey's compassion and commitment to raising awareness and adding a dimension of diversity that is often overlooked.

Fast-forward, over the years, there have been several notable Sweet Honey performances both live and virtual that have stood out for me. There are also many recordings that I love to play for the listeners but "Second Line Blues" is exceptional, particularly in the 21st Century. This deeply moving message about the need for justice, calling out Black and Brown individuals along with collective souls lost to violence, is powerful. The alternating roll call combined with the timber of the snare drum, bass, and the voices of Sweet Honey will forever lift the spirits of the souls that were taken.

To witness a Sweet Honey in the Rock is to increase the well-being of the community. There's something very special about a singing group that can carry on a legacy of performance for decades and continuously have a profound impact across multiple generations. Sweet Honey's many recordings and tributary performances leave an important footprint on African-American history.

TRIBUTE TO BEN VEREEN
Stanley Wayne Mathis

The Light Of Ben Vereen!
Here's a debt of gratitude to this very day!
A deep sense of gratitude more than words can say.
Despite my iniquities I will try my hand
Speak your name as a mantra!
Write your name in the sand.
For you Ben Vereen was part of God's plan......for me.
You were the Star that lit my way!
And as I write this poem
I can unabashedly say....
That you are an inspiration that still lights my path today.
A kid from the "Hood"in the Arts, a hard pill to swallow.
You left a road map for a kid like me with a hard act to follow.
By pursuing your passion and simply being You!
No matter the obstacles you always remained true.
No matter the challenges, inspiration pulled you through.
Little did I know after witnessing you on stage that many chapters later
I would join you on another page.
And yes, your Chimney Man in *JELLY'S LAST JAM* was all the Rage!
In *PIPPIN*, you were my blueprint when I played The Leading Player!
Your Chicken George is Legendary! Crafted with many layers.
You had MAGIC TO DO! On stage, television and films.
Yet your light shines even brighter in many other realms.
As your spirit soars your soul grows richer!
You allow those of us who came behind to dream a bigger picture.
It thrills me to give you your flowers while you're still here!
It is an honor to know you and hold you so dear.
Thank you for being a role model, a mentor, a peer.
I stand on your shoulders, Ben Vereen
It's abundantly clear!
You made a way outta noway!
And that's why I'm here...to say Thank You! Thank You...Thank You....Ase'!

Love & Respect,
Stanley Wayne Mathis

IN GRATITUDE TO BEN VEREEN!
by Rev. Melony McGant

MY HEART IS FULL of Appreciation and Gratitude today. And one of the reasons is because of the Legendary, Cultural Icon Ben Vereen.

For many years I have been a fan. After all, Ben Vereen is what is known as a "triple threat," an award-winning actor, dancer, and singer.

Tony Award, Drama Desk Award, Golden Globe Award, Emmy Award, NAACP IMAGE Award, and Honorary Doctorates are all synonymous with the name Ben Vereen.

When I met him in person by chance at Scent Elate, a small shop in NYC, I immediately thought of him as charming, charismatic, debonair, and a humble humanitarian. He touched my heart!

Over time I have learned that in addition to his icon status and many other wonderful gifts; Ben Vereen is a devoted father and family man. He is also a compassionate deep listener, an encourager, a supporter of many,
a go-giver and a gifted intuitive.

Ben Vereen truly is a Holy Man of Integrity and Grace. His Love for humanity is bountiful and I feel blessed (like many of you) to call him a friend.

As a beloved friend, Ben Vereen has journeyed with me through some of the most challenging times in my life. Through joy and sorrow, he has lifted me up, prayed for me, cried with me, and laughed with me.

And I am ever so grateful and honored that Ben Vereen has written the Foreword for *GOOD IS POWERFUL BEYOND MEASURE: An Anthology of Hope*.

If you ever have the opportunity to see Ben Vereen perform his magnificent artistry, please do. I promise you will leave feeling inspired and joyful.

WE, WHO BELIEVE IN FREEDOM, CANNOT REST

by Rev. Don Marbury

I T WAS, DECIDEDLY, NOT a typical New York Theater outing, performance or audience! Greetings through loving embraces and cheek kisses had been exchanged, and the excited shrieks of recognition and reunion had now settled into a joyous, anticipatory, white noise hum. It was as though this audience of devotees had been, once, hot-stirred into an admixture of shared love, respect, memory, and truth-seeking. And so, they tranquility awaited the coming of those who would be holding the gumbo full ladles.

"We who believe in freedom cannot rest."

In observation, some audience ingredients in this African stew pot seemed transformed, in thei rapturous waiting, to take on the appearance of body-enslaved ancestors-of-ago-centuries; braving the midnight cornfield trysts with the plantation preacher-man who risked all to teach them to love themselves, each other, and the Lord. *"Whisper only loudly enough for old massa not to hear."* Regardless of color, they all shared in and embraced the conspiracy.

Why were crashing crescendos like ocean waves coursing through the assemblage; propelling others to sit up ramrod straight in their theater chairs, their postures subconsciously defiant of the Middle Passage seating arrangement foisted upon or undergone by their ancestors?

Though no fingertips and palms tapped out a staccato beat on a goat skin held taut over a hollow tree log, feet, nonetheless, on the theater floor, thumped as their appearance loomed closer to receipt.

"We who believe in freedom cannot rest until it comes."

And then the stage vaulted them forward! And Town Hall New York City, on this eve, was transformed—transported to that little village in the West African bush. The gathering found itself magically seated after dinner in the village, and were, now, those settling around the fetish priest/griot to hear of sonorous life and living so alien from the grieving and fear cacophony hovering just outside the theater doors. That first transcendent acapella note—a gut-bucket precis in a minor key–burst forth and immediately melded with the Edenic harmonies from five Sistas, known throughout the world and throughout our Spirits as Sweet Honey in the Rock. The original members drew their name from the first song they learned, "Sweet Honey in the Rock," based on Biblical Psalm 81:16. The

Psalm speaks of a land that is so rich that when you break the rocks open, honey flows. And on this, the fiftieth anniversary of these seers, these storytellers, these revolutionary women imparted wisdom, exhorted to action, moved to introspection, tears, reflection and pause to this family gathering. Through their voices and their teaching, for fifty years, they have rendered hope that finding (perhaps rediscovering) such a land of honey in the rock is not only attainable but foretold.

Over a half-century of inspiration, through their soaring, magnificent vocal renderings, these women have risen to the stature of national treasures. They, utilizing humankind's first instruments and retaining humanity's most loving and hopeful instincts have stood against and, indeed, attempted to dispel the darkness which has sought to vanquish our shared and sacred hearts.

"We who believe in freedom cannot rest/We who believe in freedom cannot rest until it comes."

The Town Hall audience heard, believed, and through the royalty and beauty of their being and purpose, left the auditorium knowing that the human voice raised in rejoicing, admonition and love is still the most powerful force on earth!

Let the world celebrate, honor and urge acknowledgment for the shared gift of these nonpareil artists and humanitarians. Let us do all that we possibly can to ensure that their contributions and legacy continue to be lifted and honored by, especially, the music industry, the national entertainment and humanitarian award entities, and new generations of the hopeful.

None can rest until all who believe in their message of freedom, equality, justice, and love are pro-active advocates of their importance and of why Sweet Honey in the Rock are now—after fifty years of inspiration and achievement, too long overdue to receive their just

Recognition.

GENERATIONS OF SWEET HONEY LOVE
by Rev. Rhonda Afanke' McLean-Nur

WHEN I WAS 14 YEARS OF AGE, I was introduced to the phenomenal aca-pella singing group Sweet Honey in the Rock at the DC Black Repertory Company founded by Robert Hooks. I was spellbound listening to them! Their harmonies were heavenly, their style was uniquely Afrocentric, chic, and their stage presence was magically transformative.

Carol Maillard and Louise Robinson, two of the founding members, along with Dr. Bernice Johnson Reagon, were theatre and voice instructors of mine at Workshops for Careers in the Arts! They were dynamic and inspiring teachers but when I saw them perform, my world opened up to another level of revolutionary activism! These women exuded power, beauty, and vocal genius like I had never seen before! The entire audience was mesmerized but those of us who were younger felt an energy and a sacred calling to do something to make a change in the world. I began to play their music every day through college and as an adult!

Their music was imprinted in my heart. So much so that when my late son, RaShan and I were talking with a colleague of mine from South Africa and he asked "Have you ever heard of Sweet Honey in the Rock?" I shared my relationship with them and he spoke about how their music was impacting the struggle in South Africa!

We began singing some of our favorite songs like "Give Your Hands to Struggle" and "Chile, Your Waters run red in Soweto! " which was written by Dr. Berniece Johnson Reagon, the hands of oppression are the hands of hunger in Soweto! And my son RaShan joined in! I said, "How do you know these songs? You were a baby!" He replied, "you played this music everyday of my life for years! I know most of the songs by heart!" Here were we strangers from different parts of the world, three generations singing the songs of Sweet Honey in the Rock on a New York subway ride! It was an enormously uplifting and significant tribute to their worldwide message and how their music continues to build bridges and build community.

During this 50th Anniversary year, I celebrate two of the women who encouraged me personally to educate, engage and create wherever I go: Carol Maillard and Louise Robinson! Through community workshops, special concerts for children around the world and performances, Sweet Honey in the Rock has remained relevant, progressive, and true! Their lyrics speak of community, oppression, women's rights, relationships, and most of all, Love! They continue to teach us to embrace our cultural legacies with pride and always with a song in our hearts!

As life has gone full circle, I am now the President of the DC Black Repertory Company Alumni Association. And as we celebrate Fifty Years of Sweet Honey in the Rock, I invite you to join us in honoring the National and international work they have accomplished by bringing messages of hope, love and peace!

FROM A FAN
by Andrea Pearlman Richards

HELLO, IT'S JUST A LITTLE OLE ME. I am a fan, well, actually a HUGE fan, just like you may be of somebody that you are nuts about. Sweet Honey in the Rock came into my life when I was a College student back in 1987. I was attending Boston University and entrenched in the Deaf Education department. Hanging on the wall in my professor Bob Hoffmeister's office was a poster of the beautiful women of Sweet Honey in the Rock. I had never heard of them, and was fascinated to learn that as part of their ensemble was in fact, an American Sign Language interpreter, who was also a child of deaf adults (CODA).

I lived in Westchester, New York, and during the Hudson River Clearwater Revival concert, I first laid my eyes on the mesmerizing sign interpretation and poetry of Shirley Childress Johnson, and was equally enthralled with the sound and the message of Sweet Honey in the Rock. From that year on, I tried to see them as many times as I could in one year and was lucky enough to see them about four times every year. Maybe you can relate to this, but their music became one of my dear friends, helping me during poignant times. I turn to their music when I need encouragement, a lullaby, calming, and empowerment.

I played catch with my son with them, sat with my grandmother and grandfather as they transitioned out of this world with them, and even had a song of theirs front and center on my wedding day. They were the only music I could listen to for months following the tragedy of September 11, 2001. I call them my religion, my girls, my soul, and food. If there is something I'm feeling, they are the ones that bring me what I need to hear. I have learned a lot of history through them as well. I hope everyone has something as powerful as they are for me in their lives.

In 2015, the school that I was working at was forming a union. I joined Twitter so that I could be on top of the messaging and discovered Sweet Honey in the Rock active there. I began tweeting and retweeting to them and about them. A few months later, at their concert in Philadelphia, I stood in line to have my CD signed, and Carol Maillard recognized me immediately as what she said was her "Twitter fan." I humbly accepted, even though I had followed them for almost 30 years at that point, and requested her friendship on Facebook. We went out to eat and fell in love as friends, connecting, laughing and sharing our personal journey stories. Through Carol, I have come to develop an everlasting friendship with Louise Robinson as well. Twitter, you crazy platform (that I no longer engage with), I'm forever in your gratitude!

Both Carol and Louise know that no matter how much I love them as people, I will never get over the fact that they are in my life because of how they have been with me for so many years as my go-to soul support of choice. I honestly don't know where I would be today if I didn't have their music beside me and now their precious friendship.

Section Two

GOOD IS POWERFUL BEYOND MEASURE
TRIBE AND FRIENDS PHOTO COLLAGE PAGES

TAPPING INTO THE UNDERLYING CURRENT
by Andrew Zaeh, Photographer & Director

THERE IS AN UNDERLYING CURRENT always at work in this world. There in the background, it pushes and pulls through the days' tides. Silent and unseen, there are times, though, I can sense its grace at work. I can see the magic around me and feel the tingle in my belly.

I've always tried to live by 'the golden rule'; to treat others as I hope to be treated. On chaotic and stressful days, on days when the news cycle is dominated by polarization and injustice, when my anxiety is off the charts. It's not the easiest rule to live by. All too often I lose the plot and disappoint myself. Thankfully, the current is at work guiding me back to the good.

It was on one of these frazzled days when the current came to me in a human form. In the most unlikely place, a place I had no desire to go, a place I was frustrated to be in, there she was. In the moment our eyes locked, I knew the universe had delivered me a gift. This wasn't a chance meeting. This person was destined to be in my life, to enrich my life, to be a bellwether of good.

In the years since, the good that's blossomed from this chance meeting knows no bounds. Through this person and her network of good, so much enrichment and great fortune has come. The love that I've received has been truly life changing, and I've been blessed to be able to radiate that love back out into the world. I am forever grateful that the current brought us together. It's because of that chance meeting that I get to share these words with you all. Thank you, Miss Mellie Rainbow aka Rev. Melony McGant, for being an angel. For welcoming me with open wings into your circle of love, light and rainbows.

This is just one example of how good has been powerful beyond measure in my world. **In a dark moment, a moment when I needed it most, good found me and shifted my path. In your dark moments, take solace that the current is with you. It will guide you when you least expect it and need it most.**

The following pages are candid photos of what Melony McGant refers to as the GOOD IS POWERFUL BEYOND MEASURE Tribe and friends. I was given so many but have selected a variety of photos that represent the energy of this wonderful project that I am happy to be a part of!

WALK TOWARD
THE RISING SUN
FROM CHILD SOLDIER TO AMBASSADOR OF PEACE
A MEMOIR BY
GER DUANY
WITH GAREN THOMAS

Sunshine
&
Olivier

Melony McGant

YES,
WE CAN!
Love.
Act.
Resist.

The strength of a community lies in its ability to work together and support each other.

World Music
David Muir
ony McGant

Section Three

SACRED ReMEMBERINGS

EDITOR'S STATEMENT
by Shannon Wong

IN THE FIRST QUARTER OF THE PANDEMIC and lockdown, I was about to enter my 3rd year of undergraduate studies; meaning I had to declare a major officially. A few options lingered in my mind. I was going through several life changes, and a pandemic was the last thing I expected to be added on top of everything. Luckily, I had a roof over my head with all the time in the world to focus more on something I never really had the chance to – me. I found myself going back to writing to pass the time, like I did when I was younger, which led me to remember that there was a Creative Writing program offered at my college. It became my decision.

I've come to understand why I went down this road and the reason I've stuck with it till the end; being able to write (and not in the sense of school essays, proper grammar, or professionally) is a powerful thing that many of us are allowed to do. We come from different walks of life, with hardships that aren't visible just by looking at one another. With words, we're able to express our own stories in a way we want to, give space for any feelings that tend to get bottled up inside us, and we can learn to understand those around us better.

By the time I graduated, I was burnt out and lost sense of why I was pursuing this field in the first place, but this project reminded me of it and what's most important at the end of the day. I was able to see through the eyes and lives of various people through their work, several perspectives of what goodness means to them, and finding the glimmer of hope in tough situations that keeps us moving. I'm grateful to have participated in this project and to help give people's stories a home where they can be heard.

Thank you to Melony, who met me on a whim, and gave me a chance. And to all our readers, I hope that these stories can give you a sense of joy when you're in need of it, to remind you that there's still kindness in corners of this world, to give it whenever you can, and ultimately that *Good is Powerful Beyond Measure*.

A DIVINE ARTISTIC FRIENDSHIP
by Kojo Ade

I N 1969, I WAS VERY BLESSED to meet my brother and friend Anthony Chisholm during the *Black Arts, Black Is Beautiful* renaissance and world freedom movements that were happening in New York City and nationally. We discovered early in our friendship that we shared many common life interests. The arts and theater connected us in grace and power. One of those very important revelations was that Anthony Chisholm shared the same divine earth day as master artist, teacher, activist, and global citizen Paul Robeson, a great human being for whom we both shared a mutual love and respect. We both were young, developing actors and artists, open to learn from the old and new creative voices that expressed a unique direction in artistic freedom for actors, writers, directors, musicians, dancers, poets, and visual artists.

I also saw that my friend and I shared an interest in marketing and audience development, because we knew that that was an important element of communicating our artistic and cultural experience. We both shared a passion in the power of word & of mouth, to let others know about the productions we were part of, and about other important new works we saw.

At a particular time, I made a very important change in my creative development as an actor and began to explore my interest and passion for artist management, publicity, and marketing the arts. My friend Chisholm was very supportive of my change of direction artistically. I became a student at Third World Cinema which later became New Cinema Artists. I was also very fortunate to have an internship in 1973 with Irene Gandy Associates, a publicity and marketing arts company.

One of the most important lessons in friendship at that time was that friendship is like a tree growing in nature, with the grace of a love supreme having many branches. So can friendship have many new persons who share in this beautiful, life, learning journey. My brother Anthony Chisholm and I shared together, and were blessed in this earthly, spiritual oneness with the gift of friendship. Along with so many other beautiful souls like August Wilson, Phyllis Hyman, Stephen McKinley Henderson, Ebony Jo-Ann, Woodie King Jr., Melvin Van Peebles, Mary Alice, and Phylicia Rashad, just to name a few, that were also present. Anthony Chisholm and myself were very thankful to have shared that gift of friendship with everyone that was a part of that life circle.

I was also very fortunate to be a member of AJASS Repertory Theater that was based in Harlem during the late 1960s, and mid-1970s. My work in service of the arts blessed me to become one of the first African-American men to have a group sales and audience development company during the 1980s. But my preparation and development started in the 60s, and I was very fortunate to work with August Wilson on all his ten plays chronicling the African-American in the 20th century. Anthony Chisholm was an actor in four of these August Wilson productions. I also worked with

Woodie King Jr. with The New Federal Theater; Douglas Turner Ward with The Negro Ensemble Company; Dr. Barbara Ann Teer with The National Black Theatre; Lincoln Center Theater; Voza Rivers with New Heritage Theatre Group, and so many other artistic institutions.

I would like to mention two important women who were friends on my theater journey–Ms. Vivian Robinson, founder of AUDELCO, and Ms. Katherine Cook of The Wiz Group, managing director for Melvin Van Peebles group sales agency. I am so thankful and blessed to have had a village of angels and friendships like Anthony Chisholm, and so many others that live in my heart and soul memories in a love supreme always. My friend and brother Anthony Chisholm died in October of 2020. He often said he was thankful, and that in life we should keep our seat belts fastened, stay in touch with our God, and enjoy the ride.

DREAMING DREAMS TOO WONDERFUL TO DARE ALOUD

by James Aloway

(first appeared in *The Healing Adagio*)

There were days when it was difficult to imagine
That there would be a tomorrow after tomorrow;
or that my vision of yesterday
was clear enough to shine the path.

There were Mornings that came too soon
after work that seemed just through
with sunlight peeping between the cracks
in the torn window shade,
screaming the news
"It is time to start another day."
Just 10 more minutes and I will be fine.......

My back aches!
Oh Lord, help me through another day!
Did I pay the water bill?

None of this seemed
to make any sense back then,
though occasionally there was the Light.

Times when I could see
more than half-remembered dreams
of Momma's crib songs
and Poppa's hope dream for me.

I met three Queens standing tall,
with shiny thought jewels
that sometimes blinded me.

They showed me the three mountains
I needed to climb.
Each higher than the other,
all piercing the clouds.

Baby, my feet hurt!
Oh Lord, help me through another day!
When are they coming to turn the lights back on?

Standing on the curb and not lying on it
gives a different perspective on things.

I could see for miles, or at least down the street.
I can understand, believe... have Faith.
Folks heading west, while I'm moving East.
Cast a star in my eye, show me the way.

A King followed by a Queen and another Queen.
Cast a star in my eye,
show me the way–it's a new day,

Show me the way. I pray...
Oh Lord, help me Lord.

I pray...
Oh Lord, help me through another day!

WITHOUT COURAGE AND GOODNESS, YOU CAN'T LOVE!

by J Rome Andre

Without courage and goodness you can't love! You can't stand for what's right! Without courage and goodness can't win!

Originally from St. Louis, I came to New York at 15 years old. Velma, my Mom, was from Mississippi and my Father, Johnnie Eddie, was from Arkansas. My dad was a hardworking man. He held down two jobs, but was also known as one of the first Black gangsters in St. Louis. My parents were both well respected in our community. If my dad was alive, he would be 110 and my mom 97. I was born during the beginning of their turbulent relationship and was a sickly child. I was diagnosed with a learning disability and speech defects. When I was eleven, I was hit in the head with a baseball bat, causing me to have seizures. My mom corrected my stuttering by putting her gun in my mouth when I was twelve years old. I never stuttered again. My mom and dad had severe anger management problems. Both of them were well armed at all times. At an early age, I found courage to stand for what was right no matter what–love and goodness is the only way.

My parents did not accept that I couldn't learn. My dad taught me how to count and multiply by teaching me to shoot craps, how to tie my tie using a peach can, and the in and outs of the life of a loan shark. But the biggest lesson was being a man and having integrity. My mom was a disciplinarian and gorgeous. She also taught me and my big sister, Nina Rene, how to clean, cook, manners, etc. She was also employed, teaching nutrition classes around the city and state. My dad often prayed in increments of five years, asking God to give him more time to raise me because of his age. He taught me what he knew and that was a lot! Every year we went on vacation.

My parents fed and buried a lot of people in our family and community. My mom also took care of the sick. They both showed me you must have courage and goodness to love through their actions.

Two lessons I got from them that stand out. First was when I was ten years old; I was playing on the front porch with my neighborhood friends. Ms. Jackie passed by wearing blue and pink shorts and a tight wig. One of the kids on my porch called Ms. Jackie a sissy man. I was raised in an inclusive household. My parents had all types of friends. My father was standing near the front door. He stepped out, told my friends to go home and told me to come inside. He said, "As long as you breathe. Do not ever disrespect another person. Whatever someone's choice is, you respect them." I said to my dad, "I did not say it." His reply was, "You were with them and you did not stand up! You followed the crowd and that is not acceptable. She could save your life and when you see her, you call her Ms. Jackie!" He made me apologize and I gave her some flowers I picked. She accepted! But she also told my dad I was not the one who called her out of her name. I learned that day. It takes courage and goodness to stand for what is correct!

Second lesson, I dropped out of high school. I went into prostitution. That was a short-lived career move! A trick pulled a double barrel shotgun on me. That ran me out of the business. To this day I say it was an Angel! I was scared straight! So, I decided to get my GED. I ended up going to beauty school. I was the first African-American male student. The white kids hated the fact I was there. They ganged up on me one Friday. I broke a nose and busted several heads! My father also taught me how to defend myself. I ended up going to jail for assault. I was also accused of sexual abuse! They had 16 cops looking for me. One of the teachers who was white, Ms. Mary, hid me from the police in a garbage can. That took courage and goodness in her heart! She was thinking they were going to hurt me. They found me and I was locked up and charged. I was blackballed and not allowed to complete my training until after my trial. What saved me—I had to admit my sexual orientation, and the secretary of the school at the trial told the truth. In her statement she admitted, "I don't like niggers! But they attacked him first." I realized that day God sends Angels no matter what color they are. I realized it took courage for her to tell the truth and that there is goodness in everyone. Through that lesson I was able to forgive. Courage and goodness won again. Even through adversity!

I became a runaway and moved to New York with 12 dollars after my mom told me, "It's time for you to leave and don't come back until you have grown up. Because if you stay, you are going to end up in prison if you do not change your thoughts and heart. So, pack your bags!" At the time I thought she was being cruel, but she was showing me Courage, Goodness, and Love, because she was right. My dad, being very ill and blind, did not want me to leave but my mom insisted!

I needed a place and money, so I moved in with this gentleman. Eventually, he told me to get out. I moved in with my Godparents, the Hughleys. My Cosmetology license came in handy and the gift of gab! I found a room in Harlem. I used it to sleep and do hair. Finally, I got my first big break. My Godsister Mary Card called me. She told me to pack my bags and get ready to come to Detroit because I was the new hairdresser for the musical *The Gospel Truth* starring Johnny Brown, and "no is not an option." I was horrible at first. Everyone looked like James Brown! Ashton Springer threatened to beat me up and fire me several times. Jennifer Holiday joined the show. She liked me! So that kept me employed. I thought I was the cat's meow, until her wig fell in the rain and rolled down the street. I was finally close to my heart's desire.

When I was a teen, Mary Card had promised my mother if she took me out of St. Louis that she would be responsible for me. Even Ashton had to promise. My mother did not play! They kept their word. Both my parents passed away a year apart. Bettye Lavette came each time and stayed with me. She sang at both my parents' funerals. I went to Atlanta for two years, staying with Young and Stephanie Hughley. Those were hard years, but I was shown goodness, love, and compassion; it gave me the courage to stand and hold on.

For several years, I was blessed to be employed as a hairdresser and performer for directors and producers such as George Faison, Lonnie McNeil, Shelly Garrett, and Leslie Dockery. The funniest thing, I always ended up performing or being the understudy for one of the principal characters. I always knew all the songs and choreography. I took each opportunity and knew they were blessings! When I wasn't on the road as a hairdresser, I was in the studio recording my first album that was produced by Hershall Dwellighham. I was sent to take vocal classes and etiquette classes! Vivian Reed took me on and straightened me out. She instilled the importance of studying my craft and taking care of my instrument. She taught me how to breathe, move, and sing! She gave me the foundation that had lasted many moons! She showed me a lot of love and goodness.

Ronald Wyche, my mentor, was directing his musical *Satan Never Sleeps*. He called looking for my Godmother Bettye Lavette. She was living in Detroit. I asked if I could audition. He said, "Yes!" I went and I got the job, and became his new Satan. He worked with me and called his partner Melissa Maxwell to polish up the last scene. That year the show won five Audelco's. I brought home "Leading Male in A Musical!" That same year, I understudied Ken & Andre in the musical *Ain't Misbehavin'* starring Dee Dee Bridgewater. That gave me the courage to continue. More courage, goodness, and love!

One of my other hustles was the temp service. The tip of the iceberg was 9/11. I had a temp assignment next door to the World Trade Center. Being stuck there, I witnessed devastation, victims jumping to their deaths because they didn't want to burn up in flames. I witnessed both towers fall. That changed my life and direction. It made me realize the importance of having courage, love, and goodness in your heart because one does not know who they may need. After the towers fell, the city was silent, and all you could hear was whimpers. It didn't matter who the person was if they needed a helping hand. Gay, Straight, White, Black, Green, or Trans. You gave a helping hand. That's when I witnessed and knew for a fact. You must have courage and goodness in your heart to love.

The healing continues to take place, one step at a time. I've learned many lessons through my journey. Some were painful! That's the deal. As long as we breathe and live lessons will come. I look back now at my youth, how the spirit had a hand in guiding me and protecting me. Putting the right people in my life. How sneaking into a theater in St. Louis after a weed sale changed my life. I gained an extended family who continues to love me unconditionally! Ashton Springer, Mary Card, Mable Lee, Vivian Reed, George Faison, Barbara Lerman, Jon L. Evans, Ronald Wyche, Melissa Maxwell, Margaret Faison, Young Hughley, Stephanie Hughley, Kamilii Pruitt, Betty Wheeler, Heloise Mayer, Bettye Lavette, Herschel and Alva Dwellingham, Melony McGant. These mentors were angels and rainbows in my clouds and showed me love, compassion and goodness.

I've been blessed with a team of producers, Jon L Evans & Lou Rodreguiz, that truly are my brothers! They get me and my mission! I'm also part of Strafe's & The Hard Soul Meditation. I have released several albums and House singles that have hit and stayed on the charts for weeks. I'm so grateful! I'm blessed beyond measure. The healing continues to take place. One step at a time which is my motto. Through exercise and meditation, you learn to listen! It disciplines you. **I've learned many lessons through my journey. I've been blessed with the recipe of life which is: You must have courage, love, and goodness in your heart.** Then you will be unstoppable, and you will win. I'm a witness and blessings!

DR. DO GOOD
by ChiChi Anyanwu

Honored to be asked to be part of this book. Thank you, Melony McGant, for your positivity, support, and encouragement through the years.

I would like to start by saying I am the hardworking, generous, outspoken woman I am today, because of the support and love from my family. Thank you to my parents, grandmother, uncles, aunts, and siblings who raised me. Grateful for my tribe and it surely takes a village to raise a child.

I come from a large Nigerian family. My mother, Josephine, is the oldest of ten siblings and my father, Kenneth, is the youngest of his four sisters. I am the fourth child of my parents. I was a bit odd, hyperactive, and attention hungry as a child. Sometimes I acted out a lot. I learned what it was to have a "potty mouth." I would talk back to my elders, curse, run around the house butt naked, and even fist fight with the neighborhood boys . . . all at the age of seven. I even used to tell my teachers to shut up and would bully some kids. I remember being punished a lot and having to stand on a line during many recesses, instead of playing with friends. I've cleaned many chalkboards in my days. I laugh sometimes when I think about how far I've come. I was far from being "good," I was up to no good.

Sometimes my teachers wouldn't know what to do with me. However, African parents don't play that. When I acted up, I was yelled at and spanked. Not only by my parents, but my grandma, aunts, & uncles. "Takes a village," remember? My grandmother called the wooden stick she spanked me with "Dr. Do Good." To this day, I will never be an advocate for child abuse. After the fifteenth beating, I still didn't learn my lesson. Getting whipped just taught me fear, not true discipline.

A pivotal moment in my childhood was when I got in trouble after playing ring-and-run on neighbors down the street. My friends had dared me. The homeowner saw from the window. Before I could run, the door opened, and my neighbor grabbed me. He said was calling the cops and my parents for trespassing. Ironically, my so-called "friends" were nowhere to be found. Anything could have happened. I was so scared. Eventually he let me go after I apologized. But he still called my parents and my grandma. I remember my grandma being so disappointed. She didn't bring out her "Dr. Do Good" stick; nope, she did something that I will never forget to this day.

My grandma told me to follow her to the basement and to sit down. Then she spat on the floor and told me to lick it off the floor. I said "No, that's gross." She replies, "See, just because someone tells you to do something, doesn't mean you do it. You know right from wrong." She had tears in her eyes, and talked about how I come from strong people. That Nigerians are leaders, not followers, prideful people. She took out her bible and preached a sermon that night. After her heartfelt message about Jesus dying for our sins, my grandma talked about growing up in Nigeria and her journey to the U.S. She spoke about how hard my parents worked so that I could have a roof over my head. Not sure how long my grandma talked but it felt like forever. Except, I was finally listening and taking everything in that she was saying. I felt bad for letting my grandma and my parents down. The next week, after my talk with my grandma, it was like a switch went on. I had an Oprah "Aha!" moment, and was tired of being a bad kid. I wanted to be a better person and "do good." Being bad was also exhausting. I was tired of being angry, insecure, always in trouble. It wasn't until I stopped cursing, stopped hanging with the bad kids, and did better in school that I started to feel better about myself. By the 8th grade, folks would tease, calling me the "Teacher's Pet." Yes, I was and proud of it! I would always ask my teachers how I could be of service during and after class. I started helping a lot around the house, making sure to clean all the commons areas before my parents got home from work daily. Also, I kept myself busy and out of trouble by joining every school activity. I wouldn't be bored or try to act out for attention anymore. I grew to learn that "doing good" makes you feel good. Doing good is within all of us, but we must make the change for ourselves at the end of the day. It's a choice, and an inside job.

A SHORT STORY OF GOOD
Brian Scott Bagley

Once upon a child was bestowed an unending and unconditional love for everyone he met. Walking down the street with his hand in the hand of his mother, he did pull away as they passed a homeless person sitting on the corner. His mother quickly reacted, frightened, heightened, and on guard for the security of her son. The fear for something small, important, and precious that was once in her hand was now gone, infusing a stress that quickened her heart to the sounds of drumming.

She calls her son's name sharply, yet with love. Seeing her son draw closer to the man sitting on the ground, she rushed towards the two of them. The young boy in a small tender voice says the three words that would become an echoing soundtrack of his life and soul's heart;

« Excuse me, sir... »

From his pocket, he gives the sitting man, who looks up to him, a single quarter that was gifted to him by his Grandmother. He follows up his words, now with his mother holding close by almost shadowing over her son, the words..."I hope this helps. "

The sitting gentleman looks up and kindly says thank you. And hand in hand, mother and son walk away into their day. Mother, with a curious smile, asks her son what possessed you to do that? « I don't know. I just felt that it might help him. » Mother then says to her son, « That was nice of you. »

He was at the age when he was sometimes embarrassed to hold his mother's hand while riding on his skateboard in the city. But the same kind of giving was repeated. And when he held his mother's hand one last time, with tears in his eyes, trying to flow his love and gratitude into her hand, hoping that she was still aware of his presence; just so that she knows that she wasn't alone and to let her know that she is all things wonderful. That she had done amazing work, and that it was okay to let go, and to go home to her reward.

As he saw her breath whisper up towards the creator, he thought of the love, of each lesson of kindness, and good and of loss...not loss.

In the crystal clear heart of each of these moments, the base of these love actions was to continue the cycle of goodness. Not as a badge of reward to show « look at me » how good I am, but to simply be in the presence of Good, and all of its many sisters and brothers, kindness, gratitude, compassion, generosity, joy, being humble, etc. That child throughout his life would be abused and taken advantage of because of this condition. It was an enemy, it was a friend, it was a sibling, it was... but he had his condition, and could not be anything than what he was despite how the world tried him. Many times he would become hardened, but it wouldn't last. Even once retracing a day's steps to find the moment of kindness that he tried to ignore the day before.

In the end he reflected on his journey, and thought simply "at least I gave that which was given and with love." Life ebbed and flowed, but his condition of kindness was his gift and his gift to share. Now the tender voice that is heard is "good job...good job." The webbing of love and the ripples of kindnesses that began in each moment of goodness would one bring healing to the world. Or will it?

RESPONSIBILITY IS LOVE IN ACTION!

Bruce Blakey

One day a very wise young lady, with a very old soul, told me that **"Responsibility is love in action."**

At the time, we were talking about fathers. I shared my commitment, joy, and love for my family. This was a woman who grew up without a dad.

She had a strong mother who did an excellent job of instilling self-confidence, cultural pride, and knowledge, kindness, love, and a blueprint for survival in this crazy world. She has had a business, a career, and personal success.

Yet, her dad's lack of responsibility created a huge void in her life. In her eyes, the act of taking responsibility is an act of love.

I never heard it put like that before, but she was right.

We have heard this type of story often. So many lives and communities have been devastated because of a lack of fatherly responsibility.

Fathers, please look out for your kids in some form or fashion. Do what you can do, be there. TRY.

by A' Marie B

I enter the gallery of self-denial to embrace the reality of wares paraded before me; enticing me to divulge a secret that has yet to be revealed.

The desire to produce the unknown envelops me to the point of sweating blood, bursting blood vessels, in the hopes of being pitied and allowed a pass through.

It does not pan out as I had anticipated though goodness and mercy follow me.

I am forced to reconcile the inner and outer voice with no road map to lead me in full discourse, having lost sight of my inner compass many wiles ago in exchange for visions of grandeur.

The voices are hazed by the flowery presentation of a candelabra that was constructed to dispel the truth, in the hopes that a spark of Light would encapsulate my textbook prodding, narrowing my scope of unfamiliar territory.

I become further entrenched in waves of wardrobe changing episodes.

The synergistic claim embodies the essential element, clothing in eternal servitude to an existence that purports to solve dilemmas, while giving way to paths of greater depravity and valleys replete with mirages.

I long to find some shred of truth, an ounce of dignity, to allow myself a thread of pride to hang onto.

I continue to amass shelves of personalities that further malign the hue, that remains seated in quiet resolve until the time when provision runs dry and new waters are sought, to soothe the never-ending thirst collected in the aridity of people, places and things.

For now, denying that there exists such a place, where I am solely connected by reasoning, is an illusion that I have concocted to garner more knowledge.

The knowing will suffice.

Desire compels me to invest more time in the pursuit of some form of happiness that would alleviate this burning within me, searing through me, to the point of hollow protrusion, in the hopes of filling it with the splendor of jealousy, anger, envy, wrath and rage for the moment.

I see in the distance, a far cry like a beacon.

The qualities of character or conduct that engender Self-approval and esteem are found in the midst of seeming devastation and personal inner conflict. Adversity builds character and we are better as a by-product of the Goodness that we already are, in intrinsic and experiential measure.

ON SELF-COMPASSION
by Sheree Statum Carnel

As a Mother, I know that LOVE is unconditional, innate, and ancient. A Mother's LOVE is life-giving, and protective, in the perfect quantity. It is a unique quality necessary for each of her children. It has no bounds. The one time that a Mother's LOVE may be short of what is required is when she needs to give to herself. She has already given most, if not all, of her supply to others.

My prayer is that Mother gathers all the fierce, life-sustaining, nurturing LOVE she pours into her precious ones, and bathes her *own* Holy Spirit in the same. *On a daily basis.*

May we learn to practice Self-Compassion with this Prayer/Metta:

*May we be **fiercely compassionate** with ourselves, as Mothers are with their children.*

May we honor our Spirit and support our dreams.

May we protect our tender heart, as we keep it open to receive LOVE.

May we nurse our own wounds and encourage ourselves to try again, and again.

May we be honest with ourselves about our feelings and needs.

May we remember that our lives constantly change.

May we be patient with ourselves as we continue to grow.

May we LOVE and FORGIVE ourselves unconditionally.

May we always be kind to ourselves.

When we do these nurturing and loving things for ourselves, we learn even more how to do them for others. Living our lives with Self-Compassion models and informs compassion to all.

BIRTHRIGHT
by Donna C. Chernoff

It is your birthright
to know your ancestry.
This gift I give to you
commemorates
your living,
your deceased,
loved ones,
your ancestry.

My birthright journey,
began many years ago.
One old photo,
a one-hundred-year-old photo,
passed on,
a paternal grandfather,
a man my father never knew,
never spoke of,
never recognized him
as his son,
a man
I never knew.

My paternal grandmother was eighteen,
gave birth to him,
common back then.
No father's name listed,
blank on his birth certificate.
Only a mother's maiden name.

A loving and supportive father,
a quiet and unspoken sadness,
always there,

telling me something
I needed to know.

The elders,
the wise ones,
talkers of truths.
One-hundred-year-old photo,
led me,
inspired me,
to take a journey,
to find the truth,
my father's legacy,
my birthright,
and that was where my journey began.

Once detached,
pulled away,
sold away,
given away,
America's original sin.

Denied,
how to read and write.
Now knowing
is your strength,
your path to endless possibilities.

It is your birthright,
to know,
to know your ancestry.
Hold on,
never forget,
never give up,
secure your sacred legacy,
pass it on
to your children,
your descendants of future.

For we are entwined like
African rhythms,
slave songs,
gospel melodies,
R&B, hip-hop,
and on and on.
Telling truths,
telling our stories.

We are woven together
like antique quilts,
precious art pieces,
handsewn garments,
knitted, crocheted,
images in the minds,
of people
who created them,
all made with love,
leaving talks of truth,
leaving beloved memories,
leaving acts of love,
gathered together over hundreds of years.

A Dagbamba proverb states,
"Never let what you hold in your hand to fall on the ground."

It is your birthright,
your ancestry.
Speak their names.
Write their names.
Remember their names.
It is your birthright
to know your ancestry.

GROWING UP YELLOW IN CHOCOLATE CITY

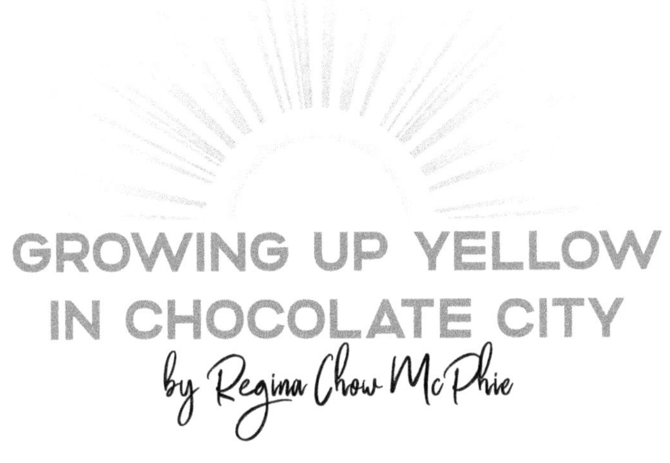

by Regina Chow McPhie

It was the summer of 1962, I was eleven years old and was walking home from the Peoples Drug Store (now called CVS). I passed a fire station where several firefighters were outside cleaning their fire trucks. They were all White. One shouted out to me "Chink, Chink Chinaman. Chink, Chink Chinaman." A couple of the other firefighters laughed. I turned around and stared at the shouter. All of a sudden, the shy little Chinese American girl shouted back "shame on your ignorance!" This really took them aback. I suspect they were surprised that I could speak English and that I, an Asian child, who exhibited no fear, had the tenacity to shame the grown man for his racist slur.

I must say I was so proud of myself that day. I had the gumption to respond to the racial taunt and come back with such a clever retort. My law-abiding father, who came to this country at a young age and became a citizen, taught us children to ignore such ethnic slurs and to not reply at all so as not to anger the persons who sometimes teased us with racist Chinese slurs. However, this time I was tired of being teased–especially from men who were supposed to have our respect and who are supposed to help us.

This is one of many memories that come flooding back to me from time to time, as I ponder my life in my senior years. I now believe that I was affected and influenced by the changing times that called for challenging the existing norm of segregation and race discrimination. Dr. Martin Luther King gave stirring speeches that called people to challenge through peaceful resistance. Everyone was touched by his speeches to rise above your normal existence. Even as a young teenager, I felt Dr. King's amazing effect on me as a minority person, who lived in the inner city of Washington, D.C., a predominantly African American community. We were all stirred by this giant orator who possessed so much charisma. My opportunity to meet this amazing personality came one day when I was a student attending Shaw Junior High School. Our middle school was supposed to be the point of origin for a march calling for increased public school funding. However, because of the last minute threats made on Dr. King's life, the venue was changed for the safety of the children. Our school was let out early. I went outside to wait for my big brother so we could walk home together. I was afraid as I noticed no one was on the street and the threats loomed in the back of my mind. A few minutes later, my cousin Nancy came out of the school and then the school nurse came running out. She asked us if Dr. King had arrived yet, and we said we saw nothing. She told us that, apparently, Dr. King and his party had not gotten word of the change in venue and she had to relay the message to him. Then a large black sedan pulled up to the curb. The school nurse ran to the car to relay the message. One back window was rolled down and the school nurse thrust her body against the car so she could reach over to shake Dr. King's hand. She was so excited and called out to us two children to come out. Although I was afraid because of the threat, my cousin and I went over to the car and put our hands in to try and reach Dr. King. I could see his face in the middle of the back seat surrounded by his entourage of large men. He leaned forward and touched our hands. It was exciting and scary. Then his vehicle quickly sped away.

Another memory is the moment of my awakening to my life's purpose. At the age of twelve, I pondered the reason for my existence and how my religious beliefs would affect my life choices. On Friday, November 22, 1963, I was home sick with a cold and laying in bed. Then my Dad called me to come downstairs. We watched the devastating news on TV about the attempt on President John F. Kennedy's life. I returned to my bed and prayed. I prayed to God to spare the life of our beloved President Kennedy, and I bargained with God that I would make my life count if he spared the President's life.

"Ask not what your country can do for you, ask what you can do for your country," rang in my ears as I prayed. These precious words from President Kennedy's speech awakened the spirit of America to live and serve; to do more for others than for yourself. I embraced his words.

Although our President died shortly upon his arrival to the hospital, I decided to keep my promise to God. I wanted to "find my calling." That opportunity came about at the Washington, D. C. Chinatown Summer Festival of 1974, where I was a volunteer member of the Eastern Wind community organization. I met Alicia Columna, a speaker at our festival. I was assigned to escort her to the VIP Luncheon. She told me that she worked at the Equal Employment Opportunity Commission (EEOC) Headquarters in Washington, D.C. She summarized its mission of enforcing Title VII of the Civil Rights Act of 1964, which prohibits discrimination in employment on the basis of race, religion, color, sex, and national origin. I found it fascinating and she encouraged me to consider working for this noble federal agency. I was intrigued with the idea of working for such a civil rights organization that helped people who filed employment discrimination complaints. I did follow up and ended up working for EEOC in many different positions for almost three decades. I loved the mission of the agency and felt it was rewarding work.

Fast forward two decades later and I'm walking in downtown Richmond, Virginia, pondering whether my contributions made any difference to the cause of civil rights. I wondered if all the tireless work–the long hours, travels throughout Central and Southwest Virginia to investigate employment discrimination complaints, negotiating settlement agreements–was worth it. It was exhausting work. I was becoming downtrodden. As an Intake Officer and EEO Specialist/Investigator, you hear complaints all day long; you interview hostile witnesses, you negotiate with unhappy employers and their aggressive attorneys, and try to resolve their differences. It was tough work that required mustering up all of one's skills in human relations, diplomacy, knowledge of EEO laws, regulations, and one's tolerance for handling the Complaining Party's emotional roller coaster of allegedly being subjected to job loss, sexual and/or racial harassment, and the other alleged harm associated with discrimination.

I must give kudos to my husband Neil McPhie, a brilliant lawyer who is well versed in EEO law and an amazing, compassionate, and humane person. He was my mentor in helping me to understand the complexities of EEO laws and regulations. In addition, he taught me the art of negotiating with skilled trial lawyers. My husband, a Republic of Trinidad and Tobago-born, naturalized American citizen, had the amazing ability to explain the most complex issues in lay terms, and he did it with a sense of humor.

Returning to my ponderings and downhearted spirit as I do my lunch time walk, I hear a faint voice calling out my name "hey, Mrs. McPhie, Mrs. McPhie!" As the voice gets closer, I turn around and see a young African American man approach me. He asks if I remember him. I stare at him and reply, "you do look familiar." The young man introduced himself and said, "You saved my job a few years ago. I am so grateful to you for what you did for me back then." He reminded me of his case and that it was a tough time in his life. He said he was put back on track and was glad that he did not lose his job back then. He thanked me again, then we both returned to work from our lunch breaks.

Hallelujah, hallelujah–– he was the answer to my prayers. God does work in mysterious ways. Just when I was feeling down and questioning the worth of my career choice, this young man renewed my spirit to march forward and continue to do good work. I was invigorated to make a difference in the lives of disheartened employees and applicants in the field of employment discrimination. Yes, Lord, it was all worth it. **If only one person benefited from my work, then it was worth it.**

LOVE FOUND A WAY
by Andrea Christofferson

One Christmas Eve we visited our dear friend Michael in Madison, Wisconsin. We reminisced about how we came to know each other.

The story began in a nursing home back in 1976 when I found a job to help get me through my last year of college. As newlyweds, Rob and I were broke but found a drafty old farmhouse to rent where we could heat with wood. Rob drove me to the nursing home at five in the morning in a rattletrap car. I had to push it through the snow to pop the clutch and start.

I wanted to be a good nurse's aide. The work was hard and I struggled to keep up with the pace required to bathe, clothe, feed, and respond to all the hall lights signaling needed bathroom trips.

It was there I met an amazing young woman, only a few years older than I was, whose spirit burned bright even in a nursing home surrounded by elders. Suzi had cerebral palsy and required help to do most things. It was hard to understand her speech at first, but she made her sense of style and determined personality very clear. Soon she convinced me to go out with her in her power wheelchair after work to a nearby pub. Eventually, she asked to visit my home in the country. My husband Rob carried her inside to warm up by the fire and onto a mattress on the floor overnight. My friendship with Suzi continued long after I left the nursing home job and we had many outings–especially shopping–which she loved. We stayed close even as I separated, divorced, and began new life chapters.

One summer, Suzi organized a trip to Milwaukee's Summerfest with another friend. Miraculously, she ran into Michael, a friend she had known back when they lived in a huge facility for the differently abled. Suzi and Michael's cerebral palsy was misunderstood in that era; their education and independence were limited. When they fell in love, wanting to marry as teenagers, their families split them apart.

Their joyful reunion led them to renew their hopes for a future together. This was not easy for two people needing caregivers, accessible housing, and living in two different counties. By sheer will and determination, they fought the system and won the right to be together. On June 22, 1980, they had an outdoor wedding on the grounds of Cave of the Mounds, where I worked. Special vans brought the bride and groom and their wheelchairs to the ceremony. Bob, my boyfriend and later spouse, was Michael's best man. Those of us lucky enough to be there cried tears of joy.

Suzi and Michael found an accessible apartment, hired caregivers, and began to pursue education and work. Their physical and communication challenges did not dampen their intelligence and wit. Suzi tested new technology that allowed her to interact with her computer via a device on her forehead. She finished her GED and launched into courses at a technical college. Michael had never been offered the chance to learn to read and worked hard to overcome misconceptions in the community. They were truly in charge of their own lives and so balanced that their strengths supported each other's weaknesses and needs. Suzi had many worrisome physical ailments but was an able manager of her and Michael's care (it's very hard to find and train trusty caregivers). Michael had more physical strength. He could get himself in and out of his own wheelchair, which gave them more independence. They loved getting out and about in their power wheelchairs.

Sadly, tragedy struck in 1993, when Suzi choked to death at a restaurant on a piece of pizza before caregivers or onlookers could help her. It was shocking and so hard to believe that she was gone.

Michael's heart was broken. But he has persisted to live a life with as much independence as possible, traveling all across Madison in his power wheelchair, bravely water skiing, and even independently riding a bus to Milwaukee to return to his beloved Summerfest. He has made many friends, ably manages his caregivers and finances, and safely navigated through the COVID pandemic.

Michael embodies joy in living everyday and experiencing all one can on this beautiful planet. He is no stranger to loss but love endures. We are so lucky to know him.

LIFE IS GOOD BEYOND MEASURE
by Mary Christopher

ife is good, good beyond measure. Our existence as Human Beings is good, good beyond measure. Before your mind starts coming up with all the reasons that Life is not always so good, or before your memory starts running all your personal unhappy experiences, let me explain.

What do I mean by Life? When I think of Life, I most often think of Creation or, more specifically, I think of Nature. Nature is Amazing and full of Beauty and Humor and Incredible Design and Healing and Wonder. I know referring to Nature does not mean the same for everyone. For some people Nature may mean bees that sting or ants who invite themselves to our picnic. It may mean big storms or weather that is too cold or hot. Nature may be a lightning storm knocking out the cable or internet connection in the middle of our favorite movie rerun.

Nature may mean difficulties or obstacles for us or our ideas of progress. Far too often, when we "mess with Mother Nature" in the name of progress, we create all kinds of problems. Our oceans and waterways are filled with plastic because of our love of convenience and lack of creativity. Neighborhoods and even entire towns are toxic due to fumes from refineries. In 2015 alone, people living in Oklahoma experienced earth tremors more than 900 times. There were an unusual number of magnitude three or higher earthquakes across the state due to fracking. Oil companies use fracking to push more oil or natural gas out of oil wells.

For me, Good Beyond Measure in Nature is Powerful. That Goodness is found in photosynthesis as Trees and Plants absorb Carbon Dioxide, and transform it into the fresh Oxygen that all inhabitants of Earth need to survive. Good Beyond Measure is the soil, water, nutrients, worms, and fungi that trees and plants use to produce the food that keeps us alive.

Consider Bees and Pollen . . .we usually associate Bees with Honey or with Pollination, which is necessary to produce so many of the fruits and vegetables we have every day. We take it for granted that our favorite fruits and vegetables will be lining the shelves at our local grocery store. We also take it for granted that our favorite Farmers' Market will be well stocked with fresh produce during the summer.

How does this happen? Almost all our favorite fruit trees and vegetable plants depend on insect or bird pollination in order to produce fruits and vegetables. On the other hand, most grasses, as well as evergreen trees, produce large amounts of pollen which is distributed by wind. Most Fruits and Vegetables are pollinated by insects going from blossom to blossom, picking up pollen from one specific kind of blossom and carrying it to another of the same variety.

If we pause for a moment and consider this process, we begin to understand how amazing it is. Bees and other Pollinators are not Robots! They are not organized or driven by embedded micro-chips. Insects do seem to have a "collective intelligence," which means a system of awareness as well as communication specific to their species and type.

We could say that Insects, and Bees in this example, are Conscious or at the very least Aware. They communicate or "share information" about the location of specific flowers with each other by doing a "waggle dance" inside the hive. With their waggle dance, Bees share the general direction and distance to flowers that have a supply of nectar. Also, Honey Bees can respond to people near their hives based on whether or not they are calm and at ease; they can react to the mood of people.

Based on the assumption that we can learn about the Creator by studying Creation, we could make some observations. Because Pollination occurs all around the World in many different climates, with a variety of plants, and pollinators, we see similar patterns of adaptive behavior. In addition, we know that all Creatures, Great and Small, make choices that enhance their survival.

Regardless of whether we agree that Bees are Conscious or that they have a Collective Intelligence or they are simply Aware, most Human Beings are blessed in some way by the activity of Bees and so many other Creatures. We survive and derive Good Beyond Measure from conscious activity throughout Creation. We can say that some kind of Consciousness "thought up" Creation and brought it into existence. We could also say that Creation, as we experience being alive in it, has existed for hundreds of thousands of years. Creation works without any thought or assistance or encouragement from us as Human Beings, so there must be something glorious going on here.

When I am out for a walk, I am aware of Sunlight, Air, Moisture if there is rain, Birds singing, grass growing, all without me doing one single thing. It's amazing! Nature is Definitely Good and Powerful Beyond Measure. Have a Glorious Day!

Dear Maze, Xander, Athena, Rheia, and Titan,

Recently, someone asked me how I came to be a lawyer and how I got involved in campaigning against the death penalty. I thought you might want to know when you get older.

So here's how it happened—I had just graduated from Waynesburg College in 1968 with a BA in French and I was trying to figure out what to do next. I got a call from a professor at the University of Pittsburgh Law School asking me if I would be interested in applying. I knew I wasn't interested in teaching French and I had tentatively been assigned to vaccinate babies in Afghanistan for the Peace Corps. I opted to go to law school instead.

As I recall, I started studying for the LSAT and got a decent score. I was admitted with 10 other Black students. I was the only Black woman. There were a total of about seven women in my class. I graduated in 1971. I think the fact that I had studied Latin and French and loved to write helped me tremendously. Many people will advise you to study Political Science if you want to do well in law school. However, a good grounding in English writing is just as important, if not more valuable.

I should note some impressive Black men who had graduated from Pitt Law in the 1950s: Derrick Bell, K. Leroy Irvis, and my future brother-in-law, who was blind, John Conley. Robert L. Vann was the first Black graduate in the early 20th century. However, although I didn't know it at the time, I was the first Black woman to graduate and the first admitted to practice law in Allegheny County.

My first job after passing the bar was Assistant Solicitor for the School District of Pittsburgh, thanks to my mentor Justin Johnson who was a member of my church. A few years later, I left the local government and went to the private sector to work for The United States Steel Corporation. I retired as Senior General Attorney after 27 years of service. I started out handling Labor Arbitration cases. I traveled all over the country wherever the corporation had a steel plant. I loved the travel until I had kids. Then the travel became burdensome. Luckily, my mother helped me out so much during that time. She often took care of your dads while I traveled.

Now, on to the death penalty–Tim Stevens was President of the Pittsburgh NAACP, which your great, great, grandfather John T. Writt founded in Pittsburgh in the early 20th century, along with Daisy Lampkin and others. Tim Stevens asked Attorney Lisa Freeland and me to co-chair The Legal Redress Committee for the chapter around 1999. Shortly after that, we were approached by Marcus Rediker a history Professor at the University of Pittsburgh to sponsor a forum on the Death Penalty.

Lisa Freeland was a federal defender then (she now heads the office in Pittsburgh). She was an expert in criminal law and the death penalty. I knew nothing about the death penalty at the time having been only focused on administrative law. The forum was an eye-opener for me. Our Keynote speaker was Rubin "Hurricane" Carter who had been wrongly convicted of murder and incarcerated for almost 20 years before he was exonerated and released. The film *Hurricane*, starring Denzel Washington, was about Carter's case; so the forum generated a lot of interest.

The forum had a profound effect on me. I was struck by how ignorant I was about the criminal justice system and how broken the system was. As a result of the forum, I was invited to visit the man that Carter had come to Pennsylvania's Death Row to meet, political prisoner Mumia Abu-Jamal. Abu-Jamal, an accomplished journalist and critic of the Philadelphia police, had been arrested and convicted of the murder of a police officer in Philadelphia. He was railroaded into prison by false witnesses and a corrupt judicial system. While he was eventually released from death row, he is now serving a life sentence and has spent more than 40 years incarcerated for a crime he did not commit.

When I started visiting death row, the inmates steered me to the innocent people on death row. Innocent? Part of my ignorance was that I thought everybody on death row was guilty. I visited Harlod Wilson, Jimmy Dennis, Walter Ogrod, and Anthony Fletcher. They have since been exonerated and released from death row. I also visited designated innocent inmates who are still incarcerated and fighting for their lives, including my client Jerome Coffey. The Abolitionist Law Center has joined my case as co-counsel and I am immensely grateful for their dedication and expertise. As a result of visiting death row inmates, I joined a local group seeking to end the death penalty in Pennsylvania, and I currently serve as co-chair for Pennsylvanians for Alternatives to the Death Penalty—Pittsburgh.

My advocacy has led me to meet some extraordinary people including Archbishop Emeritus, Desmond Tutu, Julia Wright the daughter of Richard Wright, Mireille Fanon the daughter of Frantz Fanon, Minister Louis Farrakhan, Selma James and Fred Hampton, Jr., and among others.

The use of the death penalty has declined dramatically in the last twenty years partly because of innocence projects around the country and partly because of the involvement of non-profit groups which seek to bring equity to the criminal justice system through meaningful representation by defense lawyers. It has become clear that the criminal justice system in the U.S. is fallible and fraught with error.

Most industrialized countries have abolished the death penalty. The European Union requires countries to abolish the death penalty before admission into the union. The U.S. is in the company of Iran, China, and Saudi Arabia employing the death penalty. The death penalty as administered in the U.S. is arbitrary, racist, politicized, expensive, and error-prone. It should be abolished. I hope when you grow up you will be living in a better world. This can only be accomplished when every person is valued and treated equally and with compassion.

Love,
Grandma

Summer is drawing to a close, but there's still time to go out and enjoy nature. There's nothing like a walk in the woods to clear the chaff of worry and woe. Sometimes the best teachers are the ones who say the least, and in the silence of their presence we feel innate wisdom surging up through the cracks of our own lives. The best teachers might be trees.

Feeling sad? Feeling distressed? Feeling nothing at all? Find a winding path through a canopy of trees, leave your troubles behind and let the voices of the wind lead you deep into this present moment. As your awareness begins to shift, you'd notice, gradually at first, and then suddenly, that trees are silent teachers and the lessons they offer would change our lives if we had the patience and courage to learn them.

Here's what trees know...

Grow where you're planted. We can't choose our parents, our families, our birthplace, the year we are born, our genes, or any of the other incidentals that inexorably shape our lives. Like trees, we must learn to accept the things we cannot change and thrive where we are. As a tree grows up from a tiny seedling and rises up through the challenges of its environment, adapting adversities into advantages, wisdom begins with acceptance and self-knowledge and ends with ascension and transcendence.

The invisible is the source of the visible. Unseen beneath the surface, roots grow deep giving trees the stability to stand tall and reach for the light. Trees instinctively know this, and put far more energy into root growth than branch and trunk growth during the early stages of their lives. Only when the roots are firmly established do the upper branches and leaves unfurl. We too should attend first to our inner growth before we get top-heavy with adornments and accessories.

Young and old have different needs and possess different gifts. A tiny sapling is weak and needs protection from hungry mouths and trampling feet. The same tree, many years later is able to provide protection, shelter, and sustenance for others. Our roles change as well as we age and grow. But no matter what stage we are in in life, strength comes out of our own nature, not our busy efforts.

Stand in the truth of who you are at this moment in time. Accept help when you need it, but don't stay helpless and dependent forever. Allow yourself to grow so big that others may take refuge in you.

In our struggles, we grow strong. Over twenty years ago when scientists built the Biosphere 2, a huge enclosed ecosystem in the mountains of Arizona, they planted, along with other things-- trees.

The trees inside the enclosure grew more rapidly than their cousins outside. But they had thin, weak, underdeveloped root systems. Some even toppled over from their own weight. At first scientists were perplexed. Why aren't the trees thriving in this perfect environment? Finally, they realized that the trees were weakened by the absence of the one thing not included in Biosphere 2: wind. In the wild trees must withstand strong wind and as a result develop what botanists call stress wood. Strong, fibrous wood that extensively improves the quality of life for a tree. In our own lives, it is the hardship and struggle that induces our growth and strengthens our core. As we strive to overcome the difficult people and challenging situations that jeopardize our serenity and steal our comfort, a toughness develops within us that suffuses everything we do. In light of this truth, gratitude, not resentment, is the wisest response to the forces that challenge us.

Nature is more cooperative than competitive. Survival of the fittest comes into play, but only up to a point. Life begins with self-awareness. Naturally though, organisms, both within and between species, realize that their own survival is profoundly intertwined with the survival of others. We're much stronger together than we are apart. The well-being of others becomes our own well-being. The lie of individuality is laid bare by the truth of interconnectedness. Just as the cells of our bodies work together to form a whole greater than the sum of its parts, we too are cells in a vast universe utterly void of boundaries.

Life is one amazing phenomenon – conscious, aware, perceptive, intelligent, creative, adaptive – systems intertwined within systems without beginning or end. As individuals, we are simply one momentary expression of the vast field of consciousness that expresses itself as stars, and dandelions and blue whales. To not know this is to remain profoundly ignorant of your essential nature.

Nothing is wasted, everything has value. In nature, there is no such thing as trash. Last year's leaves become this year's soil. Every individual form is derived out of material left behind by previous organisms. There is no new matter. At the molecular level, matter simply reforms and reconfigures into new aggregates and arrangements. Nothing is ever lost, there is a thin, diaphanous, veil between birth and death. Consciousness moves through the veil like the in and out breath of a sleeping God. In our own brief lives we too are formed from the materials of those who went before us. Just as the things we cast off are re-embodied. Nothing is thrown away. There is no such place as "away."

Be only who you are. Cedars don't come from apple seeds. Have the courage and humility to submit to your own nature. Don't waste time being something you are not. Without pretense or artifice, trees effortlessly express their own nature. They make it look easy. But it is not. For us, a thousand threads of desire, envy and illusion tug at our hearts and diverts us away from the simplicity of our essential nature. It takes discipline and humility to learn how to distinguish between the authentic energy of our own nature expanding and the inauthentic egoistic yearnings and desires rooted in fear, anxiety and ill-founded feelings of inadequacy. Do you want to become a singer because singing is your authentic calling, or do want to become a singer to salve a wound caused by feelings of inadequacy? If the latter is true, no amount of fame and glory will ever heal that wound. If the former is true, the music itself will bring you joy and satisfaction. In other words, is singing rooted in your authentic nature, an end in itself or is singing a means to an end, namely, self-aggrandizement? Before you embark on any arduous journey, be it a career choice, a marriage or any other endeavor to craft a life filled with joy and meaning, deep soul-searching is necessary to sort things out. Spend some time under a big, shady tree. Life isn't long enough for a thousand wrong turns.

Don't be afraid to grow. Trees never apologize for growing new leaves and branches. They don't intentionally stay small in a misguided effort to appear humble. You will not do anyone any favors by shrinking, holding back or hiding your gifts. Let what is trying to spring forth through you spring forth. Become a channel through which the creative energy of the universe can sing, yet, another song. But go slow. A tree never hurries and every moment is in keeping with its current strengths and abilities. There is no need to struggle and strain. Natural effortlessness is far more effective than hurried grasping.

Chances are there are woods nearby your home. The forest is lush, green and full of beautiful secrets. Take a day and walk alone through the shafts of light and aromatic breezes. There is so much to learn from the wisdom of trees.

KNOWLEDGE SPEAKS, BUT WISDOM LISTENS
by Ajak M. Dau

To the readers of the book titled: *Good is Powerful Beyond Measure* of our great author, Melony McGant:

I usually post on Facebook about daily life ideas, events that I attended, ethical and social advice, etc. On September 24, 2018, I posted an essay where I talked about a brother who came up with the idea of making a film, *The Good Lie*, that sheds light on the real situation and conditions in old Sudan (before independence) and how wars have affected the people, especially in the current Republic of South Sudan. Everyone suffered under Islam-Arabic culture during the time of President Omer al-Bashir, and those who ruled previously under the National Congress Party (NCP). According to my point of view, and the way I have understood the film, the actors–our brothers there in diaspora in the other continents–shared it with the world as film lovers.

What I shared that day:

"Education is the strongest tool to break ignorance. Ignorance hides the light. Because of ignorance in some communities of nationalism, some turn to encourage and support tribalism and political persons who belong to their tribe or political group. We simply don't value our unity and I think that was one of reasons why we are living like this (sustainable suffering) today whether outside or inside the country."

A great author commented on this post saying she was willing to meet me in Egypt: Melony McGant, from the USA. On October 20th I met with her. She encouraged me to build up my writing.

Who is Melony McGant? Here she is in short:

She is a traveler; she loves traveling from one country to another, one continent to another. She's visited many African, European, and Latin American countries. Smiling always (which is seldom now-a-days, not a smirk), a generous writer, keeps me in the loop, gives compliments (which kidnaps someone's negative energy). Her best optimistic books, in my point of view, are *Sunshine and Olivier* and *Seeker Dreamer*. I remember we talked about the situations and poli-social conditions in the African continent, the issues of freedom, stories of wars in different countries (Rwanda, for example), and those who died without any logical justifications in the past.

Again, on January 24th, 2022, I got positive messages from Melony McGant–as she always hits me up in my Google mail. Her messages, which are of psychologically positivity feedings, she calls for joining a supreme team to work on a book titled: *GOOD is Powerful Beyond Measure* (wisdom remembering) as she added on her message as follows:

"The point is to offer a perspective to young adults to help them on their Journeys, similar to Khalil Gibran or Rumi, and to remind the reader that GOOD IS POWERFUL BEYOND MEASURE!"

And we get to answer the question: ***What's more valuable–wisdom or knowledge?***

A short answer: Knowledge speaks, but wisdom listens.

Long Answer: Knowledge is like a book sitting on a shelf collecting dust, and has no value if there is no action. Wisdom is, perhaps, the careful exercise of knowledge.

I am honored to be among the team of authors with higher knowledge and promote the culture of writing to myself. I expect something great from our author Melony and others, and as Paulo Coelho said: "Impossible is just an opinion."

God bless you all, and may peace be upon you.

To be continued somewhere else.

A VISIT TO SENEGAL
by Luna Diagne

I will never forget the day that she called my number and introduced herself as Melony McGant from New York. My spiritual brother and friend, Arthur Seabury from Kansas City, told her to reach out to me while she was in Senegal.

I was very excited to meet her. When I arrived, she introduced me to the Faye family that welcomed her after leaving Saly, Senegal. Kewe Faye and her three sons are Melony godchildren in NYC. Melony was staying with her family. We spent the day sightseeing with Secka and Adame, from there Melony and I went to a place called Ngor, an old fishing village with a couple of beautiful hotels right across from the island of Ngor. After dinner, Melony checked into her room and we said good night. The next day we went to Dourbel and the Holy City of Touba. And, believe me, we wanted to go to more places but there wasn't enough time.

I am glad that Melony was able to meet my wife Khoudia and my two kids, Khadija and Mohammed the next day. Melony promised me that she will be back. It was a pleasure meeting her and we hope she comes back again. We Love Her Forever!

DOWN TO EARTH
by Naima Renee Dobbs

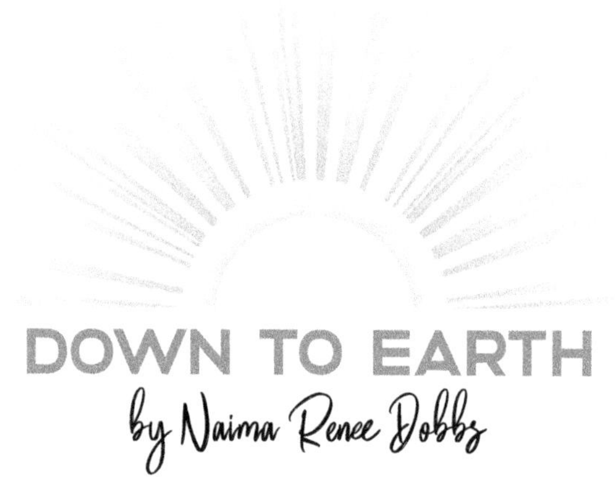

Sometimes the best advice is the counsel that we have heard so much, that the words melt away before they stick. In my teen years I began to reject the triteness of common advice, dismissing it as cliche and lacking nuance. My ideas around performance, especially in school, pushed me to fixate on existential fears. I was an anxious overachiever who felt as though my issues were so unique and personal, that I was unreachable by the common words of wisdom. "Be true to yourself," "Forgive and let go," "Self care is the best care." Okay, sure... I'll try my best, I would think sarcastically. The most profound experiences of my 22 years so far, however, brought me back to these platitudes with a more visceral understanding of their meaning.

The concept of "self care" was something I struggled putting to practice. Through my teens I understood this as having spa days, wearing face masks, retail therapy, and doing other (often consumerist) activities that felt good momentarily. School was a draining presence that left me in constant need of replenishment. I didn't understand how to fill my cup without spilling my wallet and over-tending to my grooming. I didn't understand that I was creating loops of dissatisfaction. Don't get me wrong, grooming and retail therapy have their place in lifting my spirits, but relying on them solely was not helping me overcome self-doubt.

I kept seeking advice however, by reading motivational books, turning self-help into another assignment for myself that I had to succeed at. Many books asked the reader to first figure out what was central to their beliefs and desires in their lifetime. As a high school and college student, I felt that I've been stumbling through things, following what felt right. But I'm not sure if it was true or what was just expected of me. I've felt called to do so many things in my life that I have trouble sorting through the noise of my desires. I knew that I wanted to be good at something creative and for that something to give others permission to make the best of their precious lives. Maybe a writer, an educator, an actress, a singer, definitely an artist. I suffered with indecision most of my life, and still do at times, but it helped me to realize that I was acting out of fear in making the wrong decision. I felt as though I was wasting time trying to decide things. I lived in fear of judgment from others, and since the 'others' in my life were specific to me, it felt like such a personal problem that only I experienced. Despite my intrinsic and ancient connection to all living beings, I felt alone. Since my problems felt impossibly complex, I figured that the solution or relief would have to be equally so.

In 2019, I learned about a practice called "earthing" from YouTube. Skeptical of its simplicity, and that I'd never heard of it before, I didn't really believe it to be true. The video claimed that as we receive vital energy from the sun, so does the earth itself, and supplies us with healing medicine. I tried it in my backyard when I was visiting my family in Atlanta. Took off my shoes, socks, and walked around expecting some magical vibration to jolt through my entire body, enlightening me at once of all the Earth's wisdom. I wasn't even sure what this felt like exactly or how I'd know when it was being received. Instead, I stepped cautiously around, avoiding ant hills, and dog poop, trying to focus on the feeling of wet grass on my soles. There wasn't an immediate third eye awakening moment, but I did feel a softness inside, something easing up that I couldn't quite place. I felt like a kid again. I realized I did this as a kid all the time, and never thought twice about it.

Living in Brooklyn, there weren't many opportunities to do earthing. Going barefoot anywhere in the city feels like a biohazard, even in the greenspaces. However, a similar, and even deeper, experience came to me when I went on a hike in Upstate New York with friends. We had just climbed a long way through a trail and came across a small but beautiful waterfall gurgling its way down a smooth black rock. A sudden and intense urge came over me to take off my shoes and stand by the waterfall. When I did, there was a lightness that swelled inside, like an invisible weight had been lifted off of me. As if the weight wasn't there at all to begin with. I began to cry because I was so struck with relief I felt from this simple action. I was so struck by how far I had felt from the peace that surrounded me, the peace that radiated from the dirt under my feet, and blew in the wind as the earth exhaled. My feet somehow felt deeper in the ground that they actually were; as though I buried them and they had sprung roots. I felt as though I had traveled millennia in the span of a moment, downloading information that my ancestors had once known of the nature around me. The most overwhelming message I was receiving was that I was as infinitely abundant, powerful, creative, and loving as the very earth that surrounded me. The ground from which I came– from which everything I had ever known came –was affirming me of my divine essence. How following that feeling would only bring me joy and fulfillment. As we left the hike, that feeling continued to dissolve many anxieties, calling me back home from my head, and into the magic of the present– of my presence on earth.

This experience reminded me of the 'platitudes' that I had dismissed as a teen. It was still true; it's absolutely a cliche to tell someone to "be true to themselves" or "prioritize self care.

But I now had this deeper understanding of what a cliche even was: a piece of wisdom so ancient that we have culturally become desensitized to its potency. Cliches are cliches because they are so boundlessly and fundamentally true that our complex minds reject them.

The advice I was rejecting held the very truths I needed to focus on, the wisdom that had been floating through the ages by way of nature. We can find these truths in abundance at any time, not just by walking barefoot, but by observing the nature of nature. A tree for example tries its best and cares for itself. It is true to itself, forgives, and does not question its purpose here on earth. My earthing experience reminded me that we are trees too. It is okay to be uncertain at times, even the earth is uncertain of its future. That does not stop the great flow of change, regeneration, and birth.

I saw a girl on the subway the other day wearing a sweatshirt that said, "Advice from the Night Sky: See the big picture, keep looking up, stay full of wonder, and expand your horizons." We are also the Night Sky.

As I reflect, I am learning to detach myself from parts of my past. Some of my experiences are a bit hard to relive. Writing, producing films, and giving lectures are an outlet for me to release attachments to these experiences, and to learn to view them from different angles. Speaking, writing, producing documentaries, and publishing a memoir was challenging. Simply because many of my childhood stories were tragic, so every time I told a story, I relived it. It might be hard for young adult readers to believe that I am still alive. I had to dig deep Mentally and Spiritually to bring my book *Walk Toward the Rising Sun* to fruition. While acting in Hollywood movies, *The Good Lie* and *I Heart Huckabees*, I knew I had many stories within me that I needed to share. Hence the documentary *GER: To be Separate*, and my memoir *Walk Toward the Rising Sun* in 2020 everything aligned with the aid of Penguin and Random House's Children's Books.

Values System of Nuer of South Sudan

The Nuer people of South Sudan are known for their spirituality and braveness.

Nuer people celebrate life and the new year earlier than other cultures. The festivities last for weeks. In Nuer tradition, every action an individual does is attached to the larger universe (Hoaw). Individual acts play a role in the past, the present, and the future. It's all connected. For these reasons, we have numerous festivals, and often sacrifice a cow in order to hold a feast to offer ancestral spirits the meat. In return, they watch us, they guide those who still exist in this universe.

This past year was transformational and of reawakening. Our humanity was confronted with new sets of challenges. Most of us never thought we'd be witnessing a global economic shutdown, a pandemic, climate change, and civil unrest all at once. COVID-19 forced and allowed us to stay at home, where he had endless amounts of precious time to ourselves. My solace was to think with my pen on paper for the sake of clarity, and long walks where I connected with inner unresolved thoughts. This time frame was unfortunate, but a much needed reset for me. It was a year full of self-reflection where we were forced to bring ourselves back to basics. Sometimes, letting go of the material world is necessary. So many untimely events. Kobe Bryan's passing touched me because I connected with him personally. George Floyd being murdered in front of the world reminded us/ taught us /fueled us. Fellow actor Chadwick Boseman passed. These events broke my heart into small pieces because we lost good men and leaders of our time.

The year 2020 wasn't only a challenge, there were celebrations and achievements that I cherish personally. I had my first-born son and finished my first book. COVID-19 caused me to stop traveling the world as an advocate and helped me to make a choice not to audition for movies or modeling jobs. I decided to dedicate my time and energy to my family, figuring out what it means to be a father to my son.

Cathartic Lessons Learned

My heart cries for the world, the refugees and IDPs, and immigrants. We must invest in ourselves and each other's needs. Health is key to our long-term investment. Why? My younger brothers were the last people brought to the United States before the Trump administration shut down the refugee resettlement program. They are lucky, others weren't and have been desperately waiting to be reunited with their families. Many immigrant parents were separated from their children. In 2022, it is my hope that a new administration will revisit its foreign and immigration policies, with an intention to bring back what has always made America the nation that it is. America became powerful by allowing individuals from around the world to pursue their dreams. I hope the U.S. will reform programs to offer immigrants and refugees asylum, so they can, like me, strive and thrive with integrity. I hope 2022 will bring back the humanity and integrity that the United States has always been known for.

Substance Leadership is Serving

Writing *Walk Toward the Rising Sun* helped me to express myself. In searching my thoughts, I found out that I am driven by history. For the past five years, I was a Goodwill Ambassador to UNHCR and now sit on the board of the Norwegian Refugee Council, USA office. My core goals remain the same: to serve humanity in whichever way I can, and for everyone to be given an opportunity.

MISSISSIPPI GODDAM AND THE HIGH PRIESTESS OF SOUL

by Ja'Ron Eames

I was there. At the legendary *Village Gate* on the corner of Thompson and Bleecker Streets in Greenwich Village, New York. It was 1985 and I'd come to see *The High Priestess of Soul*, Nina Simone. I've never forgotten that year. I still remember it to this day. It was the year I got sober. Drinking a half gallon of vodka—for many years, no less—put me in a straitjacket in the nuthouse. Getting sober has thus always been on my mind.

The Gate, as it was called back in the day, boasted some of the most important names in the history of music. In the 1960s, one could listen to Miles, Monk, Coltrane, Oscar Peterson, Dizzy, Errol Garner, every single one of them, for only $2.50. Even Aretha Franklin and Jimi Hendrix eventually came to *The Gate*.

Art D'Lugoff was the owner, and I got to know him well. When I interviewed him for my book *Historical Jazz Conversations*, he told me so many wonderful stories (Nat Hentoff, by the way, a syndicated columnist for *The Village Voice*, wrote the introduction to that book). Art had, in fact, managed Nina Simone for about a year. He said it was primarily for his own self-defense. She was great talent, but a bit *mashuga*; crazy, that is. We both laughed at that one.

Art also told me that Nina was one of the most significant improvisors in jazz. She took plenty of risks—and did so many things—that most singers wouldn't even consider. I really liked Art and thought that he was such a good man. He even shut down *The Gate* in March of 1965 so he could join Langston Hughes and Nina in the *Selma to Montgomery Marches* that were led by Martin Luther King.

I was fortunate enough to have seen Ms. Simone at least a few times. Besides *The Gate*, I also saw her in 1985 at the *Blue Note*, which was in Greenwich Village too. But she was drunk. In fact, she came on stage with a bottle of Champagne. She ranted and raved about life, then sat down at the piano and held court.

You could hear a pin drop when she performed her classic songs: "Mississippi Goddamn", "I Love You Porgy", "To be Young, Gifted, and Black" and "I Wish I Knew How it Would Feel to be Free". The latter was written by my friend Dr. Billy Taylor in 1963. It was originally titled "I Wish I Knew".

Hearing this magnificent lady play piano was a sheer delight. An unforgettable experience, to tell the truth. I also saw one of her last performances at Carnegie Hall in 2001. Some people are born with mental illness, but one's surroundings, especially in her case, pushed her over the edge.

Nina Simone couldn't do Broadway or Hollywood movies or become a great classical composer. That was reserved for the American beauty version of a female musician. But the world will never forget her magic. She was a genius at the piano and had a brilliant voice. She's also remembered, unfortunately, for her on-stage antics. The outbursts of rage and anger; after her fame shot to the outer limits, she attacked anyone and everyone, especially whites, who made up the majority of her audiences.

Why was Nina Simone so angry? When she was 12 years old, living in North Carolina, she gave a classical recital. It was her concert debut. The year was 1945. Her proud parents sat in the front row. They were, however, forced to move to the back of the hall so that their seats could be given to whites. That twelve-year-old girl then refused to perform until her parents were returned to their original seats. Which they did.

Now that's 'chutzpah.' But this bitter pill of racism followed her like a shadow everywhere she went. A civil rights' soul had then been born.

MEETING HIS HOLINESS THE DALAI LAMA

by Vincent Esaldi

When I was a senior at Seton Hall High School, I applied to Villanova University and was accepted with one caveat. There was no room in the dorms, and I would have to live off campus, something my parents did not want to see happen. We were told that if I attended their new Augustinians school, Biscayne College in North Miami, Florida for one year and did well, I could transfer back to Villanova with a room for me to live on campus (their reasoning was that many freshmen on campus leave, thus opening up the housing availability). They told this to a few others that indeed did transfer back after their first year at Biscayne. My parents thought it was a good idea, especially since I had an aunt, uncle, and two cousins living close by to the college.

Biscayne College came about when the Bishop of Miami offered 500 acres to the Augustinians who had just been thrown out of Cuba and lost their school there, the University of Villanueva. Their non-religious professors had also fled Cuba and they worked at any job they could get. After the school was established, they were invited to resume their teaching positions. For example, my Biology professor went from being a respectable professor of Oceanology in Cuba to working in a 7/11 in Miami, and back teaching again at Biscayne. And he wasn't the only professor I had who followed this path. Their stories of "it can't happen here and their swift exit from Cuba with just the clothes on their back" remain with me today, especially considering how we can lose our democracy in the U.S. after 2024. I digress.

My first year at this tiny sandlot college was terrific. Not only did I do well with my marks, I was also a big fish in a small pond, serving as the editor of the school newspaper, the secretary/treasurer in the all school council, and as the entertainment chairman. And then there was the off-campus activities– beach, beach, beach; seeing Ike, Tina Turner, Diana Ross (I still have her autograph), the Supremes at the Big Hotel shows on the Miami Strip, and shopping at the biggest mall I had ever seen, plus visiting South Beach before it's major transition (as a student I served on a committee to make the South Beach buildings as landmarks, to prevent them from being demolished). Dog races, horse races, AND Burger King within walking distance to our school (I was so in love with Burger King at the time. When I returned back to NJ, I tried to convince my relatives in the food industry to look into getting a Burger King franchise...at that time there were only 3 in the whole state of New Jersey).

Biscayne was a very small, new Catholic college for men (I was one of the third graduating class). We socialized with and could take classes at the girls' school, Barry College, not far away. I was in My Fair Lady at Barry College and took art classes with a nun, Sister Mary Joseph, affectionately known as Smidge. SMJ, who eventually introduced me to a girl, Weasie, who I almost married, (yes, I said married, obviously before I came to appreciate PINK crayons). I did not transfer back to Villanova.

During my senior year at Biscayne, I served as Cultural Chairman, in charge of bringing in speakers from time to time. I contacted a speaker's bureau and arranged for several speakers, but the one I remember most was bringing the Dalai Lama to a small Catholic College. It was his first time speaking in America. In his contract, we were to pick him up at the airport, drive to our school, and then afterwards someone would pick him up going to his next destination. I sent my friend Steve who had a convertible. On their way back from the airport, Steve took the Palmetto Expressway which permitted cars to travel at 80 or 90 miles an hour. I'm not sure what speed they were going but it was fast enough to have the Dalai Lama's robe flying around as they sped along. Steve said he laughed and laughed the whole trip. When he arrived, and I had a chance to meet him, he was still laughing that distinctive laugh that we hear even today. I don't remember much of what he said and I didn't have a picture taken with him. When I think of it now, I just think "WOW!" I actually met His Holiness, the Dalai Lama. By the way, someone did come to pick up the Dalai Lama, but it seemed he would have rather had another "fast" ride in my friend's convertible! I'm still laughing about that!

REMEMBRANCES FROM THE MISSISSIPPI COTTON FIELDS AND BEYOND

by Larry Evans

Walk with me Lord
Walk with me
While I'm on this tedious journey
I want Jesus to walk with me.

That was my maternal grandmother's, Eula Hall Evans, favorite song. She always sang it, especially when she "tended her flower bed," which grew beautiful roses that decorated the entrance of the front yard archway. Grandma, affectionately called "ToMama" by her grandchildren, was married to John Alexander Evans (Papa) for sixty-two years. These two extraordinary people were born in 1892 in Scott County, Mississippi. They had fourteen children and over forty-six grandchildren. My mother Lena Leo and her twin sister Rena Cleo, known as the "Evans Twins," were the youngest siblings. During the Great Migration, they graduated high school in 1945 and joined Uncle Henry in Chicago.

IN THE BEGINNING

I am a product of the American South. Chicago-born, Mississippi-bred. I had the best of both worlds. It began when I was five-months old. After making arrangements with my mother, my grandmother, and Aunt Mary took the Illinois Central Railroad to Chicago, headed to Milwaukee where I was staying with Aunt Elizabeth. My grandmother brought me back to Mississippi where she and Papa raised me and three of my first cousins; Annie Glory, Frazier (Peewee), and John Henry (Spook). We grew up like brothers and sisters. We called Grandma, "Mama," and our grandfather, "Papa." I was the youngest of the four. Annie Glory, who was a registered nurse, was smart and had the most beautiful smile and warm demeanor. She died four days following her twenty-eighth birthday. Frazier was easy going and laid back. Although small in stature, he was a force to be reckoned with whenever he got all riled up. He was my protector. We were known in the community as John and Eula Evans' grand boys, "Punto" (that's me) and "Peewee." I didn't see much of John Henry, who was much older. He would often stay with his biological parents–with his father in Louisiana or with his mother in Mississippi.

THE RURAL SOUTH

Some people might think that most Southern black folks grew up on a farm, or somewhere in the boondocks and backwoods. A lot of us were actually raised in small towns. There is the rural South and the urban South. I grew up in the rural community of Hillsboro, Mississippi (population 1,200), on a dirt road in a six-room wooden house that Papa built. There is nothing like the sound of rain on a tin roof. We called it "good sleeping weather." There were no stop lights. The only stores were Paul Chambers, Super Store, and Snowdie Chambers Convenience Store. I loved those Oscar Myers wieners, bologna, the Stage Plank cookies, green apple candy from Paul Chambers, and Miss Betsy's ice cream cones from Snowdie's. The nearest town is seven miles away in Forest (population 6,000), located between Meridian and Jackson, the state's capital and largest city. Today, my childhood memories reside on Evans Lane, named officially in honor of my family.

MISSISSIPPI LARRY

When I tell my friends about my upbringing on a farm in Mississippi, many of them look at me in disbelief as if I'm making up coming of age stories about growing up in the Deep South. The truth is–I am a bonafide country boy. My nickname at my church in Harlem, Canaan Baptist Church of Christ, is "Mississippi Larry," a name given to me by the former Senior Pastor, the late Dr. Rev. Wyatt Tee Walker. I am a proud Mississippian.

LIFE ON THE FARM

So many childhood memories: walking barefoot, picking cotton for two cents a pound, riding with Papa in a mule drawn wagon to the cotton gin, going fishing and blackberry picking, cutting bean poles, getting my haircut with manual clippers, watching cartoons on Saturday mornings (loved The Flintstones), catching butterflies and lightning bugs, Aunt Annie Bell dipping snuff and Papa smoking Prince Albert cigars and chewing tobacco, Aunt Ruby sharing family history, watching Mama quilt (I still have one of her quilts), keeping warm by the fireplace during those cold winters, roasting sweet potatoes in the fireplace, my cousins visiting from Up North and experiencing country life for the first time, tending the tadpoles before they turned into frogs, swimming in the muddy ponds, running whenever I saw a snake, shooting slingshots, bow and arrow, and BB gun, watching the sitcom *Amos 'n' Andy*, getting our first telephone, which was a party line shared with other families who would often eavesdrop on our conversations.

We used the outhouse toilet and bathed in a tin tub before we got an indoor bathroom. I remember those hot days when I would bring Papa ice cold water as he plowed the crops with our mules, Slick and Bill; those obligatory morning and evening chores of milking the cows (who also had names), marveling at how Mama would ring the neck of a chicken, or simply chop off their neck with a hatchet. The poor chickens would jump around with their head separated from the rest of their body. Their ultimate death led them straight into the skillet. That fried chicken was quite tasty with collard greens, potato salad, Kool-Aid, sweet potato pie, homemade cornbread made with buttermilk, and sometimes hot water cornbread. My favorite supper time meal was "buttermilk and cornbread" mixed together. That served as my imaginary cereal. I never cared too much for flapjacks (pancakes), chicken, and dumplings. A typical breakfast was molasses syrup mixed with butter, homemade biscuits, fresh bacon, and buttermilk. A special Sunday breakfast would consist of fried chicken or fish, biscuits, rice (with sugar and butter), and buttermilk or fresh well water. Mama would churn the fresh whole (sweet) milk from the cows to make butter. I looked forward to those special family nights when we gathered around to eat stovetop popcorn or roasted peanuts while watching shows on our black and white television set. I loved the family drama, *The Waltons*. I was the Black John Boy. We would get so excited whenever we saw someone who looked like us on television.

Remembrances of Christmas waking up with excitement to see what Santa Claus (my mother) sent me from Chicago. I used to think that Santa traveled all the way from the North Pole and came down our chimney to deliver our gifts on my wish list. Even though snow was not a common occurrence in Mississippi, I recall those rare occasions when we made snow ice cream by adding a touch of vanilla extract. It never snowed enough to make a snowman.

My first cousin Ezell and I were partners in crime. Keeping out of mischief was not on our agenda. Ezell lived a stone's throw away from us across the cornfield. We would secretly play Deuces Wild card games, drink MD 20/20, and Strawberry Hill Boone's Farm wine. Such unholy activities were strictly forbidden in the Evans household. If you were caught, Mama would use a freshly cut switch from the hedge bush and give us one of those down home stinging love-whippings. Today, that kind of parental discipline might be considered child abuse. During the "it takes a village to raise a child" era, it was customary for elders to chastise children for misbehaving. Back-talking and rolling your eyes at elders were another recipe for punishment. The elders would "set you straight" first, and THEN tell your parents, who would also have a few words, or two, with you.

PIG LICKIN' GOOD!

I remember slopping the pigs that would one day be slaughtered by Papa's shotgun on Hog Killing Day. Neighbors would gather around to witness this big event. What was once a precious domesticated animal now provided some scrumptious meals: fresh bacon, fatback meat, pork chops, ribs, ham hocks, pig ears, pig brains, pig tails, pig feet, pig liver, hog head souse, and crackling bread. We didn't need Crisco oil because Mama cooked with lard (fat) from the hog. And who can forget those smelly chitterlings? I watched as Mama cleaned those hog guts.

ANIMAL HOUSE RULES

Our main pets were cats and dogs. The cats were permitted in-house on one condition: they must feed themselves by devouring our unwanted house guests. We had well fed and healthy looking cats. Buying cat food was not an option. Dogs were not allowed in the house.

LET'S GO TO CHURCH!

I grew up in Sylvester United Methodist Church, Mama's home church, about a fifteen-minute walk from our house. Papa was a member of Lone Pilgrim Missionary Baptist Church. You had to drive there. I remember the proper way of dismissing oneself in church was to walk with a slight tip-toe with head held down and one finger pointed in the air. I enjoyed teaching Sunday school and singing in the choir. I was always uncomfortable attending those highly emotional funerals. I would dream about it for days. *Precious Lord* and *Jesus Keep Me Near the Cross* were popular hymns at Homegoing services. After a fiery and spirit-filled eulogy, the congregation would view the body one last time. The heart wrenching crying and wailing began when it was time for the family to take one last look at their loved one. You would often hear comments after the service such as, "Lawd, they looked jest like themselves," "Chile, I thought she was gonna fall over in the casket," "Girl, who was that woman who showed out at Unc's funeral? I ain't never seen her before. Hmm, well I heard she was….well, you didn't hear from me."

Mama would attend her monthly Eastern Star meetings and Papa would go to his Masonic meetings. Those traditional annual church revivals held in August and September were one of the most anticipated events of the year. Mama, along with several families, would prepare meals for those revivals, aka "the meetings." People would come from Up North–mainly Chicago and Milwaukee–to attend, driving their fancy cars and wearing their expensive-looking clothes.

I loved hearing those quartets at church concerts and listening to live gospel music on the local Radio Station WMAG every Sunday morning. My cousins and I formed our own singing group called "The Harmonizing Cousins." Mama made sure that I remained connected with my paternal grandparents, James and Elnora Ross, who lived several miles away. I enjoyed my occasional visits with them. How I loved Grandpa James' beautiful baritone voice when he sang *Hold to God's Unchanging Hands.* My father, Lewis Charles (LC) Ross, who lived in Milwaukee, was a big Green Bay Packers fan. We grew very close when I became an adult. Ironically, I was at my dad's and my mother's bedside when they passed away in Milwaukee and Chicago, respectively.

THE SOCIAL SCENE

People were ready to party hard on Friday and Saturday nights after working hard all week. Some of those same people would be on the front row in church on Sunday. Popular juke joints were the Chicken Shack and TJ's in Hillsboro, and Soul City in Forest. Hillsboro was also home of the Dale Teen Center. Baseball games were usually held on weekends in Hillsboro, especially when our men and women team played the Choctaws.

EASTER TIME

I remember reciting those Easter speeches dressed in my Sunday best that my mother sent from Chicago. I would stand proudly and recite with a dramatic flair,

> *What you looking at me for?*
> *I didn't come to stay*
> *I come to let you know*
> *Today is Easter day.*

I can still hear all of the applause. People were commenting, "Aw, you did good baby."

WHO NEEDS A GROCERY STORE?

Remembrances of those pecan, fig, peach, plum, apples, and pear trees, Mr. Clifton's apple tree, the corn field, hickory nuts, persimmons, sweet potatoes, peanuts, strawberries, muscadines, cantaloupes, watermelons, tomatoes, lettuce, cucumbers, cabbage, mustard, collards, spinach, turnips, rutabagas, white potatoes, butter beans, string beans, carrots, black eyed peas, and more. Canning and preserving fruits and vegetables were one of Mama's many specialties. Our deep freezer was always full. Papa made molasses and sorghum syrup from the tasty cane juice at our sugar cane mill. Mama baked her delectable molasses tea cakes that were popularly known in the neighborhood as "Mama Eula's Tea Cakes.

UP NORTH, DOWN SOUTH – A WORLD APART

It's quite possible to experience culture shock when visiting different parts of the United States. Whenever I would spend summers up north in Chicago with my mother, I would pick up one of those short lived weekend accents. Being exposed to Broadway plays that were touring in Chicago solidified my desire to become an actor. Chicago opened up a whole new world for me.

Of course, when my summer vacations ended, I had to return to familiar surroundings in the Jim Crow South. The days of watching movies at the Capitol Theatre on 79th and South Halsted were over. I had to go back to sitting in the colored section in the balcony at the Town Movie Theatre in Forest, Mississippi. We would throw popcorn on the whites who sat downstairs in the "good section." Even though the signs were eventually removed, "Colored Only" and "White Only" signage were the norm in most public facilities in Mississippi.

SCHOOL DAYS

Remembrances of riding that yellow school bus and playing cornet in the band in junior high. I am reminded of those dedicated teachers during my first eight years at the all Black E.T. Hawkins High School–pre-integration. Our teachers made us feel that we mattered. Public schools in Mississippi were officially integrated in 1970. I remember spending my high school years in the newly integrated school system before entering my beloved alma mater Jackson State University to study theater. During those four wonderful years, I developed an appreciation for the craft of acting, and was also initiated into the brotherhood of Phi Beta Sigma Fraternity, Inc. I also studied theater at the University of Michigan.

SO, YOU'VE BEEN ON TELEVISION?

Papa was a farmer who owned a lot of land. With my vivid imagination, I would always go to my "special place" where I would create numerous characters in my head. All of these memories and experiences paved my way to the entertainment industry.

From the cotton fields of Mississippi, this country boy from Hillsboro was blessed to perform on stages across the country, European gospel tours, and even appeared in a few daytime television serials and films. My family was more excited than I was whenever they caught a glimpse of me on one of their "stories" (soap operas). I felt like a local celebrity of sorts. Folks would say things like, "Ooh, I saw you on my Story, sittin' up there in that jury box!" Some of the popular soap operas in my community were *Another World* and *As the World Turns*. People would become so engrossed in the story and would talk about the characters as if they were talking about a real life friend. "Girl, did you hear what Erica did?" "I told ya that wasn't his baby. Chile, I can't wait til tomorrow." The storyline would drag on endlessly.

Whenever I perform onstage, I am reminded how my childhood special place enabled me to create multiple characters in my mind. My "special place" may be in a different locale, but my vivid memories and imagination are infinite.

THE LAST MILE OF THE WAY

When I've gone the last mile of the way
I shall rest at the close of the day
Lord, I shall see the great king in all his beauty
When I've gone the last mile of the way

Friday, December 28, 1973 at 2:30PM is forever etched in my mind. It was my first time witnessing a death. Papa, who had suffered a stroke years prior, made his transition just three days after Christmas. I was a senior in high school. On the day of his death, Papa and I took a walk to the fields. I can still see the image of him looking over the farmland–the land that fed three generations of his people.

Mama got her heavenly wings two weeks before my college graduation, after suffering a stroke and battling dementia. I visited her the week before her passing. I received a call a few days later that Mama (ToMama) had gone home to glory.

I am deeply grateful that Mama took that twelve hour plus train ride one winter day in 1957, and brought this country boy to Mississippi where she and Papa shaped me into the person I am today. I am who I am because of a sense of family and community that was instilled in me at a very young age.

No matter where I may roam, or wherever my journey takes me, Hillsboro/Forest, Mississippi will always be home.

While I'm on this tedious journey, I want Jesus to walk with me.

MY 65TH YEAR ON THE PLANET
by Dale Fielder

As I reached my 65th year on the planet, I am at the realization of less time ahead than behind me. I find myself thinking quite a bit about death and making preparations for the new life to come. Wrestling with all the feelings of failure in all the things I wanted to have accomplished by now, I am brought back to seeing all the goodness I have witnessed on Earth in these 65 years. Starting with the unconditional love from my parents–I was a surprise baby, born after raising my siblings and they were in their fifties. I knew without doubt I was conceived in Love and was bathed in it for the remaining 32 years of the 58 years they walked this Earth in marriage. Through their example, I have learned that no matter what challenges, difficulties, and disappointments I created, they would still love me, and I experienced how that always sustained me.

What I have learned about life comes down to one powerful point: that throughout all the Universes, no matter what time or dimension, known or unknown, **there is only <u>Good</u>**. Goodness is the essential nature of the Universe. There is no such thing as "badness" or evil. These are created by humans: miscreations or distortions of the true essence of universal life which in human terms can be described as *Divine Love*. "Goodness" has always been, as God has "always been." Fear came later and was also created by human beings. Fear is not inherent in Life Itself. It was a result of us using the *Divine Life Force* from a place of selfishness, etc.

One of the principles I live my life by is ***"Fear is a temporary loss of confidence in the inherent goodness of life."*** I try to remind myself of this every day. What I have learned is that I have a soul that gives my life animation, gives me the ability to 'exist' on earth, and in the physical realm. This soul (for want of a better term) is a *Divine Spirit* that lives within me that comes from my father/mother God, whom I will henceforth refer to as The Creator. This 'spark' of the Creator's body or essence was given to all beings throughout the Multi Universes. I learned to respect the fact that a similar *Divine Spirit* lives in another, even when they do not realize it, and is creating chaos or evil constantly through their actions in the outer world. This led me to learn that what occurs in my life that I perceive as challenge or as "badness" is a direct result of my own actions and miscreations. I have learned through my spiritual practice that to further evolve and grow, it was not enough to merely realize and understand that fact, but my God-given duty was to also clear my miscreations. How? By focusing on *The Light* which brings feelings of "goodness" within myself and then outward (that is the nature of Love, in that it seeks to expand). This "feeling goodness" began to remove the feelings of fear, where I could now see the inherent goodness of Life in any situation. Using my spiritual practice of holding my miscreations in the light of the Violet Flame, I can transmute my miscreations back to their original state of God's Infinite Perfection.

This is the knowledge I have learned through 65 years of seeking answers. That *Light, Goodness*, and *Love* are supremely spiritual and *Divine*. They come from the Creator and are how we are intended to walk the earth. By their very nature, they seek expansion. In other words, goodness is exponential and is why Christ's only commandment was to "*serve your fellow man through Love.*" This became The Golden Rule to do unto others as you wish to be done for self. When you give to another without thought of return, what is returned to you is "tenfold" and exponential. For me this is The Way to live this life; in Love with it all.

I DIDN'T REALIZE WHAT I'D MISSED UNTIL I FOUND IT

by Sunya W. Falayan

The COVID pandemic marked a seismic shift in the world, how we related to one another, made us reevaluate our usage of resources, how we viewed work; and perhaps most importantly, allowed us to think about who we were as people. Being the textbook introvert, I reveled in the time alone—swimming and gliding in and among my own thoughts. I was able to process the time of great sadness and loss for many— with gratitude and appreciation. As a result of my endless musing, I decided to pursue something I had been considering for a number of years but had not prioritized it. For that reason, I had not taken any action or made any moves toward making it happen: I decided to pursue an artist's residency in Mexico that I had heard about 5 years prior. Little did I know that decision would lead to a seismic shift in my own life.

I had been reevaluating my relationship with work; the effects of capitalistic expectations on my body, mind, spirit, and time, for a number of years. As a twice divorced mother of two, and a domestic violence thriver, I was now at retirement age with no egg in the nest, and no retirement portfolio. Bereft of the financial assets that would have been mine if I had been able to hold onto my homes. What I did have was a modicum of freedom and a strong sense of self: my children were now grown, no financial obligations to my grandchildren. I was free of the sacred responsibility of taking care of my mother (my beautiful and inspirational mother had advanced Parkinson's Disease and she was my sole responsibility for the final 5 years of her life). I had come to the end of my divine placement at a historically Black college, where I had volunteered 20-30 hours a week for at least 7 years (another Divine Assignment), and I knew my assignment was coming to a close. For the first time in my life since I was 21, I had no obligations of time to other people. This was wholly and completely MY TIME!

The joy and excitement was palpable. It was time to make a move!

One of the benefits of working through the trauma of divorce was the development of an artistic practice in dual tracks: I already played the flute, and over the years I learned African drums and dance. I also learned to become a textile surface designer. These activities and pursuits were also my own therapy, and over the years I continued to invest in those skills. I also realized that making the decision to work part-time was one of the ways I helped cultivate joy in my life and parenting. It allowed me to pursue my art practice, homeschool my youngest child, to develop a creative way of thinking about my time, and resources. So, I gathered my materials, applied for the residency in Mexico, and released my faith!

I arrived in Chapala, Mexico in June of 2021 and immediately fell in love! I arrived at night, but when I went outside the next morning, I felt as if I had stepped into a technicolor movie. (I think about the scene in the Wizard of Oz, when Dorothy leaves the black and white scenery and steps into Oz). I loved the air, the singing birds, the cobblestone streets, the street food, the vendor's stalls, the tapestries, weavings, cacophony of sights, colors and sounds. I dived into my work, blueing my hands, the tarp and outdoor spaces where I worked. I walked next to the healing powers of Lake Chapala, and found myself in the land, food, culture, and people. There is an African presence hidden in plain sight throughout Mexico. The Indigenous cultures and history are humanity centered. People are generally kind, welcoming, and the culture is familial and helpful. I met beautiful people from around the world who welcomed me into their communities. People saw beauty in my gifts, welcomed me as family, and encouraged me to let go. So, I began to let go of the programming I had been born into: a culture of hustle, grind, work, little rest, and uneven sleep. Even though I worked part-time, I was still programmed to work at something all the time. I began to realize how exhausted I was not only from my own work, but from my mother, grandmother, and the expectation of Black women to work, to care and be responsible for making everything happen. I didn't realize what I was missing until I found it, and I found it in Mexico: the peace, joy, freedom, color, and healing I didn't realize I needed. Before my residency was up in August, I had secured an apartment in Mexico, and made plans to move. It happened in December of 2021.

In this process, I experienced a reevaluation of my spiritual practice, as well as a renewed and deepened faith. My faith and imagination have always been expansive, but I have experienced a growth and security within myself that has allowed me to envision new ways of making income that are consistent with my values. This allowed me to move beyond fears I had around my security. Sometimes we have to move our minds, bodies, expectations, and perhaps the setting we're in— to experience the abundance God has for us. To live in joy, peace, healing, and love is our birthright. The more we avail ourselves of the good around us and in us, we can experience the power of returning that good to others, creating powerful change beyond measure. God is good, in joy, and the gratitude I move!

FOUR YEARS TO FIGURE IT OUT

by Owen Gambill

Finally, college graduation. I accomplished what I've been working towards for almost all of my life. Through all of the ups and downs, the Zoom classes due to the COVID-19 pandemic, and the countless all-nighters filled with work and studying, I can now call myself a college graduate. But what's next? As I enter the so-called real world, and while I still do feel uneasy about the future, it's amazing to think how far I have come since I started college four years ago.

While I ended college with a degree in Film and Media Studies, I originally started out as an Economics major for the first two years. It was agonizing, spending this precious time working towards something I was not energized by. I was pretending to be someone that I was not, for the sake of a "reliable" or "steady" career. It took a supportive family and a group of friends to help me realize my true passion and what I wanted to work toward. Recently, I've been kicking myself for wasting those two years of my life on something that I will never benefit from, but I've recently been able to find a newfound appreciation for that time.

I've been told that college is a time to figure out what you DON'T want to do in life, and I've always used that as an excuse for not knowing what the future holds. I was giving myself so many reasons to not switch to a film major and stay in economics until I came back to that idea. While it was a decision filled with uncertainty, switching my major and focusing on my passion was the best thing I could have ever done.

Over the past couple of years, I have been able to work on a number of different documentaries and narrative films that have made me into the person I am today. I was fortunate enough to help document and film the University of Pittsburgh's Center for Vaccine Research as they worked to defeat the COVID-19 virus. Another amazing documentary I am currently working on is following the restoration of the childhood home of Pulitzer Prize-winning playwright and Pittsburgh native, August Wilson. (I actually met Reverend Melony McGant at the grand opening of the August Wilson house in August of 2022). August Wilson, originally named Frederick Kittle, grew up in the historic Hill District, which was Wilson's primary inspiration for his plays. Wilson wrote The American Century Cycle, a series of ten plays that chart the African American experience throughout the 20th century. Through this project, I have been able to learn so much from the residents of the Hill District and the life that August Wilson led.

Finally, in order to graduate with a film major, one must create a short film that can be entered into festivals and used in your portfolio. For this final assignment, I collaborated with my long-time best friend, creative collaborator, and fellow Pitt grad, Aditi Sridhar. Aditi wrote a beautiful screenplay, *Aloo Poori*, that follows the story of a mother and daughter during their last day of living together in a small town in Western Pennsylvania. *Aloo Poori* roots itself unapologetically in South Asian culture, addressing the prevalent stigmas surrounding mental illness in the South Asian community. Working together on this project with Aditi enabled me to learn so much about a culture that I had previously not known much about, making it the most meaningful and enjoyable project that I have ever been a part of.

If it weren't for those first two years of college, when I was figuring out what I didn't want to do, I would not have been able to be a part of such beautiful projects and films that inspire me to be the human being that I am today.

GENESIS
by Rev. Dr. Sedrick Gardner

Amplified Bible Genesis 1:31

"God saw everything that He had made, and behold, it was good. He validated it completely. There was evening and morning, a sixth day."

This scripture from Genesis is the first thing that comes to mind when I think of "good is powerful beyond measure." After all everything that was created by God was deemed good and, in some interpretations, good and very good. That is the premise and the principle of it all. So anything that I deem as other than that, or bad, is simply my interpretation of what is deemed by God as good.

The interesting point to this scripture is that there was also night and day within this creation. Hence, I gather why our perspectives can be both good & bad based on what we experience and how we view it. So even within God's goodness, things may be perceived as darkness and light.

The good thing is that we know anytime there is darkness, it disappears when light is introduced. It stands without saying that light is the most powerful energy. Scripture also tells us that we cannot worship two deities simultaneously. This simply means that we must make a decision to align with lightness or darkness. Lightness being the more powerful energy, it stands to reason that it should always and in all ways be our aim. I've been asked more than once if God is good all the time. And if so, then why is there so much bad that I see in the world? At those times it is challenging to convince the person that they are not seeing bad. What I usually retort in saying is that at some point, something has happened to you that at the time of occurrence seemed to be the worst thing possible. After time and space away from that situation, and witnessing later, it catapulted you into a better place. Would you still deem it as the worst thing in the world, or the thing that made you move to a better place? Usually, they say I'm glad I'm in the place I am now, and no longer in the place I viewed as bad.

This is the reason that our question to God should not be "why, why me, or why now God?" The "why" is too big for our brain to comprehend at the moment. It often takes time to figure out the why. The more appropriate question to God at the moment is: "What is the lesson in this?" You can usually figure out this question with deep contemplation and recognition of repeating patterns. This question gets you to focus on the goodness and the light of the lesson being taught. This lesson usually comes to teach you about different people and circumstances in a noticeable pattern that can be discerned with honest contemplation.

Jesus implored us to love our enemies and do good for those that may persecute us. At first glance this seems like absolute craziness and weakness. The truth is that it is meekness at its best alchemy. Because meekness is translated as "not sweating the small stuff," and reserving your energy for when it's really needed for the major storms. If you engage in every battle, take on every argument, your energy will be depleted when it is necessary to tackle the major obstacles of life.

Loving your enemies changes your thoughts about them, and the separation is eliminated in your mind. Doing good acts and kind gestures for them will change their image of you in their minds. Eventually, they will cease to see you as an enemy with your continued kind deeds. This is the only act that can free the energy from darkness to light. Goodness is powerful beyond measure.

Here is the most challenging lesson to discern. No one is against you. All the difficult situations and people in your life are what your soul has drawn to you to learn the lessons that it knows you need for your growth. This is how you expand your consciousness. If you perceive them all as a friend that has come to help you grow towards expanding your consciousness, you will begin to learn the lessons of your soul's unfoldment moving to the next classroom level more expediently. After all, with all that is going on in the world these days, who has time for remedial learning and not advancing to the next classroom?

I am willing to learn the lessons that my soul is drawing to me at every moment with courage, conviction, and conviviality. I call it all good. I name it all good. I experience it as all good because I chose light as my principle. Light removes darkness and gives me insights. Insights allow me to intuitively find my way back towards light regardless of what happens outside of me. I have found productive things to do in the night time, one of them being to sleep through it. When I awaken I know the next day will bring light. I can take the perceived dark places of my life and find productive things to do as I call forth light. And there will be light, just like in the beginning when God first called it forth. Light was allowed to manifest, which meant that it already existed in the invisible void of God. I allow light today because good really is powerful beyond measure.

MY DISCOVERY OF HARLEM
by James Gillard

"Jim, get upstairs now, it's getting late."

That was the familiar voice of my mother reminding me of the uneasy balance of giving your child space, but also setting parameters. It was the mid-70s and it was a time that represented friendships, new discoveries, and danger—all intertwined in this village of Harlem. Long gone was the Renaissance Era. Harlem was in a time of economic woe reflected in many urban spaces throughout the country. Heroine, dilapidated buildings, poverty, and crime became all too familiar sights in the community.

At the time I didn't understand the magnificence of this place, it was just home to me. Yes, there were names I heard in my journeys to school. Names like Langston, Billie, Baldwin, and X. But that wasn't the Harlem I could touch or feel, not as of yet.

My Harlem experience came from how others viewed me. Like the times when I would visit family in the South and they could sense something about me, slightly different. Swagger, a Harlem swagger that was unbeknownst to me. The way I talked, walked, or just observed. They would always say, "Yeah, that my cousin from NY, Harlem." So, in a confident way, I didn't need to know the history. In some way, I felt as if I was making history—just because of this place Harlem.

Mind you, I grew up in Lincoln Projects on 135th and Madison. My world at the time was about as far as four avenues—Park, Madison, 5th, and Lenox. It was a concrete jungle filled with about 15 buildings. Within that space I saw life, experienced love, played ball, and at times, experienced sheer terror. In essence, this was my Harlem; filled with soulful encounters with the elders who reminded us of the blocks that Malcolm walked, men and women who could party hard the night before, and still get up and go to work. Then there was the stark reality of innocently playing on a street corner that was next to the same spot where a dead brother or sister lay. Yes, it was a Harlem that was rich with black life; good, bad, and indifferent.

I guess this is why Racism was a distant thought. My life didn't consist of feeling oppressed or unworthy. In some ways Harlem sheltered us from the world outside of 110th Street. I encountered few white people unless they were teachers at my elementary school or a salesperson. As I stated, this was a Harlem to me that was only about 4 avenues.

In my early teens my world expanded (7th and 8th Avenues), and things soon changed. I could travel, venture out beyond my 135th home, and 125th to 155th became my new home. I went from catching bees and playing scalies, shooting the dozens, to chasing girls and hanging out a bit later. Really much later—"Sorry mommy." At about this time in life those early names of those voices from years past began to come to existence to me in different ways. Langston, the great poet laureate of Harlem's words, was introduced to me and I listened. His work lead me to Baldwin and Wright. Suddenly the Harlem I had not known of became a lot more touchable. I still couldn't fathom the depth of this place.

Summer times changed and the street developed a rhythm. Young brothers were doing something new with music. Our local park became a gathering place for a concept that would bring about beauty, individuality, and a whole new creation that would change the way we view ourselves and the way we are viewed: HIP HOP.

It was the late 70s, the time of albums, microphones, and young brothers telling stories in rhyme. The block had changed. Hot peas and butter, Red rover, Johnny on the pole, and catching bees evolved into catching girls, dressing fly, rapping, and the only place that could showcase your new found style. It was the new neighborhood jam.

Jams in the park were full of life, break dancing, kangols, and girls. Girls loved hip hop, and this was our time. Stories were told about life and Harlem in rhyme. The Bronx was also feeling this new energy. Although hip hop started to flourish, Harlem's economic woes stayed the same. Desolate buildings and brownstones littered certain blocks, Reaganomics affected our programs of childcare, community centers, and numerous other social ills. Hip Hop reflected this shift with edgier lyrics. Materialism and the introduction of a little rock that destroyed the fabric of the black family.

Harlem has now become the poster child of what's wrong in America. An economic social disaster. But this was the opinion of outsiders. I delved into the short stories of Langston and began to read *The Autobiography of Malcolm X*. And amongst this turbulent backdrop, I fell more in love with Harlem.

The crack epidemic ravaged this historic community. It's been said that in the early 80s—mid-90s, more drugs came through Harlem than anywhere else. Urban legend, but as a youth growing up in Harlem, I had a drug dealer friend on about every corner. At this same time the city began to sell abandoned property (brownstones) for 1 dollar. There were some takers but not many. Although you could buy the property for a dollar, what was not told was how much you had to pay to get the property refurbished. This set in motion the introduction of a new population. A population which had laid in wait causing uneasiness to stir about amongst the native Harlemites. Politicians with hidden agendas didn't help the situation. Uncertainty filled the air and Harlem was introduced to a new word: gentrification. Harlem was headed for a second renaissance, one which consisted of economic vision, trimmed down, and sleeker culturally. Langston, Billie, Baldwin, and X became monuments of a distant past.

Harlem, at one time, was the Mecca of the black experience. It now is a village of status and economic focus. But I continued to study, document, and listen to the voices of this community. Voices that share stories of awe, pain and, oh yes, a style like no other.

As I continue on in my journey, my goal is to document these stories of the Harlemites who still reside here, and to continue to discover those voices who I only read about but now I experience. This is the continuous story of my discovery of Harlem.

REVOLUTION
by James Gillard

A special call to my young brothers and sisters

The world views us as Helpless, hopeless, unfocused, undisciplined, thugs, gangbangers, immature, lost, angry, arrogant, promiscuous, rude, scary, bullies, and the next generation. They label us as meaningless.

But what happens when the world views us as Helpful, hopeful, focused, disciplined, champions, independent, mature, secure, joyful, confident, polite, encouraging, self-assured, and the next generation?
Then we become World Changers.
IT'S REVOLUTION TIME!
Can anyone hear us? Is anyone listening?
We are the voices of Youth.
AND THIS IS OUR REVOLUTION. Not a revolution of taking back property, but taking back who we are. And letting the world see—that our revolution occurs in the mind.

The revolution is not about how you look, where you're from, or what you wear. It's about what you do, how you live,
And what you give.
The revolution is not about tats, braids, or weaves it's all about words, thoughts and deeds,
It's much more than just holding down the block It's about holding down your family,
It's about learning the truth.

The Revolution is me, I'm the proof
The Revolution is not about bottles guns or knives it's not about beats, samples or rhymes
It's about lives, ours, AND RIGHT NOW WE WANT TO LIVE, STOP THE VIOLENCE. Please listen.

DREAMING THE WORLD INTO BEING
by Sylvia Galbin

We are co-creators with spirit. We have the power to shape the world in many ways, both individually and collectively. Using this power consciously to create good is our sacred duty.

The tools for doing this are our intentions, words and, of course, actions. Words are powerful because they create. When we say "I do," a union of two lives is created. Words are used to create in the material world but, more importantly, words form our thoughts. The words we tell ourselves shape our beliefs, emotions, and actions. We can use words to create good, but our unconscious mind, which contains all our fears and imagined evil, is also hard at work shaping our world. Using our intention to consciously choose words & thoughts that will create good outcomes can change how we feel and also how things turn out. When many people do this, a force begins to exert, which can reshape our collective destiny.

Creating good takes work! We can replace unconscious thoughts with ones we choose. We can resist the messages of others and of our own minds that we're allowing unconscious fear to be pictured outside us in the world we are creating.

Yes, we can imagine a better world! If we observe our thoughts and the words we use both in our own minds and in the world, we can create good outcomes for ourselves and for future generations. In this way, we can harness a powerful force for good.

From "Flowers of Darkness" a collection of unpublished poems by Sylvia Golbin

NIGHTMARE

Like watching a bad dream recurring,
I stare fascinated,
as the fabric of my life unravels.
I slip through spaces in the weave
which the cold scissors of our anger cut
leaving bone and sinew showing
and the echo of a scream
piercing the silence of eternity.

Never before have I seen such roses:
(blood red plumes, lush in full promise of bloom).
And then the unseen thorn
and the red blood blooms on my finger
(surprise eclipsing fear)
I stand transfixed:
a trapped deer in the blue forest.

And then white sheets, cool sterility,
and the luxury of fear
as starch pure nurses hurry on their rounds
like dreams, bleached and dried out
In the morning sun.

Is this what we reached for,
nosing each other in the swirling realms of sleep
As dreamy blue rose petals
darted like swallows
on the horizons of our minds?

So come,
when morning tidies up
the rooms of night,
let's give her our quilt
and let her nimble fingers
mend its ragged edges with
the colorful cloth
of hope.

From "Music of the Heart" an anthology of unpublished poems by Sylvia Golbin

WISE WOMAN

We have lost the way.
We wise women.
We have forgotten the path to the well.

In the mists and twilight
She is waiting;
In the faces of our children
She is waiting;
In the shadows of our organizations
She is waiting
To emerge.

She is waiting to teach us once again
To be the guardians of earth;
To show us the path that is ours.

So let the tears flow
And the mountains roar!
She will be heard!
She will be recognized!

With the wisdom we will heal.
With the wisdom we will serve.
What a lot we have to learn.
So much resistance to overcome;
It is a Herculean effort or the simplest thing.
You decide.

Music has the remarkable power to bring people together, transcending cultural, social, and linguistic barriers. Musicians often use their craft to foster a sense of unity, harmony, and connection among individuals and communities. Through their compositions, performances, and collaborations, musicians can promote understanding, empathy, and togetherness.

The act of creating music itself is a collaborative process that requires musicians to work together, listen to one another, and synchronize their efforts. This collaborative spirit often extends beyond the stage or studio and can inspire unity among listeners and fans as well.

Particularly in the jazz genre, musicians frequently engage in improvisation and collective improvisation, where each individual contributes their unique musical ideas to create a cohesive whole. This process mirrors the ideals of unity and cooperation, demonstrating how different voices can come together harmoniously.

In 2019, I met Taiwanese Vibraphonist Chien Chien Lu while doing a tour in Europe with my friend and jazz trumpeter Jeremy Pelt. It seemed that we immediately clicked on a personal level. Night after night of concerts, I realized what an amazing talent Chien Chien was. We had the opportunity to have many conversations about music and realized that we shared musical vibes. I told her that she should make a record and let me produce it. Although Chien Chein didn't think she was ready to record, she trusted me to produce it and develop her sound. There were a lot of rehearsal sessions to find the right musicians for her music, and we did a lot of shows to figure out the overall vibe that we were going for. We recorded her debut album "The Path" in spring of 2020 and released it in September 2020. What started out as a musical relationship started to develop into a strong, trusting friendship as we discussed music and life equally.

Musicians faced unique challenges during the pandemic. It was no different for me. I was doing my best to figure out how to survive with no work and wondering what the future would be like. It was a challenging period and initially, I had no idea of what to do. For the first two months of the lockdown it seemed like I did a lot of cooking for the family and watched Netflix.

Finally, Chien Chien Lu and I had a phone conversation and decided to start practicing together. We would meet about 3 times a week to practice, which also led to writing and releasing new music. So many musicians were doing livestream shows so we decided to join the bandwagon. Chien Chien helped me transform my basement into a nightclub vibe and also built a stage in my backyard to do outdoor concerts. For these shows, we used musicians from Chien Chien's band and from my band which later would help to form our "Connected" band.

During this process, there were many things going on in the world. In addition to COVID-19 virus, there was the killing of George Floyd, the Black Lives Matter movement and an increase in Asian Hate Crimes. Chien Chien, being from Taiwan didn't really understand the race dynamic in the US. To be honest, it is also difficult for me to understand or explain to my children. We both questioned why police officers would unnecessarily kill a person just because he is Black, why are people attacking people just because they are Asian, and why there often appeared to be disharmony between Blacks and Asians.

The world seemed so divided. While writing and practicing, Chien Chien and I had so many conversations about the division in the world and tried to make sense of it all. We laughed, argued, and cried about things. It was a very emotional time for us both which transcended in the music we were writing. The two of us decided that the music we were creating had to have a purpose other than showing off our technique and virtuosity. Considering all the divisions in the world, we decided that we wanted to do a project that would help to unite people and cultures around the world.

Naming our band "Connected," it comes from our belief that we are all connected brothers and sisters regardless of race, religion, cultural background, sexual orientation, political association, etc. This is a project that stems from the love of mankind and is totally inclusive.

As we fast forward to July 2023, the band that we had created "Connected" was nominated for two Golden Melody awards (the Taiwanese version of the Grammys) for "Best Producer" and "Best Instrumental Album." We won the Golden Melody Award for the Best Instrumental Album!

Goodness is an energy that is contagious and spreads. It makes me happy and fulfilled to see and hear the response to our "Connected" project. The audiences are the most diverse I've seen for Jazz performances. Oftentimes there are people in the audience crying from emotion, thanking us for the messages in the music. For me, music is more than technique and virtuosity, it's about connecting people and letting them feel something. One of the greatest compliments that I receive as a musician is that my music made someone feel something.

My wife and I also try to model for our four children the importance of Goodness. We believe that Goodness, kindness and love makes everyone's life a more beautiful existence. As parents, it is our duty as human beings to do whatever we can to spread this goodness, and in turn we will also receive beautiful energy from the universe. Collaborating with Chien Chien Lu and the creation of "Connected" has shown us all that Good Is Powerful Beyond Measure!

I REMEMBER...
by Prof. Donald Muldrow Griffith

remember walking down a street in Chicago after school thinking, "I am certain I can do anything in the world, but I cannot figure out or decide what I should do or which direction I should pursue." My parents were always and my university buddies were sometimes encouraging people, demanding and supporting me on my journey to somewhere.

University time arrived and I went to fulfill entrance exams for admittance to Loyola University Chicago. The room was full of students applying, like myself, although I possessed a singular identity in the space. It did not matter!

A long time ago, I was crossing a downtown Chicago State St. intersection with my mother, Edith, and I asked her why was Daddy so demanding of me and seemingly passive with my sisters? My wonderful Mother, very nicely explained: "Your father is supporting and preparing you for your future. This is why he presents you with so many challenges!" I was quiet, but appreciative of her caring explanation.

In the examination room, as I flew through the pages, I experienced a light flash on the right side of my head. Suddenly, I realized what my parents had done for me! I could handle the questions on paper with ease, because of them! Their never ending demands for good grades, requiring reading and written reports annually during summer vacations, and for the remaining time during the day afterwards could be spent outside, playing with my school buddies! If I wanted Aunt Jemima pancakes when I went shopping with Daddy, I had to be able to pronounce the name, otherwise, no pancake mix. And on and on and on!

But the flash brought understanding, respect, and appreciation of my parents' determination to see myself and my sisters rise in knowledge and gradual understanding. Now, I am in university, but I still did not know what to do with myself! As usual, time marches on, although sometimes it seems to move in slow, step by step progress.

The university stumbles continued, through my lack of continual interest. After all, I was on the track team, with some of my track-school friends, and this was enjoyable. Much more so than classes! I learned lessons, but one especially stuck with me. I ran the high hurdles and one day I raced against another good hurdler from another university. I was in front for most of the race. Then I mistakenly attempted to glance to the side to see his position and he eased by! I lost my focus and the race, disappointed my coach, teammates, and myself. But I learned to concentrate until the job is finished and that lesson has been helpful during the course of my life.

I studied education and psychology. Eventually, I managed to graduate. The state of Illinois offered me a therapeutic position at a large mental institution in Chicago. I took the oral and written tests and was appointed. I was doing something, earning a nice sum of money, but I still did not know what I wanted to do. Was I just doing something? I wandered from there to a private hospital, worked at a Catholic school and home for children, and eventually as a probation officer for imprisoned juvenile offenders. I remember walking down the street thinking, "I am so busy earning a lot of money, but I have no time to spend it!" So what? The years were passing! I was just doing something, but I still did not know what I really wanted to dedicate myself to, something with meaning for me!

Among many and various books and articles, I read *Yes I Can: The Story of Sammy Davis, Jr.* I read the document from cover to cover, non-stop, as I should have done in school, but didn't! I was inspired by his achievements and influenced. I saw Malcolm X on TV as he courteously and intelligently dealt with questions from inquisitors from the "other side of the fence." Man, he always handled them in great fashion. A wonderful source of inspiration and knowledge!

I had wanted to be a theatre artist at the back of my consciousness for a long time, and slowly this aspiration began to surface. After completing my daily positions as a therapist, I began studying voice with Martha Larrimore and acting with Edward Clarke at the Chicago Fine Arts Building during the evenings. They were very demanding but highly instructive leaders. I was progressing. I also regularly visited the Art Institute of Chicago across the street to educate myself, appreciate art, and be inspired by it. My acting teacher, in time, insisted I attend ballet classes with Edward Parish. I reluctantly accepted his insistent requests. Thank Heavens! Doors began to open in modeling, theatre, commercials and musicals.

Accompanying these upward steps, I eventually met Oscar Brown Jr. It was an eye opener for me in theatre, politics, and maturity. He was a wonderful human being indeed! After opportunities in Chicago, it was time for me to find out whether I could "play with the big boys" in Los Angeles, California, or New York City. Meanwhile, I lessened my therapy shifts, as I dreamed and prepared for my big movement! Fortunately, my artistic developments provided substantial earning and I was enabled, through my Chicago experience, to head toward my dream realizations. Though I received warnings from my ballet teacher and a radio announcer of classical music on W.G.N. Radio regarding future societal racial obstacles, which I had read but ignored, as there wasn't anything I could not address or handle! I was eventually off to New York City.

The city opened its doors for me, from Lincoln Center, theatre, TV commercials, modeling, staging fashion shows, being a spokesperson for industrial shows on a national and international scale, dance concerts and musical productions. Although I was very fortunate in New York City, I eventually increasingly grieved at the non-appearance in many artistic and commercial events, in which I participated and observed. Few or no sun-tanned people were involved, such as myself!

Berlin eventually beckoned with an invitation. My friend and director Tod Jackson encouraged me to depart the USA and seek humane social relief and artistic promise in Europe. In Berlin, Germany, to be specific! I took his advice and remained in Berlin, Germany until today, where all is improving and well!

Good fortune had been my life long companion, unbeknownst to me, until awakening during my later years. Parents, grandmother, sisters, family, friends, teachers, readings, and prayer, have supported myself and others since our mutual beginnings, known as born days. So today and furthermore, we are able to run, step, glide and stumble, while maintaining our forward balance and continuing in our directions, wherever we are located.

Onward and Upward, Despite All! Maintaining and developing progress in whatever land we inhabit! Thank you everyone for everything, then, now, and during whatever futures we obtain, always!

BEYOND DOUBT
by Femi Sarah Heggie

I went to the East Coast to attend Sarah Lawrence College. I was alone in NYC. My parents had died when I was a small child and I had no relatives here. When my grandmother died, I was sent to Los Angeles to live with an aunt. I was beaten, molested, and found solace only in school and in the music of Aretha Franklin. "One of these days," I told my twelve-year-old self, "I'm going to leave here." I was able to do that on graduation from 12th grade. I couldn't get out of there fast enough.

Coming into New York City after college, I found a new love, the theater. I was in my early 20's when I became active as a working stage manager. Fortune was on my side. A lot of people dreamed of working at the now famous Negro Ensemble Company. It wasn't so much a dream of mine. However, I was lucky to be accepted there in their first year. I don't think I realized what a wonderful opportunity it was.

I began to venture out and stage-managed other theaters. I also had a side gig braiding hair in African corn rows. With the help of friends, I was hired for several celebrities including Stevie Wonder, Valerie Simpson, Nina Simone. I had a dream of braiding Aretha Franklin's hair. I loved her and felt she was anointed with a voice that expressed how I felt. Her music was a source of comfort since I was a child.

My three brothers had died during my growing-up journey. I related to the pain in Aretha's expression. I used to wish I could sing my pain into listening ears. I met Melvin Van Peebles along my journey and became very close to him. He was one of the smartest people I knew. The only man of color to have two shows running on Broadway at the same time. "I'm going to meet Aretha and I am going to braid her hair," I'd often say to him. "You are always talking the Spirit stuff," he'd say. One night while at his production, "Ain't Supposed To Die A Natural Death," I saw her. I couldn't move. Melvin knew. He called me over. He introduced me. As I look back on it, I get the feeling that Melvin orchestrated the meeting.

"I've been looking for someone to braid my hair," she said to me.

"You've been looking for me," I answered. I gave her my telephone number not believing that I'd ever hear from her.

"Hello, may I speak with Femi?"

"Who's calling?" I asked.

"This is Aretha," is what I heard next.

My heart began pounding.

"Wow!" I thought.

"For real?" I asked. She laughed.

"Hi," I managed to say.

She wanted to know if I could meet her and asked that I bring my resume. I always believed "What mind can conceive, we can achieve." It had been proven repeatedly to me but THIS, this was the ultimate manifested dream.

When I first met her, she was sitting at a Fender Rhodes playing "Bridge Over Troubled Waters." That song to this day is at the top of my favorite songs by the Queen. I started out braiding her hair and soon became her personal assistant until she left New York. I traveled with her to various states, islands, and countries. I got to be of service to her and I was so grateful. I always reflect on this when I start to question our input into "manifestation." It was a dream I had long before I met Melvin, or anyone else who helped me along the way. It was a dream that I kept to myself and exposed only 20 years later. I am convinced that as we can conceive, we can achieve. Visualize your dream, feel its reality, never stop. It will show up and say in a language only you will hear and understand, "You've been looking for me, here I am."

ONCE MORE THE PORTER

Think you then that I cannot hate you White Brother,
That for every crime you propagate
I cannot post another?
Know you that my heritage is African Dark hate?

Think you American neighbor, I hold life so dear,
That I ignore the might of mace
And turn to you tear,
That for dignity, I would not enter the grave's embrace?

Think, you Emasculating employer, I cannot recognize your wile,
'cause I sweep with a long handled broom
And grind my toothful smile,
I cannot hate you in my darkened room?

Hear then Brother, my reason why;
Bile beneath the sugar destroys the fly.

KSU 1955
Kent State University

———————————

SEASONAL RECALL

And the warm wet smells cling to the sides of trees
Reminding me, in October, of May months quick
Behind the red-brown fuzz formed soft and thick
On the extended branch when one looks off and sees

April timidly smiling above the tired snow of yesterday.

And October, still warm from September's rich browning,
Drowses among mellowed colors into snow. The winds squeeze
The unresistant leaves and slow wrinkles in the waters freeze
Into washboards of clouds where crickets used to sing.

And I remember May, in October today.

KSU 1956
Kent State University

MORNING COVENANT

I opened my eyes
In the middle of a clear bright morning,
Where shining clusters of light reflecting the bright, young day,
Spring-like in glowing patches,
Bounced merrily from window to wall to window again.

And all the while,
God sat outside, high on a soft cloud pillow savouring
The morning the morning that wrapped it's warmth around him and me,
Waiting for the coming of the noon.

So I opened my ears to the morning
As it filled my room Shinning Out Loud
As it lit up the shadowed corners where night used to be.

And God yawned and stretched in slow God-like pleasure.
I yawned warmly, rolled over
And went back to sleep.

KSU 1956
Kent State University

BEBE'S HAIR

Blown soft by green winds
Ebony swirls, tremulous their stirring
Brush against a slim gold brown column
Evenly, - long dark shuddering forest.

KSU 1957
Kent State University

LAST SUNDAY MORNING

Whatchu standin' over there crying fuh?
Bettah git on out from down here fo' dey come back
Down here wit dem dawgs and dem hoses and dem lectric thangs.

Guess you ain't hurd what the sherif say,
Say wasn't to be no congagatin down here
Afta da-splosin.

Say wudna bin nobody hurt much no way if
all lem nigras hadn't crowded up in the church
when the bomb went off.

Lawd ham mercy, way dey carried them babies
outta dere all hurt and broke up
Chile, I ain't never seen nothin like it
in all my natural born god-fearing life.

But the thing that really got to me was
the way that woman was crying so pitiful and holding onto
that little white shoe.

***September 15, 1963: A bomb set by white supremist terrorists exploded before Sunday morning services at the 16th Street Baptist Church in Birmingham, Alabama. Four young girls were killed, and many other people injured.*

POLICE REFORM
by Gerald Henderson

olice and criminal justice reform has been a hot button in this country for some time. Even prior to the death of George Floyd, protests against police misconduct have taken place in the form of Black Lives Matter, Colin Kaepernick famously kneeling during the national anthem, marches for Trevon Martin, and the list goes on and on. These protests have been in response to the treatment minorities have received at the hands of police in a police encounter. As we know minorities are more likely to suffer disparate outcomes than their non-minority counterparts. "The coercive force used by law enforcement to maintain public order is one of the most important responsibilities entrusted to our government," from which law enforcement derives its authority. "It is a sacred trust," which each officer serving under the colors of law should have. For the most part, it has been my experience that the vast majority of officers serving recognize this obligation and take the oath seriously they have sworn to uphold.

However, in any organization, there are those who abuse their authority and run amok with impunity. Many face no accountability due to a policy called qualified immunity which undermines the integrity and confidence in the legal system. Qualified immunity is rarely spoken about outside of legal tenets. It is largely unknown to the average citizen. Qualified immunity is designed to protect public sector workers (police in particular) from frivolous (or meaningful) lawsuits while performing their official duties. The standard that the Supreme Court set meant that a plaintiff seeking redress would have to show that a case previously existed with very similar facts to the plaintiff's, and that a reasonable police officer should know that his conduct would amount to the use of excessive force. "In other words," as the Libertarian Cato Institute puts it, "justice in civil lawsuits alleging police misconduct turns not on whether the state actor broke the law, nor even how serious their misconduct was, but simply on the happenstance of whether the case law in their jurisdiction happens to include prior cases with fact patterns that match their own."

This fact holds the individual officer unaccountable for the actions taken in a civil proceeding. This also leads the courts to give the officer the benefit of the doubt in situations, civil and criminal.

Unionization of many police organizations also can create impediments to reform. Many of the union contracts have very specific clauses that prevent immediate termination for serious violations but rather call for progressive discipline, which only after a series of violations does the officer face termination. The officer can then go through the grievance process for minor discipline up to the termination. These unions provide the officer with attorneys representing them in matters of arbitration which allows the officer to challenge the discipline the officer may receive for varying misconduct. The union absorbs the cost, the officer merely pays the monthly union dues. Additionally, the officer is indemnified by the police department; we have all heard the stories of the officer who cost the department/city thousands of dollars by willful misconduct but remains on the job.

The shielding of officers who engage in misconduct does desperate harm to marginalized people, and minority communities. It sows the seed of mistrust and non-cooperation with investigations into criminal activity. All are counterproductive to the motto "To Protect and Serve."

Abuses of authority also occur for economic reasons. An officer can create his/her own overtime by simply making an arrest or writing traffic citations. Each of these actions required an appearance in court which many union contracts have pre-set hours of overtime the officer would receive for the appearance. Some jurisdictions' contracts have set hours for preliminary hearings, then pre-trial screenings, then trial. It can be ten hours or more at the overtime rate for a case going to trial. Many times, these (flimsy) arrests occur in poorer communities due to the fact that the defendants cannot afford well-paid legal defense, which would have the potential of exposing some degree of misconduct. As I stated earlier, MOST officers are quite compassionate, thoughtful, competent with a straight moral compass, and true to the oath they have sworn to. They do not need qualified immunity or union protections to do the right thing. But it is time to get rid of it and contractual agreements that protect those that engage in misconduct. All must abide by the law, and officers should be held to a higher standard. Additionally, the courts should do away with peremptory challenges, which allows prosecutors/defense attorneys to play games with the jury pool. The peremptory challenges result in the exclusion of potential jurors without need for any reason or explanation allowing attorneys to "rig the jury" in cases where an officer is on trial. All should be accountable before the law and tried by a jury of one's actual peers.

The good news is that it appears the protests have brought a significant light to this very dark place in the justice system. They have introduced a flood of activism and subsequent education on these matters. Police culture, the silent "blue line," is starting to have a dialogue with citizens they serve and protect. Command is taking seriously the complaints received and taking action when misconduct appears. Most importantly, communities are coming together, speaking with one voice, and educating each other concerning rights afforded to the citizens through video and conversation. We can make a difference and create change.

THE INTERNATIONAL ENTERTAINER
by Victoria Horne

In the Spring of 2010 on a Sunday morning, I drove solo along the Northeastern Coast of Florida. I hadn't lived in Jacksonville, Florida for long. I relocated from Harlem, New York City. Mandarin, which I now call my new home, was a neighborhood located in Duval County. It is located on the eastern banks of the St. Johns River, across from Orange Park. On this particular day, I was ready to explore my new surroundings. I headed for the freeway, onto I-95, heading north. The day was all mine. Learning about new people and places is what I've been doing my whole life. I was ready to learn something new, ready for adventure, and to explore.

One summer, when I was five years old, my grandma Edith R. Horne brought me to Jacksonville for a short vacation to visit my great-grandparents and my mother, who I didn't live with at the time. We traveled by train from New York City through most of the South.

I used to hear my folks call the train "The Super Chief." My grandfather often rode on those trains. He was a porter before he settled in New York City. He ended up owning his own shoe shine business, servicing people when they need a good shoeshine. I used to visit him at the Grand Central Station at his booths.

My great-grandparents came from Sumter, South Carolina, and moved to Jacksonville in 1935. They lived on Church Street in the downtown section of the city. I really don't remember much about them on that journey. I just knew there was a lot of love and harmony in their home. One day when my great-grandmother Marie Black, (Toby, they used to call her), had a pot of hot boiling water on the stove. I, being the curious child, accidentally turned over the pot onto my left arm when she wasn't looking. You could hear me howling all the way back to New York City. Grandma Black spread butter on my arm to ease the pain so that I wouldn't have a scar. My great-grandparents also used to raise chickens. I used to hear my great-grandmother say, "I'm gonna wring that chicken's neck." That meant that we were going to have chicken for supper.

When it was time to say goodbye to my grandma, I headed back home on the train to Harlem. It would be several years before I'd return to Jacksonville. We arrived at Penn Station safely. As I was getting off the train, my shoe got caught between the platform and the train door. A friendly porter came to assist, and Grandma always came to the rescue.

This time my destination was to visit Kingsley Plantation. The Jacksonville Airport and directions to Savannah, Georgia, were visible. Before I reached the airport, I noticed the sign that said Kingsley Plantation. I knew Heckscher Drive was where I'd exited, where I'd turned left at the sign for Kingsley Plantation. I'd travel past the Sisters Creek Marina and St. Johns River Ferry Landing. The view was like a painting and the sun was shining brightly. There was not a cloud seen in the sky. I passed sailboats and the St. Johns's ferry boats that take you over to St. Augustine, Florida, the oldest city in the country built in 1565, then back to Fort George Island. I've visited several castles in my life, but I never visited a plantation. I've seen a few in photographs–and in the movies. This was a day I'll never forget among several visits I've made to Fort George Island and the Kingsley Plantation.

The Kingsley Plantation and My Family Roots

Yes, I am the great, great, granddaughter of Peter Brunson, out of Sumter, South Carolina, born in 1799. On the census he named the country in Africa where his mother was born. The city or town in Africa that Peter's mother came from was Mukunow in Tanzania. The distance from Senegal to Tanzania is 5,916 kilometers. The air travel distance is about 3,676 miles.

According to Daniel L. Schafer's book *Anna Madgiggine Jai Kingsley: African Princess, Florida Slave, Plantation Slaveowner*, Senegal was the last seaport where slaves were put on to ships and sailed to America. Two miles from Dakar, Senegal, "The remote and fortified stronghold known to European traders as Gorée Island (Gorée from the Dutch word for good harbor) had been home to slave merchants since the middle of the fifteenth century." Anna Madgigine Jai Kingsley was from Yang Yang, Senegal, an ancient capital of the king of Jolof and believed to have been Anna Kingsley's home prior to 1806. I found the story about her so interesting that I wanted to share it with you.

When I arrived at Fort George Island, I found myself traveling down a dirt road that never seems to end. There were oak-palm cypress trees. The moss hung over me, high above me. I was amazed at the sight of these trees.

I've read that Zephaniah Kingsley, the plantation owner, planted these trees to line the road to make a path to the town. Now, these trees appear to have taken a life of their own. While I was driving along this road, I thought about the slaves and slavery. I thought about how they might have felt walking up and down this dirt road. Having the comfort of being in my car made me think about things I've taken for granted. I had a feeling as if I were back in 1790 when Zephaniah Kingsley Jr. petitioned the land. The power of nature surrounded me. It had its hold on me. While driving in silence, my mind was thinking of the history here. How could any man want to enslave another? It is beyond my comprehension. Oh yes, it was for greed, money, and power!

It was about 2 miles before I reached the plantation. I was able to park my car and have a walkabout. One of the very first things I noticed was the slave quarters. The huts were situated in a semi-circle. Originally, there were 30 huts. Only a few remain there now. It is believed that the Spaniards built them out of cement by grinding oysters and coquina shells into a consistency of powder mixed with lime. I was fascinated by the process of how they were made and how they formed their structure. I ran my hands over one of them. You could get a good idea of how the slaves lived in their tiny quarters, spending time with their families when the day's work was done. Singing songs from their homeland and sharing stories of their heritage in the evening under a moonlit sky.

As I continued on my walks on the grounds, I saw the well-preserved plantation owners' house. It's said to have been built between 1797 and 1798. It is cited to be the oldest surviving plantation house in the State of Florida. The attached kitchen and barn still exist. The free black slaves and private owners lived on the plantation until it was transferred to the state of Florida in 1955. In 1991, it was acquired by the National Park Service.

Walking slowly towards the river I found a place to sit on the grounds near a tree where the river flowed. For the moment alone I felt peaceful. I thoroughly enjoyed my surroundings. I closed my eyes and thought about Anna Madgigine Jai Kingsley, how she and Zephaniah Kingsley Jr. first met. It was a true love story. It was told that Zephaniah Kinsley had some business to attend to in New York, but he never returned home. He died in New York, and Anna Zephaniah became the owner of the Kingsley Plantation, but not without a fight to prove she was legally married to Zephaniah Kingsley.

According to Antoinette Jackson and Allen Burns in *The Kingsley Plantation Ethnohistorical Study for the National Park Service*:

> "The first records and archaeological information of the first generation of Slaves brought from Africa to Fort George were Igbo and Calabari from Nigeria and other areas from Guinea and Zanzibar. The crops that were grown on Kingsley Plantation were Sea Island cotton. This crop was very valuable because of its long silky fiber. It had to be worked by hand. This particular cotton was being sold from the 1790s up until The American Civil War (1860-1865.) Indigo was the original cash crop of Fort George's Island, where Kingsley Plantation is located. The green leaves and stems produced a rich blue dye that was highly valued throughout the world. The banana-shaped pods are the seed pods, and the plant also produces small pink flowers. The plantation was self-sufficient, so all food needed for the planter's family and the slave's community was grown here. Okra is one example of a crop with African roots that became a staple of southern cooking. Other provisional crops included beans, potatoes, peas, sugar cane, squash, gourds, and many more."

It was getting late, and I had to return home. Why I'm sharing this story with you is to tell you growing up poor doesn't mean you can't follow your dream. I am fortunate to have been able to travel and perform in many different countries. So, my message to the younger generation is up and coming. Anything is possible if you want it to be.

HALO: HAPPINESS AND LAUGHTER OVERFLOWING
by Joseph H. James, Jr.

The old saying about laughing and laughter is that it's good medicine for the heart—healing, soul-refurbishing, and mind-cleansing.

BEGIN THE DAY WITH HAPPINESS!

Happiness is a gift that does not come freely to all. There is a very real mix of rich, depressed, miserable people all over the world, because money and material things do not translate into happiness. They do give people a sense of comfort and security, but true happiness can still be elusive. As human beings, we all will experience suffering at some point in our lives. But misery is a choice, a personal choice. I am not saying you will never be beset by misery, but that it is a choice to stay that way.

Think of happiness as a seed, planted inside you. Let's call it the "happy seed." Well, in order for it to grow, you'll need to water it with a daily amount of love—*self-love*, joy—*unconditional love for self*, gratefulness—*being grateful for life*, and peace—*keeping self-doubt and confusion out of your spirit*. And the number one lesson about happiness is it's your own individual responsibility, no one else's.

I AM A WINNER! YOU'RE A WINNER! THE RACE WAS WON WHEN WE ENTERED THE WORLD!

Remember. *We are all winners!* We start out our lives as winners. There is no such thing as, "I didn't ask to come into this world." Well maybe you didn't, but your actions show that you wanted to be here. Because you had to *win* a race! Yes! *You* beat out millions of other sperms traveling down the fallopian tube to get to the egg that developed into the human being that only you could be. That's why it's important you know that you came into the world *as a winner*. You won that most primal of races! Whether you were born into a family of wealth or a family of poverty. You are still a winner and will always be a winner!

LAUGHTER IS CONTAGIOUS

An infectious smile is like a virus, only in a positive way. When your smile or grin spreads across the landscape of your face, it also spreads across every barrier and language. A baby's laughter is just as contagious as an old person's laughter. It is a beautiful thing to see, hear, feel, and experience. You have lived through yesterday, be it good or bad. You are standing in the present moment of "life." Let it embrace you with the happiness you so richly deserve.

KNOW THYSELF!

In order to be happy, you have to know what makes you happy. Each one of us is different. For me, the smell of lavender calms me and balances me. And the smell of orange blossoms makes me feel fresh and joyful. The sound of music comforts me. Soul, Gospel, Jazz, House, Rock, and Opera are my music choices. Meditating and listening to self-help and healing tapes are a part of what keeps me in a positive mood. Watching the beautiful sky and variations of clouds deepens and exercises my cognitive emotions. Seeing the colors orange and yellow gives me energy. Taking a hot bath, playing in the sand on the beach in the summer or the snow in the winter, and deep therapeutic massages are things that relax me. So, learn to embrace things that enhance your smell, sight, hearing, and touch. Remember there are layers to happiness. But it should always start from inside!

The reason why the word *overflowing* is in the HAPPINESS AND LAUGHTER OVER-FLOWING acronym (HALO) is because you need to learn how to compartmentalize joy, happiness, fun, and laughter. Learn how to store it in your memory, so when you need to use it, you'll be able to pull it off the shelf and from the files of your mind and heart. Keep it sacred and guard it. Don't let anything or anyone rob you of your joy and happiness.

CHILDHOOD MEMORY

I remember when I was around nine years old, and my parents bought me a beautiful purple banana bike with whitewall tires. It had a bell on it and a night light. That was one good looking bicycle! One hot summer day, I rode my bike down to the dime store and left it against the telephone pole as I ran into the store to get candy. I was only in the store for five minutes because I knew exactly what I wanted when I walked in: a pack of Banana Now and Later, a box of Boston Baked Beans, Hershey's Chocolate Bar with Almonds, Bazooka Bubble Gum, and Strawberry Twizzlers.

When I came out of the store, my heart dropped because my bike had disappeared. I turned about in circles, trying to see which way it had gone. My head began to spin as I looked around for my most treasured bike. I quickly ran to the corner and as I looked a block and a half down the street, I saw this older kid with no shirt riding away with my bike. I yelled and said, "You stole my bike. Bring me back my bike!" as I ran down the street after him.

I ran after him for two city blocks. I saw him look back as he laughed knowing that he got away with stealing my bicycle. He got smaller and smaller as he vanished into the traffic. I slowly stopped running and sat there on the curb, panting and trying to catch my breath. I held my head down and cried my eyes out. I felt so mad, angry, and violated. I sat there for an hour hoping he would bring my bike back to me, but it was gone and he was gone and neither would ever return.

Finally, I got up and walked home with a bag full of candy but no bicycle. I was distraught and highly upset that someone would steal something from me. When I got home, I ran onto the porch into my mother's arms. She said in her usual loving way, "What's wrong baby?" I couldn't even get the words out, as I gasped, mumbled, and cried. Finally, I mustered a way to formulate a sentence, "Somebody stole my bicycle from in front of the store."

My mother was calm knowing that the bike was gone forever. She took a tissue from out of her pocket and wiped my face and nose. She said, "It's ok!" But it wasn't ok, I thought. I loved my beautiful bicycle and now it's gone, stolen. She asked me, "Are you ok?" Her very calm question seemed to bring me a sense of comfort in knowing she wasn't mad at me. Then she looked at me and said, "It's just a bike! Don't cry over anything that won't cry over you." That statement stayed with me my entire life. Material things won't ever cry over you! That diamond ring or bracelet you lost or was stolen from you is shining just as bright on someone else's arm or finger. So, I learned at an early age to be grateful and appreciate material things but never worship them. Moral to the story is never allow material things to possess or rob you of your joy. Guard your happiness because you deserve to be HAPPY!

THE PANDEMIC

Some people will say it is a mental sickness to talk or laugh when you are by yourself! I totally 100 percent disagree! What this global pandemic has taught me is I have to learn to enjoy alone time and look in the mirror and smile at myself, laugh, talk, encourage, sing, jump for joy, dance, cry, and shout. After all, it's my life. It's a beautiful feeling to just be happy or be in a happy place, knowing the secret formula to turning on your "happy button."

Thank you, God for the sunshine and for blessing each of us with the capacity to discover our HALO!

SACRED GEOMETRY
by Joyce Morrow Jones (Orisanmi Kehinde Olesanya)

When absorbed with disharmony in our life, it may seem impossible to observe and perceive the concept of destiny which is always manifesting. Sometimes, it's welcoming to not see, because then, it is easier to accept that life isn't perfect, or that perhaps that a current situation was inevitable. Yet, it only takes a moment to ponder Sacred Geometry which is all around us—the flow and movement from a concentric realm of manifestation. Perhaps, if our presence can dwell in that space, there is room to perceive Divine Order in the unfolding of destiny and our Highest Good.

Sacred Geometry moves in patterns, starting from a central position and graduating outward. Where are you in that flow? How can you create a space in that center to ground yourself?

If it helps, find an object that reflects a pattern. I prefer flowers. In a moment of mindful meditation, examine the flower without judgment. Feel the textures of the stem, leaves, and petals. Embrace the energy of its color, how does the color make you feel? If there are imperfections, acknowledge them. Make note of any patterns or layers. Bring the flower close and then position it farther away; does that positioning change your perception? If a single flower, place it in a vase all by itself. Observe how it stands alone in its own beauty, essence, and worth. Gradually begin adding other flowers. Each time, note how this composition adds or detracts from where you started. Perhaps, you decide to remove a few or make the bouquet more luscious. Consider each step as part of your mindfulness. Did you keep the initial flower in the center? Or has it become incorporated within the composition? Can your flower still hold its energetic presence in the bouquet?

Flow with this process of being the "creator." Each step, or decision was yours to make. Whatever choices you engaged in, it really didn't change the nature of the flower. The flower remained true to its creation and aspect. Its Divine be-ing remains unchanged. From the encoding of the seed, to its dormancy in the dirt, and throughout its nurture and progression—that flower became what the Divine Creator intended. The environmental conditions that the flower may have endured can influence it but doesn't change the nature of the flower. Acknowledging the concept of destiny through our spiritual mindfulness allows for the fertile ground and the flower of our destiny to thrive and manifest.

Extend this mindful meditation to aspects of how you perceive yourself and your destiny. Can you see the patterns of sacred geometry? How can you express that in a tangible way? Consider writing in a journal using metaphors, symbolism, or analogies. Over time, go back and see how your perception changes during different situations and how your understanding of your destiny is evolving.

A movement and mantra that comforts me involves acknowledging my position in a Divine flow to greet the day: Begin with several cleansing breaths and speak the following, while turning towards each position raise your arms, then place to your side. Take a few cleansing breaths in that position.

I Honor the energy of the North
I honor the energy of the East
I honor the energy of the South
I honor the energy of the West
I honor the energy of the heavens above (looking above—arms still stretched upwards)
I honor the energy of the earth below (looking down—arms bowed towards your feet)
I honor my place in the center, I am in the Divine Flow (arms wrapped around your body. Take a moment in this position to envision the flow of energy from each of the six cardinal directions).

TO DO GOOD FOR OTHERS
by Rosario Jorge Do Amaral

I was born and raised in the Dominican Republic with a severe and rigid family environment. Despite a lack of affection, we always had dedication, love, integrity, and teachings from our parents.

My dad was of Lebanese origin and my mother of Spanish, French, and Italian origin. Even though they came from different cultures, they lived well and respectfully, teaching their four children the importance of having a united and loving family.

My paternal grandfather died young, at 42 years old, leaving a family of nine children. My dad was eleven at the time. My grandfather's brother was his partner and when my grandfather died, he took all the family assets and financial resources, leaving my grandmother in poverty. My dad, seeing his mother's situation, took a professorship in mathematics, which he adored and excelled at.

This story marked me deeply in my childhood. I respect and admire my Dad for having to work hard to support his mother and siblings. He gave up his engineer dreams to send his two brothers abroad to be doctors.

My paternal grandmother, an extraordinary woman, lived with us until she died. She was always protected and supported by all of us. I was always happy to return home after school and smell the sweet aroma of my grandmother in the kitchen preparing delicious Lebanese dishes.

We grew up in an atmosphere of goodness, unity, peace, always wanting to do good for others. Our house was modest, though we never lacked anything. We learned to give little value to things, appreciate what we had without pretensions, consumerism, and sharing everything we had with others.

We had the privilege of sharing with my maternal grandparents who had the same principles and values. Every Sunday we had lunch at my grandparents' house with mom's seven siblings, their children, and my great grandparents. These times were also schooling moments where I learned a lot.

During this time, I visited neighborhoods of disadvantaged families, frequented religious groups that helped poor communities, bringing them both spiritual and material support, following what I had learned with my parents to have a happier and meaningful life.

Thanks to my upbringing of love, values, and integrity, I became the woman I am today. Passing on these values to my daughters, I hope that it will continue onto future generations.

LIVING WITH LUPUS AND OTHER AUTOIMMUNE ILLNESSES...

by Queen Alena D. Jones Smith aka Lana "LJ" Joseph

Inspired by my beloved beautiful Queen SisTar Melony McGant

My inner child is playful, kind, and extremely carefree.
I learned later in life to just let things be
and enjoy life's journey and the people I meet.
It's not always easy to look at situations clinically.

However, in doing so, a person can deal with things more at ease.
For me, it's a helpful way to navigate this awesome journey called life.
Every human being has the power to assist another person.
I do my best to assist my fellow sister or brother.

Even though...
there are days that I can barely hold a cup
and I have to use a foam hot n cold cup
because it's a bit lighter.
I am grateful to have hands to hold anything!
There are days that my finger joints won't allow me to write or type;
so, I use my voice recorder to unleash my thoughts.
Writers must write!

And... There are days that my head is in a fog.
I can't get my thoughts out like I want to;
or I can barely get out of bed.
The inflammation in my feet won't allow me to get up right away.
However, I do not like to complain about my down days.
I always want to focus on the positives.

I have lived and battled Lupus
and other autoimmune illnesses,
for more than 14 years. Diagnosed.

We are all in this world for a purpose and reason.
We have the opportunity to change negative narratives.
There are times that we cannot change others' mindset.
That's okay, I believe that goodness is contagious!

Though I suffer Lupus, Fibromyalgia, Rheumatoid Arthritis,
Costochondritis, Hypertension, and Neuropathy;
I am grateful to be alive.
There are days when 3 or more illnesses will flare-up simultaneously.
I push through the pain.
I conquer the fear of helplessness.
And….I have never been fond of pity parties.

I will always choose good and I choose to be a blessing.
I choose to assist anyone on my life's journey.
I am optimistic about human beings as a whole.
There are many ways to show positivity through giving.

My mother always said, "It is better to give than receive."
I didn't realize what she meant until I became an adult.
We are here on earth to share what we can with others;
even if it's just a smile or a kind word to someone.

Respectfully, I am blessed with assistance;
especially from my beloved husband,
King "Artist" Rodney Smith.
He works incessantly to provide and care for me;
while educating other healthcare providers.

Every day…
I continue to work hard; beyond illness.
I refuse to use my multiple autoimmune illnesses
to get in God's plans for me to create…
and to be a blessing to humankind.

Any act of kindness towards another human being is good.
We don't agree with everything another person believes.
And that is perfectly alright; we can agree to disagree.

I was born to serve…
My Father… Master… God/Yahweh
His Son…Jesus/Yeshua…

When Spirit commands.
The Most High...The Universe...
and Mother Nature is working in unison.
When my work here on earth is done,
I wish to be pleasing in His Eyes;
that is my ultimate blessing.

I pray to always inspire...encourage...motivate...
uplift and love on those who accept me as I am.
In God's Eyes, I am perfectly imperfect.
I am a constant work in progress.
I have good days like many human beings.
I have physically challenged days,
like other human beings.
We are all going through something!
I pray for Humanity.
I pray for you and me and mine.
When God awakens me,
I know that my journey is not quite fulfilled.

I hope to leave a legacy of love.
And I continue to pray for world peace.

WORDS TO LIVE BY!
by Adam Khan

In a world that's spinning, here's a few words of advice, to guide us on our journey, to make our lives precise: Do good, spread kindness, let compassion be your voice, remember to have fun, and rejoice in every moment. Comparison is futile, for we each have our own story, unique backgrounds, journeys, leading to our own glory. Set high expectations for yourself, let your potential soar, but be mindful not to burden others, and disappointment store.

Life's perception is shaped by profound experiences, listening and understanding, the greatest lessons found. Compassion, self-awareness, humility be your guide, embrace growth and learning, with hearts open wide. Live within your means, find true contentment in modesty's nest. Seek friends who share goals, dreams that are real, together, supporting each other, your aspirations reveal. Give purpose to each day, let no moment be in vain. Avoid empty relationships, where love cannot sustain.

Craft a routine, a rhythm, that brings structure and peace, and with a written plan, life's challenges you'll cease. But above all, to all those far and near, listen with an earnest heart, for understanding others is where connections start. Care about causes beyond yourself, make a positive mark, and in doing so, your soul will forever embark. With the radiance of the rising sun, wake early, embrace the day. Let positivity bloom, darkness fade away.

Measure what truly matters, seek depth over height, be good to all, spreading love with all your might. So let these words guide you, like stars in the night, in wisdom they're rooted, shining ever so bright. Do good, have fun, with these lessons profound, May your journey be enriched, as life's treasures you surround.

THE MONARCA BUTTERFLY: A TRIBUTE TO LIFE

by Martha Llanos Zuloaga

feel very small within an enormous display of greenery, strength, and majesty of nature. I have been walking early in the morning in an immense forest, between imposing pines, cedars, and oaks. I continue advancing and find, with astonishment, closed paths full of fallen dry leaves, and some trees that are not green. They are of a rich copper color. Signs read: "Sacred Tribute to Life."

The atmosphere offers a great silence. I hear only the sounds of birds and the wind. I was there after an exhausting trip as co-pilot in the cabin of a typical Mexican sheepfold truck, with ropes on the sides, and after riding a horse for an hour. All this! To be among the first to enter this place, marked on my list of life pilgrimages: The Monarca Butterfly Sanctuary in Michoacán, Mexico.

The Monarca Butterfly is simple, humble, without as great a variety of colors as others, but compared to the normal period of life that most butterflies live (one month), the Monarch can live up to 9 months. They have greater inner strength and ancient wisdom, which give Monarca butterflies a better chance of coping with difficult situations.

Within the various families of butterflies, the Monarcas are a tribute to life because, to hibernate, they fly almost 5,000 km every year. Many come from Canada or the United States to land in Mexico, whose forest reserves have welcomed them by preparing their forests to provide the best habitat for this species.

When winter begins, these butterflies know that death is lurking. They migrate large groups, singing to life, and nature with their persistent flutter, until they reach the forests and the sun which welcome them. They also come together in a harmony of generations and mutual tributes–the wisdom of grandfathers and grandmothers, guiding young generations on the routes of flight. These grandparent guides are protected by the young ones, because they know that most of them will not return. Then, young butterfly couples find homes for reproduction within the forest.

I continue walking with slow and thoughtful steps, always accompanied by the Monarcas that flutter with the heat and the glare of the sun.

In this Sanctuary, I discover that the dry leaves fallen on the ground were dead butterflies, creating carpeted roads with their remains. Likewise, the copper-colored trees were not another species of tree, but the same pines and cedars in which swarms of butterflies perched, covering all the branches and changing them with their presence.

At sunset, I contemplated for the last time that forest transformed by the Monarca butterfly. I have always liked butterflies but I totally identified with these tireless travelers–small beings that surround the trees with affection. I thought of stories of whispered pilgrimages in the pines. I smiled and said to myself, "Tiny but powerful, free, wise, and enthusiastic." It was an unforgettable trip sharing wisdom, freedom, and enthusiasm with a twin sister, the Monarca Butterfly.

Recorded by Sweet Honey in the Rock

Years ago, while I was at a meditation program at an ashram, I frequented South Fallsburg, New York. When my meditation teacher said during her afternoon talk "trust in your blessings, and always flow like sweet honey from heaven," I was profoundly touched by that phrase. It resonated with me and I started to hum a melody. Well, of course, being a member of a vocal ensemble that had the name "Sweet Honey" in it, it had a special meaning for me. The Melody continues on my journey back to New York City. And this is the poetry that accompanied the song I eventually composed. It was recorded by Sweet Honey In the Rock.

Oh la la oh la la
La la la

How many roads I've traveled
Too many alone
Circling round my truth
 Trying to find a home
At times all around me darkness so hard to see
That grace is his ever present
 always guiding me

If I just take the time still my mind,
look into my heart I find
the inner melody inside
 is calling out to me
It's saying
Trust in your blessings call will flow like sweethoney from heaven
Trust in your blessings and all will flow like sweethoney from heaven

Now
every moment is a new beginning
I can make the choice to change
 and know that I can grow
 and give and live and learn
 that life's a loving lesson
let me always hear your teachings
 and your music
bless me as I walk this path
I'm reaching for the highest.
 Yes!
I'm trusting in amazing grace
flowing from a holy space
telling me my rightful place
is anywhere I am
 so you should
Trust in your blessings and all will flow like sweethoney from heaven
Trust in your blessings and all will flow like sweethoney from heaven

So many roads to travel
but I'm not alone
when I walk and I live in truth
 my heart is my home
God's light takes away the darkness
 easy to see
that grace is all around me
 always guiding me
 if I just take the time
to still my mind
look into my heart I find
the inner melody inside
is calling out to me
 it's saying
Trust in your blessings
and all will flow
like sweethoney from heaven
Trust in your blessings
and all will flow
like sweet honey from heaven
 Oh la la oh

WILD LAVENDER

Walking up the hill with you –
Passing tress and first signs of Spring –
I love this moment with you.
You are precious as the sunlight
Goes through the leaves of the oaks.
You are taller and stronger than you know but by summer
You shall see, you are the golden tree.
Wild lavender tumbles down the hillside.

DREAMS OF A PRINCESS

When she's in her kingdom, she smiles all the time.
Long hair, doe eyes, she listens everyday for her Prince.
Hundreds of blossoms bloom in her garden, as if winter never came.
And the spring never ends–
Twirling about, in her white dress awaiting the night fall and the moon to rise.
A shooting star ignites her eternal love.
Waiting no longer.

FREEDOM FALLS

Freedom falls in between the wave and the crash–
Where the salt kisses the shore.
Every breath in the nowhere,
Before bliss.

SWINGIN DAYS

Two ropes support my wings.
And take me places.
Cotton sky –
Tree tops are my grass, and the birds are my compass.
I swing free and I'm happy.
Built on the love of my love–
For my smile.

LE RENDEZ-VOUS DES AMIS

Sitting outside far from the madness –
A corner breeze blows against my cheek.
The birds sweetly sing to me:
"La joie de vivre."
Plenty of bricks to go, but I find joy in the reflection of your spectacles.

LET THE STORIES BE TOLD RIGHT
FOR MY GRANDDAUGHTER KACEY AND HER GENERATION OF PITT BLACK COEDS!
by Rev. Don Marbury

I, The Rev. Don Marbury was asked in early 2020, by the then-editor of the University of Pittsburgh's, "Pitt News" to write a retrospective, op-ed piece on the Black student Computer Center takeover which had occurred 50 years before. I find it especially significant and poignant for the article to now be included in the marvelous book, *Good Is Powerful Beyond Measure* because nearly 55 years later, my granddaughter will be matriculating at Pitt as a freshman in the Honors College. The inspiration, the nexus for this book, is the University of Pittsburgh student confidant, counselor, door-opener and way-maker, the late Betty J. Tilman. Were the late Sister Betty still on this side of the universe and still making dreams happen at Pitt, she surely would have been one of the first persons I would have had my granddaughter, Kacey, seek out. Nonetheless, the Spirit of Betty Tilman wafts as strongly and lovingly over Pitt as it always did --even as it did way back when Black students demanded equality and commandeered the Computer Center; in the clear knowledge that there was surely one Black woman on campus who would support and be so proud of their commitment and bravery. The life and contributions of Betty J. Tilman represents the essence of why "Good is Powerful Beyond Measure," is such a must-have book. Therefore, for Kacey and her generation of Pitt Black coeds. I authorize my op-ed for inclusion in this marvelous anthology! Rev. Don Marbury, on this 15th Day of June 2023.

June 23, 2020

Googling the January 1969 Black student takeover of Pitt's Computer Center, I came upon a document that showed the actual sign-in sheet of the students who had participated in the seminal event. I pored over the list as the faces of those classmates who participated came caroming through my head in vivid memories of each signatory. And then I was abruptly and ruefully reminded that I would not find my name among the signatures on the document.

Since I was a commuter student at Pitt in 1967, and had part-time jobs to help pay for my education, and though I was on an academic scholarship, I missed a great deal of the campus cultural and social life. In addition, there were only a few Black students enrolled. I preferred the comfort and safety of my Black Hill District, a community located adjacent to Oakland. It was not as though I had never had contact with or had an adversarial relationship with whites. My Schenley High

School pulled in students from Pittsburgh's rich ethnic conclaves. Students from Polish Hill and the Italian and Greek enclaves had all been my classmates, and we had gotten along relatively well.

But there was a certain naivete that characterized my teenage walk, despite my life experiences. I suffered from a kind of racial emotional schizophrenia. Every summer up until I was 15, I spent time in the red dirt hills of rural Alabama, Georgia, and the cities of Atlanta and Birmingham where my parents had been reared.

I wasn't myopic about discrimination and oppression. I've experienced having my Southern cousins push me into the street in order to allow whites walking abreast to traverse unhampered on the sidewalk. I'd drink from "Colored Only" water fountains, sat in the segregated colored balconies of Birmingham movie theaters, and been accosted by stereotypically racist Southern sheriffs. But it was the late '60s, and I believed that America was on the cusp of a racial and social upheaval. Hope characterized my raison d'etre. I was a Northerner, a Pittsburgher, and I had not, somehow, projected, sought to compare or intuited the palpable racism of my Deep South experiences with the covert, unique "Steel Town" brand and its bedrock foundation of institutional discrimination.

I diligently followed the daily details of the burgeoning civil rights movement and hung on to Dr. Martin Luther King Jr. 's every word. I was a talented, African American university student who loved the King's English; I could articulate and write it, I was told, exceptionally well. My personality also enabled me to be unintimidated in white settings and to interact comfortably.

My parents rarely talked about being raised in Klan country or the constant degradations of their Black life experiences. Besides my integrated high school experience, my world was still decidedly Black. My community was Black. My church was Black. My friends and social interactions were Black, but Pitt, circa 1967, was so very white in all aspects.

In 1968, my sophomore year, everything turned into a maelstrom of social and political upheaval. Some Black men and women stepped up, those who had far more knowledge of the history and overall status of Blacks in America than me, and they were generous in sharing their discernment. I became one of the original members of the Black Action Society. People like Curtiss Porter, Jack Daniel, Bebe Moore Campbell, Luddy Hayden, Tony Fountain, and Joe McCormick contributed to me becoming the involved person I am today; as any of my family members, friends, pastors and formal educators. Through their organizational skills, planning and campaigning strategies with the Pitt administration on African American student equity, I, at once, found myself evolving into a political, cultural, and racially self-aware being.

The knowledge they inculcated through the Black Action Society, nationally recognized civil rights guest speakers, campus teach-ins, and Black empowerment reading lists transformed me. It made me angry and ashamed at what I had not been made aware of about the plight, throughout history, of Blacks in America and throughout the diaspora. I was an English major, and at the time I was serving as the features editor at The Pitt News. I was the only Black student working on the paper and was on a track to become its news editor during my junior year. The Black student population seemed very proud of my representation and the articles, mostly about Black student activities, that I was able to write.

My journalist role notwithstanding, on that January day in 1969, I breathlessly rushed to the Computer Center after hearing belatedly of the BAS takeover. I stood outside the demonstration, desperately, and guiltily wanting to be inside the barricades with my fellow students. Dennis Schatzman, a friend and takeover leader who was standing near the barricaded entrance to the Computer Center, noticed me on the outskirts. Sensing my pique, he shouted words to me that would forever direct my life path. Dennis intoned words to the effect that they needed me "inside" the University's established structures to ensure that the truth would be told. I will never forget him hollering, "Make sure the story is told right!"

Later, on becoming the first and, to this date, I believe the only Black editor-in-chief of The Pitt News, I was able to monitor, editorialize on and ensure that the stories about all things related to the University and especially its Black student population were as Dennis advised "told right." I found purpose, resolve, and my destiny on that day in January 1969; though I still lament, nearly 50 years later, that my name is not on the scroll of those who laid their physical selves and futures on the line.

MAKING THE WORLD GO 'ROUND
by Ellyn Long Marshall

Dammit! She'd fallen asleep with the television on again!

Blaring morning TV trumpets rudely awakened her, and it was to the same distressing newscasts that'd depressed her to sleep the night before; imminent world and civil war, tolerated political and individual corruption, skyrocketing inflation, violent crime, the spreading pandemic, moral and environmental decay. She clicked it ALL off, rolled over, and squinted to seek visual escape through her bedroom window. ***Dammit! The Weatherman was RIGHT, it's STILL a mess out there!*** Icy raindrops bordered an unpromising charcoal sky, mimicking the depressing newscasts. ***IT'S ALL TOO MUCH!*** She shivered and lay back, pulling the covers over her head.

Why even get up? To do what? To go outside, where unstable pedestrians and manic drivers compete in a menacing terror pageant? To shop for overpriced groceries for a meal to be 'tolerated' by post-COVID taste buds? To do 3 weeks of laundry in much too costly machines–laundry that will probably need washing again next week? NO, DAMMIT–WHY? In that moment, it seemed the whole wide world was crumbling to an END and the filthy debris was falling heavily on her. She couldn't get up. **DAMMIT!** That "Nasty Ol' Despair" had been slithering around, and was now seductively draining "Sweet Sister **Hope**." And she could feel her Life Tank dwindling to near empty.

Instinctively, she fought back for survival, taking slow, deeply nourishing **Breaths**, and **Prayed** herself **Back, Back to That Moment**. And prayers answered. When she opened her eyes, she was timelessly transported and staring through a *different* window.

She was looking out from a hospital bed, where, decades ago, she'd recuperated from hernia repair and tubal ligation. It's not that she was depressed nor anxious back then. (Although, she HAD only casually informed, rather than discussed with her traveling husband, her decision to have her tubes tied). And a stay in the hospital was certainly no stranger to her–both daughter and son had been Caesarian deliveries. She lay there back then, mind wandering aimlessly, taking those same deep Breaths to soothe painful stitches.

And then, IT Happened–Rather, SHE Happened! At that timeless point, she experienced a complete realization of her purpose and of the essence of life. This STUNNING 'Happening' illuded all her senses (perhaps her Third Eye). But somehow, she absorbed full awareness and knowledge of the all-pow-

erful ENERGY, that results in and regenerates All LIFE. he realized that THIS is what some call 'GOD.' Most Importantly, she simultaneously realized that SHE was an Essential LINK in that 'GOD,' or ENERGY, that every living creature is a link in this; AND that only when the links CONNECT can this LIFE (the World) thrive and be regenerated. She further realized that this CONNECTION–via thought, word or action, is actually LOVE. That it is more contagious than any virus, and it IS our purpose and responsibility to SPREAD it! Not like on TV, -but in every Little Thing we Think and Do. **WOW! It was SO Clear and Simple!**

The **Impact** of her **RE-Membering** transported her 'back' and, just as suddenly, the window was her own bedroom window again. It still had the view of that rainy, gray sky, but now, somehow, it softly urged her to wear her bright pink sweater–to brighten up the day.

She got up, (grateful that she could, when so many she knew couldn't) and dressed brightly. Then put on her favorite Chaka Khan to accompany a light breakfast. 'Sweet Sister Hope' had been revived and she felt her Life Tank refilling! Scooping up her shopping list and bag of dirty laundry, she went out to take care of **Her Purpose** at hand. And she did that–and everything–with Love and a Prayer, that she would continue to Re-Member how crucial it is that she Lives and Spread a Love Pandemic.

Before she left her apartment, she glanced out the window and thought she saw a tiny patch of blue in the distant sky. She smiled and thought, **"What's LOVE got to DO With It? Only EV-ERYTHING, Miz Tina! It Truly "MAKES THE WORLD GO 'ROUND!"** And, eventually, her **"Dammit!"** became **"My Goodness!"**

atiently sitting on the front porch steps. Cracked and broken, yet full of hope. Full of undying faith, anticipation, and childhood optimism. This time he can feel him in his bones. This time he will show up. It's always a gamble of course. A risk he was always willing to take. And so, there he sits all dressed up in his Sunday blue polyester two-piece suit, which is missing a middle breast button that holds the heart in place like a safety pin; *"Three-piece suits are for babies."*

He turned eight six months ago. This suit looks exactly like the a man he called "Daddy" wore the last time he saw him. A button down unbleached white wrinkled, permanent pressed shirt ,and clip-on long blue tie. *"Bow ties are for babies."* Long pants slightly uneven at the hem, pre-fab white pocket square. Matching navy-blue striped socks, elastic, quietly fraying at the top as the story unravels.

Old disappointments mended at the heel and toe. His black patent leather dress shoes were busting at the seams from a sudden growth spurt. Face shining like new money from Vaseline, hair parted down the side, cake like icing with Murry's Pomade. He sits patiently on the front porch project steps. In his lapel, he wears a plastic red rose. He wears his heart on his sleeve. He has to pee, but he can't right now. He wants to be there to greet him when he walks up the block. So, he sits waiting, tapping his foot to keep from peeing himself, watching the parade of fathers and sons, and daddy/daughter moments coming and going on a perfectly sunny Father's Sunday.

He was itching to hold his hand and aching to hug his neck. To feel that five o'clock shadow that only daddy's have. Hoping he's not gotten too big to be picked up anymore, wanting to be a baby again. Playing the fantasy reunion over and over in his head. Fighting back any dread of the last "Daddy No Show." As he puts his hands in his pockets, he realizes there are holes that need to be mended. Mama will take care of that later, she always does. Good at picking up broken, torn pieces and stitching them back together. But for now, he will pretend his pockets are full of positive outcomes and of gold. This morning in church, he asked God for his Father on Father's Day. Hungry for food, but starving for a Daddy Day even more he sits patiently rocking, tapping his foot so not to wet himself.

His mother calls for him to come inside but he refuses to budge. He's not moving cause he knows, he just knows he'll be here. He didn't call or anything, or say that he was coming. He just feels him in his bones.

"What father would forget his own special day?" Laying next to him on the project porch steps, awkwardly embraced in last Sunday's comics (a poor boy's wrapping paper), is a gift he bought with money his auntie gave him for his eighth birthday. Another "Daddy No Show" event. It's a gift set. Cologne, deodorant, soap on a rope. Mennen Old Spice was too old fashioned, so he knew he had to upgrade. Old Spice is a gift for Grandpas from babies. He knew this gift would please him. With this gift, Daddy would show him favor. And so, he sits wetting himself just a little, wanting to cry, but needing to pee more. Determined to see this thing through, he sits faithfully waiting. With the faith of a mustard seed, he waits.

The sun wanting to witness the outcome begins to lose interest and starts to retire. Again, he hears his mother call but he doesn't respond. He just sits, faithfully waiting. Finally exhausted he grabs the gift and rises to his feet in defeat and turns to go inside. He opens the screen door. It aches and groans with apologies. Then suddenly, he hears a man's voice; strong, yet understated. Like Clark Gable or Garry Cooper in some black and white movie. Or better yet Billy Dee Williams in Mahogany saying something like, "Ain't you gone say hello to your ole man on Father's Day?" The little boy turns and leaps all at once off the project porch steps in one fell swoop, into the arms of a tall black man in a blue two-piece pinstripe suit. *"Three-piece suits are for babies."* He flies into his arms, almost knocking him backwards, unabashedly wrapping his legs around his waist, his arms around his neck! He deliberately runs his cheek across the man's five o'clock shadow. The man smells of cologne. "Not the cologne I got him," he thinks boastfully to himself. The tall black man wears a silk red rose in his blue lapel. "Mama's gonna Like that!" Yep, that's my daddy! And all is forgotten and forgiven!

At that point the little boy knew that every once in a while God, and even Santa, come to the projects. "I missed you, Daddy!" The little boy cries, voice breaking into tears of joy and relief. "I missed you too, Lil Man," the tall black man says. Music to a little black boy's soul. The little boy thinks to himself, "This is the best Father's Day EVER!" And as he himself grows old, it becomes the only Father's Day he chooses to remember.

LIGHT VS DARK
by Nasser Sundiata Metcalfe

When I think of the vast power of goodness and how powerful it is, I find myself compelled to consider the power of bad as well. After all, light requires darkness to be seen. So, in order to truly qualify the power of good, it seems we must simultaneously examine the weight of its opposite. Our suffering through bad experiences typically leads us to process and appreciate the good ones that much more.

The balance of good vs evil or light vs dark has been an inherent aspect of our lives since the beginning of human existence on Earth. This is evident by daily occurrences that every living creature on this planet is subject to, and none of us is powerful enough to change it. Each of us, regardless of geographical location, other differences or distinguishing qualities we may possess, experience half of our days in the light and the other half in the dark. There are some places in the world where 24 hours of daylight is constant for half a year, then nighttime for 24 hours in the other half. Even in certain environments, this balance of nature, light vs dark, exists.

So, if the very realm we occupy is governed by a deeply contrasting juxtaposition at its core foundation, then wouldn't it make sense that all of its inhabitants carry the same balance of light vs dark within us? Seeking the answers to such questions has been the hallmark of humanity throughout the centuries, and only a handful of enlightened beings ever come close to figuring it out. We are all as capable of selfless acts of kindness, as we are of destructive acts of cruelty. Where the balance lies between the two and which side is embraced more depends on an individual. There are a myriad of factors that determine this and they are usually shaped by one's life journey.

As we traverse through our individual life cycles, we tend to seek answers as to what our true purpose is here. For some it is to spread goodness, for others it may be the opposite; even if they carry a logic that they use to justify their actions by thinking that they are doing a form of good, regardless of whether it causes pain to others. Our real purpose in life is to learn. Earth is one big classroom. As inhabitants of the planet, our lifetime is dedicated to being her students and getting our lessons. All of our experiences, good, bad, or in between, carry valuable lessons for us if we are open to seeing them as such.

When I was an adolescent, I experienced a bout of depression so deep that I actually attempted suicide. Luckily, my mother found me after I took a whole bottle of pills and rushed me to the hospital. Even though I was physically well enough to be released after a day or so, I was kept for the better part of a week for observation; in case I might make another attempt on my own life.

During this week I had a number of visitors, family and friends, who came by to wish me well. I was touched by the outpouring of love but there was one particular visit that impacted me more than the others. Although my parents had been divorced for years by this time, my father was always still very present in my life and visited me daily during my hospital stay. One particularly quiet evening, in the darkness of my hospital room, I laid in bed and looked up to see my father entering the doorway as visiting hours did not apply to parents. There was no particularly deep or revelatory conversation. In fact, this could have been any other moment we might have had under regular circumstances. We watched television and chatted like we always had.

At one point Dad asked me how I like the hospital food. I told him it was okay. He then inquired if there was something else I might like, to which I said sure. We decided on a nearby Burger King and after a few minutes Dad returned with a bag containing a couple of whopper meals. We ate and continued to watch television. Eventually, we finished and Dad bid me farewell saying he would see me tomorrow.

He departed, and I was left in the darkness and quiet of my room again. I experienced a major revelation that would forever change the trajectory of my life. It finally clicked that there were people who cared and that my life truly held value. Suddenly, I felt tremendous guilt for being selfish in putting my loved ones through such emotional trauma, and the things that had been bothering seemed insignificant. Before I knew it tears were streaming down my face and as I bawled uncontrollably. I knew that I was releasing my pain and would never be reckless with my life again. I haven't had the slightest inclination toward suicide in the decades since.

This is why good is powerful beyond measure, because just like the flower that grows in between the crack in concrete on the sidewalk, even in the face of the worst of our troubling times, there is good to be found if we are fortunate enough to see it. There will always be dark times, but they can also feed the goodness that always surrounds us if we allow it. For that reason, goodness will always win in the end if we believe in it.

FINDING SUCCESS WITH NOTHING
by Dale A. Miller

I began my life having nothing. I found early that to succeed while having nothing, I needed to develop "hard work and dedication" to achieve goals–and nothing valuable comes easy. "Nothing" to me is being poor, having no assets, food, shelter, clothes, or relationships. Being poor, I had to learn to accept family responsibilities. I had a younger brother and sister who relied on me for guidance. Mother was disabled and father left us with nothing.

Solace came to me when I went to school. I stayed in the library for many hours. I read topics that informed and prepared me to make good decisions. I eventually realized that to make the best decisions, I must have an education. In this modern age, a bachelor's and a master's degree are paramount to achieve a background that will last a lifetime and make me a person who began with "nothing" important.

I was born on April 1937 in Bridgeton, PA on my grandfather's farm to a young single mother. My father was unknown and we only speculated his background. As a very young boy, I had to assume control of family functions in support of mother, younger brother, and sister. At age 12, my mother was hospitalized with mental illness. My siblings and I were sent to live with relatives for a short while, and subsequently settled with my grandfather on his farm.

After graduating from high school, I left the farm and began a quest for a professional baseball career. This led me to enter the famous "Negro American Baseball League." Over the course of two years, I played with Kansas City Monarchs, Detroit Stars, New York Black Yankees, and ended with the Indianapolis Clowns. I was drafted into the army the same year with a promise of continuing baseball there, which did not happen.

When I was discharged from the army, I returned to New York City, and entered a civil service job in the Postal Service. I served 33 years and ended my tenure as the manager of a large station. While there, I got married. My wife and I produced five children, seven grandchildren and great-grandchildren. I also began my pursuit for an education and received a bachelor's degree in business. I was short of a Master's Degree in Humanities and Religion because of a dispute and disagreement with my thesis submission. I retired and began a new job with the New York State Insurance Fund as a senior safety officer with OSHA related responsibilities. I retired after 17 years of service at the age of 77 years old. **After medical setbacks, I began a new healthy lifestyle and continue it today.**

FINDING LIFE'S PURPOSE
by Jean Miller

My father Alfred H. Dickson, of African American descent, was born in Virginia and migrated to Lowell, Massachusetts in the late 1930s to accept a chauffeur's position from a prominent banker. He was a single man, spending his spare time painting pictures and was a master in watercolors. Many of his paintings won awards and are on display at the prestigious Whistler House Museum of Art in Lowell. I have several of them in my apartment. They have become conversation pieces among my visitors. My dad was also a boxing trainer/manager at the YMCA in Lowell. He was responsible for the professional careers of many young men.

My mother, Evelyn B. Johnson, was born in Bangor, Maine, and was one of ten children. Her mother, my grandmother Edith M. Johnson, spoke French and was an advocate for the National Federation of Afro American Women in Bangor. My grandfather, William A. Johnson, was an active Mason and one of Black Bangor's most famous entrepreneurs. He opened a store called William A. Johnson's Everything Store, selling everything.

Meanwhile my talented mother and her four siblings were asked to join the Bangor Symphony Orchestra, where they played classical music on the weekends. After graduating from high school, my mother moved to NYC, and lived in Harlem for ten years. During that time, she was hired by W.E.B. Du Bois to be part of the staff of the NAACP'S monthly magazine, The Crisis. Years later, she moved to Lowell to care for her ailing sister, who was recovering from surgery. She met my father through a mutual friend and married after a brief courtship.

I was born in Lowell, Massachusetts, many years ago. Dad was 55 and mom was 40. He was still a chauffeur and a very successful artiste. But my mother was having seizures and was diagnosed with epilepsy due to a traumatic accident during childhood. Her doctor made the decision that she should no longer work. So, she became a stay-at-home mom, providing a beautiful single-family home with a front and backyard for me to play in. However, we were the only Black family in an all-white middle class neighborhood, so there was no playing going on in my yard. I never came in contact with the white children in my neighborhood before age six. Up until then, I spent weekends and holidays with my cousins in Boston and entire summers with my grandma in Bangor, Maine. My preschool years were beautiful and full of wonderful childhood memories.

But life for me was about to change. Summer came to a joyful end and school began that September. I began my life outside of my home as a kindergarten student at the same time Southern racism and Jim Crow laws were making headlines in the country. The adults in my young life failed me because they sent me to school and never prepared me with knowledge I needed to know as a Black child. I knew nothing about racial discrimination or that being black would get me beat up every day. They didn't realize that they were sending me into a lion's den to be slaughtered.

I was supposed to socialize and play and learn my ABCs in school, but my skin color got in the way. We were black and white kids who had never come in contact with each other. I was never bitter toward them because they were white, so I couldn't understand the reverse. The N word, along with other racial slurs, were always heard but never addressed by adults. I never shared my school issues with my parents because they were quiet people living in a white neighborhood and trying not to make waves. Also, my mom was epileptic, and I didn't want to be responsible for her having seizures. I had no allies or family friends I could approach. So I stayed quiet and friendless for six years.

I finally graduated sixth grade, going on to junior high and high school without any incidents. I never had a social life while in high school, so I was not distracted. I studied hard and was on the national honor society roster every month. I passed my college boards and got accepted at Howard University. On the night of graduation, I received five awards in different categories. Classmates that ignored me for four years congratulated me on stage and invited me to hang out with them over the weekend. Lots of fun parties and celebrations. School was finally over, and we were all going our separate ways. For that last weekend, I was finally accepted and treated as a classmate.

I started out in kindergarten as a small Black girl who faced blatant racism alone for twelve years and now it was over. And my classmates would never know what a wonderful lifelong friend they could have known.

Fast forward to age 63: After CCNY, marriage, children, college graduations, employment, retirement, and grandchildren, I found myself as an empty nester with six adult children who no longer needed me in the same way. Now comes the midlife shift in my lifestyle, where my purpose begins. I joined the Kennedy Senior Center in Harlem and met some wonderful people who have become my very dear friends.

I also joined the Hansborough recreation center and was introduced to the pool. I decided it was time for me to learn how to swim. The Harlem Honeys & Bears Synchronized swim team, who practice in that pool, taught me how to swim. Later, I joined them and became a bona fide swimmer, participating in the team's synchronizing routines. I won gold medals in the individual competitive events, and both on the local and state level. I also entered and won gold medals in three master's competitions.

The youth Learn-to-Swim program was another component of our team. Children met with us twice a week after school. I had the pleasure of teaching them and other youngsters how to swim. Two of my granddaughters joined the youth program at very young ages. They remained in the program for several years and became excellent swimmers. That was a special bonding time with them, and they realized how much fun young people can have with seniors.

I am also the administrative director of Dr. Glory's Youth Theater—a marvelous performing arts program where young people are trained in theater arts and have an opportunity to perform in front of an audience. Dr. Glory Van Scott is the founder and artistic director.

Today, I am living my best life with a positive outlook. I've learned to listen and not give advice unless asked. I don't overthink everything, becoming more spontaneous. I am grateful for my husband, children, grandchildren, great grandchildren, and friends. They are all gifts to my life. **But most of all, my real purpose in life is to be happy. And that comes from inside when you choose mind over matter. I practice it every day as I watch my life continue to expand.**

HINDSIGHT 2020
by Lewis Nash

On May 25th, 2020, Memorial Day, the world witnessed the racist, barbaric, inhumane torture, and murder of George Floyd in Minneapolis. On June 4th, I watched the first of three memorial services being held for Mr. Floyd from the living room of my house in Phoenix, while sitting beneath a wall filled with photos of my deceased parents, grandparents, great-grandparents, other relatives, and ancestors. You see, this was my parents' house, where many joyous family gatherings and celebrations took place. As I watched the service, listening to the songs and words of the various speakers, my feelings vacillated between sadness, anger, encouragement, and hope.

When the service drew to a close, everyone was asked to stand in silence for eight minutes and forty-six seconds–the length of time that police officers had remained with their knees on Mr. Floyd's neck and body. I stood, faced the photos of my ancestors, acknowledged them and all they'd endured during their lifetimes here in America, bowed my head, and immersed myself fully into the present moment. Tears streamed down my face as I experienced the nearly 9 minutes, reflecting on how Mr. Floyd suffered before he took his last breath. I took several deep breaths to calm the emotions I was feeling, and suddenly it hit me–that what I was doing at that moment, taking deep breaths, was something Mr. Floyd was prevented from doing so! After the incident in Minneapolis happened, my two adult daughters reached out to me from New York City to express their shock, outrage, and concern. They realize that in America, it could very well have been their father with a racist police officer's knee on his neck.

I would venture to say that most Black men in America have experienced some uncomfortable moments with law enforcement. I've had my own tense encounters with aggressive police officers, and these encounters often begin to occur very early in our lives. When I was a 16-year-old high school student in the early 70's, I was called a nigger by a white Phoenix police officer on a street near my high school. I hadn't done anything; he just felt the need to express himself. That same year, I was called a nigger by an older white student at my high school during a physical education class. During the summer of 1979, while a student at Arizona State University, I made my first trip to New York City. I was excited about just being in New York and finally getting a chance to hear my drumming heroes like Max Roach, Art Blakey, and Elvin Jones! I stayed in Westchester County, NY at the family home of one of my ASU classmates. She was a Music Therapy major named Joy DeNicholas, who remains a friend to this day. Her sweet mother, Mrs. DeNicholas, treated me as if I were her own son.

I would travel back and forth from their home in Yonkers, NY, down to New York City for drum lessons with my teacher, Freddie Waits, and to hear the legendary jazz masters that I only read about.

One evening after hanging out in NYC, listening to music with my good friend, saxophonist and jazz educator Allan Chase, I headed back to Yonkers on the Metro North train. Because of where the house was located, the closest train station was in a town called Bronxville, NY. I would exit the train there and walk several blocks to the house. As I was walking from the train station on this particular evening, a police officer pulled his car in front of me, his lights flashing, cutting off my path. He instructed me to stop, got out of his car and asked me, "Who do you know in Bronxville?" I felt a bit of trepidation, as I'd of course had "the talk" with my parents years earlier about dealing with these very common occurrences in the lives of young Black people in America. Anyway, I explained to the officer that I didn't know anyone in Bronxville, and that I was walking to a house in Yonkers. He took my ID, told me to stay put, and he went back to his car to examine it. It took a while, but eventually he came back, handed me my ID and let me go on my way. Perhaps someone had seen me walking through the area on more than one occasion and decided to alert the police. It didn't really matter, the tone and tenor of the encounter wasn't that of a courteous inquiry, but more like a forced detainment and interrogation.

In any case, recalling these incidents is not the point, as I've forgotten many of them. The point is that when one regularly experiences derogatory or discriminatory comments, and at worst potentially life-threatening encounters, it becomes necessary to develop a thick skin and survival skills. Living in New York City during the infamous "Stop and Frisk" policy, the "Central Park Five" incident, and many of the well documented instances of police violence against Black males, I knew what was happening, and that under certain circumstances, it could happen to me. If it was only about dealing with hurtful racial epithets and ignorant comments, that would be easy. These are only the tips of the icebergs of the systemic racism that exist in the criminal justice system, housing and employment, health care, education, the business and corporate world, government, and American society as a whole.

Often we try to ignore or repress much of the subtle and not so subtle racism and bigotry we experience, otherwise it's possible to become consumed by it. Black jazz musicians from earlier generations were masterful at navigating this terrain. Some stood up, spoke out, and challenged norms, but often are at the risk of losing their jobs or even their lives. In the course of my life and career, I have had many conversations about life in America with my peers and with most of the Black men and women in the jazz world who nurtured, taught, and groomed me. Understandably, a common thread that runs through the experiences of Black musicians in America across generations is the similarity of experiences in dealing with racism and developing the necessary survival skills. We learn to live our lives without becoming consumed by anger or depression. I had these same conversations with my parents, older relatives, Black teachers, and elder church members.

So many institutions, corporations, and organizations have released statements in solidarity with the Black community and in support of the right to peaceful assembly. I'm encouraged and heartened by what I've read in those statements, and it's beautiful to see so many Americans of all ages and ethnicities passionately participating in nationwide demonstrations. Conversely, I realize how relatively simple it is to put out a statement, while the difficult work still lies ahead. A sincere statement can ring hollow when not followed by action. How many individuals and institutions will continue to challenge the status quo after the headlines fade and the news cycle changes? How many will demonstrate the commitment, perseverance, endurance, and tenacity required for the long fight? We've been hopeful and optimistic in previous situations in recent years, only to be let down once again.

I do remain cautiously optimistic, however. People still protest and ask what they can do. They're pledging to hold themselves in their personal and professional circles accountable. They can educate themselves on the history and origins of these problems, so they're armed with facts AND passion. Going back to what we called "normal" before is not an option. We must expose and eradicate the systemic and institutional racism in so many areas of American life. Those in power in the criminal justice system, police departments, politicians at the local and national levels who make public policy, educational institutions, nonprofit and philanthropic organizations, corporations, small businesses, our families and friends…Everyone has to be held accountable. We have a golden opportunity to listen to those who are hurting or marginalized, to have empathy, compassion, and to dedicate real time, energy, and effort to bringing about change. Let's be bold enough to create a society that truly values love, respect, generosity, kindness, and equal justice under the law for all its citizens.

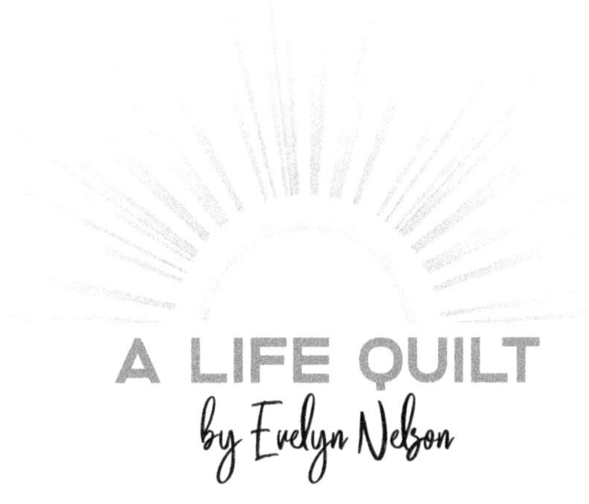
A LIFE QUILT
by Evelyn Nelson

As a young girl, I grew up on the rural, segregated Eastern Shore of Maryland, the daughter of a Methodist Minister. However, our family was originally from an urban so-called integrated section of Pennsylvania.

I thrived in Maryland among the myriad of cultural traditions and religious values of this tight-knit Black Community. There were activities such as: "church campground meetings" where parishioners stayed up for three days singing hymns and praying; "Hog- killing times" for farmers; planting and harvesting crops in season for the community; and "Quilting Parties" for the ladies.

From that time on, I have never forgotten the blessings of those early beginnings, especially when a group of the town's women gathered on Monday mornings to make a quilt for Sister Brown or Sister Smith or whoever needed a warm bed covering at the time. I watched eagerly as the ladies gathered around a quilting table with their supplies of small fabric squares and shapes gathered from old shirts, warn- out dresses, coats and printed flour sacks. With needles and thread, they artfully sewed together all these pieces by hand until they had created a beautiful warm quilt by the end of the day.

From this point on, I began to develop what I have named my "Life Quilt". First, as a little girl, I cut and sewed clothing for dolls by hand, using fabric left over from garments my mother made for herself, my sister Gloria and me. Her interest in sewing came from a necessity to make ends meet, as a poorly paid preacher's wife. Here was a a great example of of using "lemons to make lemonade" as she developed skills to create masterful garments for her family.

Next, I started making garments for myself as well as for my friends. As time went on and I was ready for college, I informed my parents that I did not want to go to school to become a doctor as they expected but wanted to go to school to become a Fashion Designer....... and I did!

I made the right choice and have been blessed to be able to express my talent, fulfilling my life's purpose and passion in creating the career I have chosen for my "Life Quilt". As a fashion designer, my career has developed as an entrepreneur "couturier" for a private clientele, an Off-Broadway costume designer, a high school fashion design teacher, as well as a fashion design college professor. There were other job experiences for me such as: tour guide at the United Nations, realtor, hair salon manager that created detours from my career path, but were welcomed as additional pieces adding more variety to my "Life Quilt".

Blessings come in all forms over the course of a life time as have mine. We have been given tools with which to work through all experiences whether easy or challenging. The pieces of my quilt when sewn together create a variety of blessings and experiences which I consider Good and Powerful Beyond Measure.

Just like at the end of the day when I saw the women complete a beautiful, warm and useful quilt with pieces they had collected, I have been collecting the beautiful people and wonderful experiences and blessings which make up my "Life Quilt" to create a masterpiece of sharing my talent and blessings.

People come into your life for a reason, a season or a lifetime. When you figure out which one it is, you will know what to do for each person. When someone is in your life for a REASON, it is usually to meet a need you have expressed. You have manifested them into your reality. They have come to assist you through a difficulty; to provide you with guidance and support; to aid you physically, emotionally or spiritually. They may seem like a godsend, and they are. They are there for the reason you need them to be.

Then, without any wrongdoing on your part or at an inconvenient time, this person will say or do something to bring the relationship to an end. Sometimes they die. Sometimes they walk away. Sometimes they act up and force you to take a stand. What we must realize is that our need has been met, our desire fulfilled; their work is done. The prayer you sent up has been answered, and now it is time to move on.

Some people come into your life for a SEASON, because your turn has come to share, grow or learn. They bring you an experience of peace or make you laugh. They may teach you something you have never done. They usually give you an unbelievable amount of joy. Believe it. It is real, but only for a season.

LIFETIME relationships teach you lifetime lessons; things you must build upon in order to have a solid, emotional foundation. Your job is to accept the lesson, love the person, and put what you have learned to use in all other relationships and areas of your life. It is said that love is blind, but friendship is clairvoyant. We don't meet people by accident, they are meant to cross our path for a REASON.

Muhammed Ali, Maya Angelou, Harry Belafonte, Lerone Bennett, Jr., Howard Bingham, Sam Cooke, Ossie Davis, Ruby Dee, Katherine Dunham, Minister Louis Farrakhan, Aretha Franklin, Jim Hadley, Austin Hansen, Sr., Lena Horne, John H. Johnson, Martin Luther King Jr., Malcolm X, Toni Morrison, Gordon Parks, Rosa Parks, Paul Robeson, Moneta Sleet, Fred Watkins and James Van der Zee used their gifts to bring about goodness and change in the World. I've learned a lot from these humans, as well as from my own parents, Hattie Collins and Samuel Collins, and Barbara Rasheed, my beautiful, brilliant, compassionate partner and wife of 47 years. Be humble. Be kind. Be patient. Carry yourself with dignity. Do your best. Have confidence. Listen deeply. Love what you do. Pay attention. Share your gifts and goodness. Walk with integrity. I have always wanted all that!

Looking back, I think this was also what my parents wanted for me and my brother Michael. Because of Jim Crow, they had come from Belhaven, North Carolina, looking for opportunity and work. At first, we lived in Harlem but then we moved to the Lower East Side to the Baruch Houses between Delancey, Columbia, and Houston streets. I was able to walk to elementary school P.S.97, and I attended junior high at P.S 22, then went on to Seward Park high school. In high school, I worked at Chase bank and afterwards I got a job with Con Edison. It was a good job with a pension. Except I wasn't happy.

So, I asked God to help me, to give me something that would make me happy. "God, I know you are busy, but please give me something special. Tell me, what is my gift?"

I was still working at Con Edison. One afternoon we were digging holes in the street at 60th and Broadway. A guy gets out of a cab with a beautiful 16 x 20 photograph. I asked him what kind of camera shoots a photo like that. He said he shot it with a 35-millimeter camera.

I bought a 35-millimeter camera and began to carry it everywhere. Sometimes my life flashes back before my eyes. I see the baby picture of me in the window of photographer Austin Hansen's Harlem studio and the many photos my father took of us in the family photo albums, some clearer than others. Now I realize that God had already planted the seed through my father.

I quit my job at Con Edison and enrolled in the Black Journal Film Workshop/NET, Channel 13. Then I decided to take a class at the Afro School of the Arts from Joe Harris.

I interviewed with Jim Hadley and he hired me. He said, "I am not going to teach you how to shoot, I am going to teach you the business of photography. First of all, there are a million photographers who don't develop their own films. That's where the money is, in developing your own film." He taught me how to make contacts, how to stay in touch with clients, and the importance of location scouting. To this day, I write down interesting and unusual locations.

Jim Hadley rode a motorcycle. He was so dedicated that once after a motorcycle accident, I saw him shooting a model while on crutches. The famed model and restaurateur B. Smith was a rep for Jim Hadley early in her career and, in 1972, Jim Hadley sent me to shoot the first Black model for Camay Soap for an Essence Magazine ad.

After about a year and a half, I left Jim Hadley to take a job at K&L Color Lab. I learned everything I could about developing film and six months or so later, I asked Joe Harris to hire me. He told me, "I'll try you out for a month but don't quit your other job." Little did he know I quit my other job the next day!

I ended up working for Joe Harris for a year and a half, first as a photographer's assistant, cleaning the studio, acting as a gopher, processing film, and assisting in shoots. Later, I was an assistant photographer and actually shot jobs for him. More and more I learned that our teachers are everywhere. I didn't personally know the great singer/songwriter and entrepreneur Sam Cooke but I always carried his words "Observation Baby!" with me. As a photographer and a student of life, it describes my journey. If we pay attention, we can understand that just as people speak, nature talks to us too. Animals, birds, bees, the wind, clouds, every leaf, fish in the sea, raindrops in the sky, flowers, trees, all vegetation–even the air we breathe is teaching us.

Because of Jim Hadley, my philosophy became, 'The more you learn, the more you earn' and 'shoot for your client, but also shoot for yourself.' I continued my freelancing, taking portraits in my Harlem Studio, and took a job at LIFE Magazine.

Me at TIME INC. Imagine that! LIFE, PEOPLE, MONEY, and SPORTS ILLUSTRATED magazines. I thought to myself, "I know I can do this. It's God guided." I processed film, blew pictures up, shot photos for the company newsletter, and often ate with other photographers like Alfred Eisenstadt. I knew and appreciated the work of James Van Der Zee, but there was another renaissance man who would come to greatly influence me.

One day, I was walking down the hall and I saw a name on the door...Gordon Parks. He was distinguished, handsome, and Mr. Cool Complete. I would see him enter the building, but we hadn't had a real conversation.

On this day, he invited me into his office. We talked and he wrote down his phone number. It was EL5 0361...Gordon Parks gave me his phone number! I couldn't wait to tell my wife Barbara. After that, I often walked him home. We would talk about life and what was going on in the world. On many Saturdays, I would edit his photos and color transparencies. I admired his humbleness and discipline. I'd go to his house and eat kielbasa and cabbage. Gordon Parks said to me: "Tyrone, you are a part of the family. You are officially my Godson." I was so honored when he invited me to shoot stills with Fred Watkins on the Solomon Northup Odyssey film. I was equally honored when his family asked me to be an Honorary Pallbearer at his funeral. Like my parents and all of my ancestors, Gordon Parks now lives in me.

I worked at TIME INC for 24 years and nine months. During this time, I was freelancing and had my own portrait studio in Harlem. My photo of Martin Scorsese & Michael Jackson was in PEOPLE Magazine and PARIS MATCH. My photo of Paul Schaffer was in PEOPLE Magazine. North General Hospital was my client for many years. I left TIME INC to take a staff photographer position at EBONY/JET magazines in 1999.

Observation Baby! Another man I greatly admired was John H. Johnson and his commitment to the Black experience. I had been freelancing for JET Magazine a year or two when I was asked to shoot him receiving an award. I remember walking him back to his limo. "I want to work for you," I said, and he smiled. Eventually I worked full time as an EBONY/JET staff photographer for 13 1/2 years. I covered major events as well as movers and shakers of the Black world.

People ask me if I have a favorite photo. I don't have a favorite photo. They are all special. Gifts from God. I do remember the great Muhammed Ali bought me breakfast at Salaam's at 116th in Harlem. Aretha Franklin was beaming with joy at her birthday party. I was nervous shooting Lena Horne and she said to me, "Calm down and I'll give you a kiss." I immediately calmed down and she kissed me on the cheek.

From actors, athletes, business owners, CEOs, boxers, children, elders, ministers, musicians, politicians, presidents/presidential inaugurations, schoolteachers to flowers, trees, hummingbirds, and butterflies, every opportunity to use my gift is a blessing.

I've been given this gift of photography from God. I love documenting moments in people's lives. My images of family days, birthdays, weddings, retirement parties, births, funerals and family portraits will live on forever. **I could not have done any of this without my wife, Barbara Rasheed. She has inspired and supported me and continues to be a beautiful partner on our life journey. We've been married for 47 years and together for 52 years. This is God. Without Her, I would have nothing. My reality has exceeded my dream. I had no idea where God was taking me. And I Am Not Done Yet!**

POSITIVITY = GOOD BEYOND MEASURE
by Tawnya Farris Redwood

Positivity and Love are powerful tools that help develop purposeful lifestyles, life progression, and legacies.

Positivity, like light at the end of a tunnel–sometimes referred to as tunnel vision, can be a powerful, motivating force that provides focus that is needed for task completion and dream fulfillment. Another way to think about positivity is to embrace it as fuel to the roots of goodness. Positivity requires mindfulness, commitment, and determination. It is best utilized when undergirded by love.

So many have heard and have been indoctrinated with many positive messages throughout their lives. These messages are intended to guide and direct lives in ways that foster higher self worth, confidence, awareness and to assist people to grow into their highest selves. The following are popular and love-filled positive sayings that have become mantras for so many:

- It's better to give than receive.
- If you can't say something positive, don't say anything at all.
- Be helpful, not hurtful.
- Work hard, stay humble, be kind, keep smiling.
- Put your best foot forward.
- Winners never quit.
- Never stop learning because life never stops teaching.

And for the record, yes, negativity exists in the world because everything in our world works in opposites. The true beauty of opposites is having the ability to choose. We can't always have the impact on our life outcomes that we desire, but resisting negativity and making positive choices on purpose will result in less distress and disappointment.

I vividly remember being confronted with choosing to be positive early in my life. I'm of small stature and my legs are really, really skinny–just like my Momma's were. She was hugely self-conscious all of her life about this. I almost fell victim to this same negative self-image that hugely affected hers. However, she wasn't having any of that! So, this single parent, minimally educated powerhouse of a woman proceeded, not only to protect me when she thought I needed it, but she also loved, supported, strengthened, and championed me. She made sure that I was equipped with the internal and external resources that I needed to succeed. Mission accomplished!

My grandfather was 97 when he transitioned and was the oldest living member of our family's church home at the time of his death. He had attended our church from the tender age of 10 and was a deacon from as far back as I can remember. His dedication and commitment directly influenced the strong church upbringing of my entire family. There was an extremely rare Sunday that after Sunday School that me and my cousins would not be seated on the pew directly behind the deacons. We would have to be certifiably sick to not be there.

So when I began being bombarded with ugly taunts and criticisms about how skinny I was, specifically my legs, it started me on the road to low self-esteem. Thankfully, I was Blessed to be able to draw from and depend on not only my Mom, but also my faith, inner strength, and the knowledge that I was good enough. That the GOD that I serve doesn't make mistakes, so I could rely on HIM to get me through any trial or tribulation. Please know that at the younger ages, I couldn't articulate what I understood, but I was definitely steeped in my belief and understanding that I could achieve anything that I put my mind to and "That that this too shall pass." I set out to prove to myself that in spite of any so called infirmity that I could: be popular, earn a spot on the Jr. High cheerleading squad that would transition to the Sr. High squad, that I maintained through my high school graduation; that I would run track for two years in high school; that I could roller skate, hike, dance, and participate in any activity that I was interested in and experience no physical limitations because of my "skinny legs." And, in my adult life I came to the understanding that those who are unfortunate to not have use of their legs, no matter the size, would most likely be happy to use, if they could, these really skinny ones of mine.

So, like all of us, I was Blessed with many gifts that I have been allowed, encouraged, and empowered to share widely. Along with some flaws (physical and otherwise), which I have been allowed to overcome, and others that will require a lifelong effort to mitigate or even eliminate.

Most importantly is that, throughout all of my ages and stages, I have learned to seek and embrace positivity in all forms from as many people, places, entities, and experiences as possible. I highly recommend that young people adopt this same position. Be mindful that every thought, word, and action that emanates from you creates your past, directs your present, and affects your future.

So activate positivity by choosing to: think positive on purpose, speak positive on purpose, be positive on purpose, and live positive on purpose. Be a blessing on purpose: love and show love on purpose, be love on purpose. Then trust and believe that what you send out through the universe will come back to you tenfold–plus some! **Making positive and love-filled choices on purpose means building a meaningful destiny that is Good and Powerful Beyond Measure!**

SILENCE, GRACE, AND GRATITUDE
by Louise Robinson

I am a person who sings for a living and one of the greatest sounds for me, is the sound of silence! When I was a little girl, I used to sit in the closet. I loved the fact that I could open my eyes wide and see nothing. Even better, I could hear that sound...silence! I was too young to understand that I was meditating. I was just enjoying the silence, allowing grace to transport me into a happy place! I may not have had the language for it, but I surely had the heart for it. It's funny how when you're young. you may do things without understanding what you're doing. You may not know to be grateful or to revere God, you just know it made you feel happy and that you want to do it again.

Now that I'm older, I understand what it means to be born again. I understand what it means to be still, to know what it means to welcome, and appreciate Grace. I also understand that silence is the gift that allows us to hear the voice of God over our own voice. Someone asked me to consider coming up with three words for 2024 instead of resolutions. My three words are: SILENCE, GRACE, and GRATITUDE!

SIMPLICITY OF TRUE GOODNESS
by Louise Robinson

Every summer, during the last two weeks of August, we would pile in the car; my mother and father on the front bench, me in the middle, my sister and brother at each window. I had to sit in the middle cause I was the youngest. I didn't mind much because we were on our way down south to Grandma Pearl and Pop's house, and that was very exciting!

It was always hot and we didn't have air conditioning in the car, so all the windows were wide open as we rolled at 60 mph with our eyeballs blowing back into our heads. This was the vacation we looked forward to every summer. Being at Grandma Pearl and Pop's house was the complete opposite of our life in New York City, in the Bronx, in the projects. Don't get me wrong, I loved growing up in New York, but my grandparents house was the total opposite. Cabbage and watermelon patches, corn fields, well water and every kind of fruit tree you can imagine. We could just walk up to a tree and pluck a peach, plum, cherry or apple. We were in heaven!

We'd play by the spring until we could smell my Grandma's chicken and pound cake made with warm butter kept on the window sill. We would visit and pick up cousins all the way down from Baltimore, Hampton, and Newport News; until finally we all carpooled over the river (James River) and through the woods to Spring Grove, but we called it " the country." Porches and screen doors, neighbors houses you couldn't see unless you knew where to turn off the dirt road. It was a good life, a simple life, a life that afforded every opportunity to be near nature, live off and enjoy the land and family, slow down, smell the southern air, observe stars, listen to silence and know the SIMPLICITY OF TRUE GOODNESS!

GOOD MEASURE

The souls about you, do they glow?
Bright glow? Glow rather low or hardly any glow?

Who loves or hates? Who down and who elevates? Who gives? Who takes?
Who reciprocates? Who withstands or who breaks? Who attracts and who retract? Who does
and who spews?
And no matter, who keeps right and straight?
Even in abysses of uncertainty and fear, who will do ill and who will illuminate?

And of the aforementioned, you are who?

Glow cannot be without love and traverse cannot without good.
Soulless do not shine.

Glow generates in love, its degree of intensity in proportion to good and its meter the soul.
Souls measure goods. Great goods pronounce glow.

Procurers of love and good, your soul endowed from design to being and purvey love and good
you glow.

Do you not lighten up in the grace of love and good?

A gaze upon love and good sunbeams the deepest space, all time.

REMEMBERING

Born 1969 in Palestine, I recall a magical time as a kid with all my family around me, living, praying, eating together, playing with neighborhood friends, and the beautiful voices emanating from the minaret reminding us of what is important, binding us together.

These images, sounds, and recollections live in a fragile bubble of light always. It was always apprehended by the piercing carnage and chaos of a grand nefarious darkness, ongoing, unchecked; that is the occupation of Palestine. Fear quotas present as break-ins, kidnappings, beatings, and imprisonment of family and neighbors, and confiscation, theft, checkpoints, and murder are the norm to this day.

There is no forgetting the images of occupation armed forces regularly violently crashing into our homes, particularly in the middle of night, the helmet's flash-light blinding my six-year old eyes, shadows of military figures pointing rifles at us. It was not a light of clarity, but blinding.

Given the choice to remain and collaborate with the occupation forces meant spying and reporting on other Palestinians or risking the death of their children. My Father and Mother opted to migrate to the United States in 1977. For the occupation forces, it was a no-brainer to get us out; it was ten less Palestinians on the land.

Bless his soul, my uncle Azmi (1933-1988), an artist and oud player, with his wife Bonnie, a woman of Jewish descent, helped my father and our entire family settle in the United States. His lovely wife, two daughters, a son, and three grandchildren survive Azmi.

It was one step forward to the US and numerous steps backwards in life. We found ourselves in a new land, already at a disadvantage, but alive and together. I, for example, was on my way to second grade in Palestine, a writer and reader of Arabic and mathematics. After immigrating, I was in a Queens, NY kindergarten learning the English alphabet and singing along to "Humpty Dumpty had a great fall."

Everyone in my family was set back, particularly my father, the **Mukhtar**, the head and leader of his village, reduced to menial laborer for most of his adult life, exerting long hours to sustain us. Immense challenges lay ahead within the new land's anti-Arab, anti-Palestinian, and anti-Muslim sentiment.

That is history, the beginning of my story. I share not to draw sympathy nor anger. I wish the opposite, to remind of courage, resilience, and faith in dire circumstances, to thank my father Atef D. Rum (1930-2021) and my mother, who survived several military occupations and sacrificed greatly to ensure our lives.

My father and mother, uncle and Bonnie shed magnificent light in most blinding times to illuminate our way to safety, survival, and growth. I am forever indebted to them, and along my personal spiritual journey to illuminators including Howard B., Paul K., Mike M., Marguerite R., Nara G., Steven G., and others, who have brilliantly shined selflessly to inspire my own light to glow brighter and share it likewise.

GOODNESS AND WONDER: WHY WE BELONG TOGETHER

by Jan Schmidt

Miracles, goodness, and wonder have followed me all the days of my life. That my husband and I ever got together and are still together after thirty-five years is at the core of this extraordinary luck. Two stories Arthur and I tell about ourselves make clear the beating heart of how, with all our outward differences— male/female; Black/white; tall/short; East Coast urban/Midwest rural—we share an underlying twin-ness. It's experiences like these that allow us to cross the divides and connect on a simply human level.

Jan's story. When I was in sixth grade, my friend took me on a day trip with her parents from our small town in Wisconsin to another maybe two hours away. On the drive back, her dad stopped at a restaurant. I froze. I'd never eaten at a restaurant, after all, this was in the 1950s and people didn't eat out like they do now, especially not my parents with six children.

Sitting in the back seat, lost in culture shock, I stared out the window at the birch trees with their peeling white bark. The only thing I knew about dining was from eighteenth and nineteenth century novels. I imagined crystal goblets, giant platters of foods, and, lined up beside each plate, a series of forks. How would I ever know which one to use?

When we got out of the car, I followed, an obedient child, a prisoner of my own fear. I would never tell anyone, as talking about how you felt was not something we did in Wisconsin.

Inside, the diner appeared like a mansion. Once we were seated, the waitress handed me this big plastic-covered thing she called a menu. I opened it. Lists and lists of food. Some with pictures. A whole section called desserts. One long jumble of unimaginable wonder.

My friend's father asked what I'd like to order. His words came at me from outer space. He must have seen the confusion on my face, as he pointed to one that read *half chicken, mashed potatoes, and vegetables.* I gulped. When my mom cooked dinner, she used one chicken for eight of us. How was I supposed to deal with half a chicken? I looked up, petrified. Her dad ordered for me and I felt faint and stared into the blank white surface of my ceramic plate. Next to it lay only one fork—I was saved.

I don't remember anything more, except that outside my world lay a greater world that I wanted to learn about.

Arthur's story. When Arthur was about twenty, having grown up in Harlem and eaten mostly at Chinese or fast food or small family restaurants, he went on a trip to Paramus, New Jersey with a crew he was working with. He was studying to become a hairdresser. This was before he was a successful hair stylist, the first Black in midtown at prestigious Henri Bendel's. This day they were learning to make chignons and practice hackling, which meant mixing and blending hair, mostly synthetic, in various colors, and untangling wigs or hair extensions.

At the lunch break, they drove to a mall with a Steak and Beef Restaurant. Big, bad, Harlem-ite Arthur walked into the immense dining area of this chain eatery lit by elegant chandeliers with multiple dangling crystal prisms. At the time, he says, he felt like a kid with a few pennies at a candy store and gasped, "Oh, God, this is just like Hollywood."

His co-worker cringed, looking around to see who else might have heard what he'd said. "You're embarrassing the crap out of me. Don't you ever say anything like that again."

This would have made me die on the spot, but Arthur says she didn't squelch his amazement; he even appreciated her passing knowledge to him. Of course, he didn't say anything, as telling others how you feel was not something folks from Harlem did either.

We often laugh about our naiveté and that, no matter how much we've seen and done, no matter how hip, or cool, or successful we've become, things continue to arise that we have no clue about. The older we get the more we realize that, as the philosophers say, *I don't know* is the path to wisdom. Underneath our differences, what was apparent was our desire to escape from the confines of our up-bringings, our blinkered visions of reality and yet, keep alive our wonder at new sights and insights. A wonder itself that wonder could survive the world's indifference and sarcasm.

BE YOU, BE TRUE, BE IN INTEGRITY, BE IN FAITH

by Rev. Dr. Ingrid Scott

"In the coming world they will not ask me—Why were you not Moses? They will ask me—Why were you not Zusya?"— Zusha of Hanipol Ukrainian rabbi (1719 - 1800)

Growing up, I always considered myself the black sheep of the family! The youngest & only girl, I considered that I had missed out on being gifted as my two older brothers were both talented. Whilst it never stopped or hindered me in any way, I was never envious of either of my brothers or anyone else for that matter, as God in me, always gave what I needed in order to rise to whatever the challenge in whatever way was necessary. I came to understand that we're gifted in so many diverse ways, that my gifts won't look like yours or vice versa. But what matters is that we live in a way that expresses our most authentic self, and in doing so we're giving kudos to God.

We live in times that constantly bombard us with images and messages of all the things we need to have or to be, in order to attain "perfection," or to be considered successful. It's challenging to hold out for, or onto, one's individuality and the right to be our truest expression of ourselves. People are often striving to be like someone else, whether it's an "influencer" they follow on social media, or some celebrity; they overlook what it means to be themselves. If we're trying to be like everyone else, then who will be us? Who'll be you if you're not? That's what Zusya was reminding us.

"This above all: to thine own self be true, And it must follow, as the night the day, Thou canst not then be false to any man," — Shakespeare

This has guided me throughout my life; as someone's daughter, sister, friend, and wife. There were always others, who thought that they knew me better than I knew myself; and hence, always thought they knew what was best for me. If you try to please and acquiesce to each different version of how they'd like you to be, you'd never get to be yourself. It's not about being selfish but about acknowledging that you're here on this earth as a representation of the Divine, which is always unique in its expression. Never duplicating anything twice; not even your fingerprints!

Therefore, always check in with your heart as to whether what you're doing or how you are expressing is absolutely you. Sometimes it can be scary or overwhelming trying to authentically express yourself. Whether that's in how you dress, your gender orientation, or the career/vocation you choose. I have found when fear tries to undermine my confidence to cling to this powerful and unchanging truth: *"For God has not given us a spirit of fear, but of power and of love and of a sound mind. 2 Timothy 1:7*

A solid and stabilizing reminder that I'm one with God and all that God is, who is the same yesterday, and today world without end. So, I'm more than equal to whatever is before me.

"Integrity, it's not a 90% or an 50% thing, you either have it or your don't" — Unknown

I remember being amused when I came across this quote many decades ago but realized it to be an infallible truth. There's no halfhearted way to be in integrity as it defines and shapes our character and our life. It holds us accountable so that our actions are congruent with what we say our beliefs and values are. We either act in accordance 100% of the time or that we're not in integrity. Everyone decides for themselves what that looks like for them, and the chances are that your definition of being in integrity will look completely different from someone else's, and that's okay. You must discern for yourself what are the appropriate words, actions, and attitudes for you to be living your life in integrity.

But all of this is encompassed in one word: FAITH.
1.The faith you have in God in you to be you.
2.The faith that allows you to be true to yourself.
3.The faith that allows you to let the mind that was in Christ Jesus be in you and operate in you in Integrity.

STORY OF AN UNKNOWN, LOCAL, HARDWORKING, CHANGE-MAKING SCHOOL SOCIAL WORKER

by Arthur Seabury

Can you believe this? *Time* magazine wrote a feature story on me! An unknown, local, hardworking, change-making, school social worker. The initial phase of the pandemic in my community caused a response captured from the local news channel running this story about my work; titled "Hogan Preparatory Academy social worker an ally for students experiencing homelessness," which can be found on KSHB 41's website.

This story set off a chain of memories, exposing me to many whom I've kept in the dark about my early life. In 2021, I was awarded the Distinguished Alumni Award from my high school in Sedalia, Missouri. In 1975, I was reminded how I left there in total shame. It happened like this: I was the Student Body President (the first African American) to hold the position. This was 1975, and this school was 93% White. Many were still fighting the Civil War in their minds in those days. Funny how we have come full circle now as we watch the country start to move back to voter suppression and denial of civil rights.

I was also the first Black Drama Club President and had just returned from Argentina as the first African American Exchange student from the school. Things were falling into place until I was falsely arrested as an accessory to a felony. It seems I was across the street from a crime and did not tell who it was. I was arrested and stripped of all honors connections to school functions. I'm sure some of you know this story. We were going to be bold and perform Room 222 at our Fall production. This would be the first Black play performed in the historically White establishment. It was not to be.

The most embarrassing result of the charade was that I lost my scholarship and let all the community down. There were jokes made about me because Richard Nixon had recently been impeached as well. They compared me to him, being impeached because of stolen tapes. Apparently, there was tampering with a vehicle attached to the charges that the assailants were charged with. Because I was extremely poor, I took a bargain, and joined the Navy under the delayed entry program. All charges would be deferred if I could get an honorable discharge in a minimum of four years. To be in boot camp days after graduation. This was a letdown to the youth who looked up to me as hope, hope in a desert!

My neighborhood, no matter how small the community, was filled with every type of criminal and or crime. I was in an area where the red lights were burned nightly. I had friends who went to jail and reform schools regularly. God and good logic kept me from going too far. I would be known as the studying kid, the kid most likely to succeed. My mom was a functional addict and alcoholic. My dad was an over the road truck driver with a big anger problem. He was violent and physically abusive to my mom. Boy, the things I had to endure as a young helpless man. He didn't understand addiction and would try to beat her clean and sober. My mom stayed with us and they were together for 56 years. Codependency is a real condition. The emotional scars that addiction leaves on the innocent will manifest itself in many anti-social ways. My mom died on Valentine's Day ten years ago. My dad is 90 and feeling the wrath of loneliness. Ironically, I still love and adore him despite the abuse.

I went through Dental Technology school in San Diego and was given orders to Cherry Point, North Carolina. One of my fellow students was marrying a Marine in Cherry Point and we switched orders. I went to Roosevelt Roads in Puerto Rico instead. This was amazing for me. I was under 21 and in the states could not go out to bars, but in Puerto Rico there were no restrictions. I met some very good and some very sketchy people there. Three such amazing people I met there were Melony McGant, Herman Pike, and Gerald Celestin.

Herman was getting close to retirement from the Navy, and I was a kid full of bullshit and youthful misinformation. Emotionally and mentally, I was immature, but Herman took me under his wings and helped me to develop into a man. Herman was originally from Kansas City, Missouri, and was connected to my way of thinking. He and I had so many discussions, helping me open up my eyes, taught me what it was like to be a sailor, and a mature man. He moved back to San Diego after retiring, and I followed soon after. His saga was to continue in San Diego and to this day, we are still close. I was sent to the USS Ogden LPD 5 out of 32nd Street Naval Base in San Diego. Our friendship grew even stronger while I was on long cruises. I would visit him as soon as we returned to the Continental US.

One other very important connection from Puerto Rico was Melony McGant—this beautiful and young sophisticated Black woman from Pennsylvania. She was classy and way out of my league, but I went to work trying my best to be in her circle. She was refined and very astute. No one-liner would ever impress her. We were mutual friends with Herman Pike, and I settled on being a friend without my ego having to be fed by her. We also stayed in touch and made our friendship come full circle.

We followed each other on social media. I became addicted to her "Breathe" messages that were released regularly. She would encourage and send me kind words often. Some people were just placed in the paths of others, and only God knows why. I guess I could say by this time in my life, my self-esteem could handle a friend like her being closer than other friends, but we have both moved beyond that area of our lives.

Gerald retired and stayed in San Diego as well. He was from Haiti and became one of the closest friends a man could have. He also recently had a stroke, but we stay in touch. He is working hard and improving daily. Gerald introduced me to an African shop that we both frequent. He introduced me to Luna Diagne from Senegal. I would stop and hang out with him on my way home from San Diego City College. Yes, I finally made it to college. The G.I. Bill covered it. Ain't God Alright!" I became a very good friend to the owner Luna Diagne through my Hattian brother Gerald Celestin. I spent many hours hanging out with these charismatic brothers. We were kindred and inseparable.

After living about ten years in California, I moved back to Kansas City. When I returned, I was able to become a member of F.O.R.I (Friends of Reggae International). I worked with the Rasta

Dave Clark. He promoted Reggae festivals all over. I was able to invite Luna and Gerald to stay with me during a few of the festivals. Luna was able to connect, sell some clothes and statues in the meantime. One day I got the message that Luna had gone back to Senegal, West Africa. The technology once again kept us connected. Luna and I Facetime regularly. Friends and brothers for life.

I finished my education with a BS in psychology and Master's in social work from University of Kansas. I became a Drug Court Coordinator for Jackson County, Missouri. I then became a family counselor for the Scott Greening Center for adolescent substance abuse until I went to work for The Urban Community Leadership Academy Charter School. Then to Hogan Preparatory Academy, both in Kansas City.

One day, Melony told me she was going to Senegal. I was so excited in my spirit. I made her promise me she would visit Luna Diagne there and he promised to receive her.

They made a connection, and I am sure this is just the beginning. Recently, I have been a part of an innovative charter school program in Kansas City. I have received several honors and awards in my tenure. In 2016, I received the Outstanding Educator Award from CMSU (currently UCM) and in 2019, the Excellence in Education Award by the Missouri Charter School Association. I was placed on a billboard in several locations in the city to allow all people to see. I had a feature story run in two parts with KSHB-TV 41 in Kansas City. I am a board member for Missouri School Social and now, I am looking for my next adventure!

I am sure there is a new connection for me or perhaps an old connection coming full circle. I am trying to write a book and this story is my start. Connecting to the people placed in your path is such a blessing. Be very careful how you treat people. They just may be instrumental in your life! Thank you.

GOD IS GOOD
by Grandmother Marian Dawn SkyWeaver

Before I could start writing this page for Melony McGant's book, ***GOOD IS POWERFUL BEYOND MEASURE***, my son Rob came in all excited. "Mom," he said, "I must tell you something. God is Good." He said it with excitement in his eyes and voice. Remember I told you I got a ticket for parking where the other employee parked? Well, today, I parked in another parking lot, while the others parked in the same place. Someone broke everybody's windows and into their cars. If he had not gotten a "no charge" ticket, his car would have been broken into also. I smiled at him and said, "Yes, God is Goodness!"

I thought of various times I experienced the power of God's Goodness in my life or had been a part of that Goodness experience in someone else's life. The power of that Goodness is inside the oneness of all. Within the essence of Goodness are words like Vibration of Love, integrity, wisdom, faith, respect, intimacy, honor, courage, unity, conscience, mercy, joy, care, forgiveness, belief, prayer, ceremony, thoughtfulness, kindness, etc.

I want to take a moment to write a little about the "Vibration of Love," within the essence of Goodness from my viewpoint. Remember we each have a point of view, and there are at least 360 plus viewpoints in the circle of life to choose from. One item or view at a time with at least 360 plus meanings, values, worth, suggestions, intentions, indications, wishing, plannings, proposing, etc.

As I looked at the words "Vibration of Love," I saw colors, lines of all sorts, had all kinds of feelings, various words & definitions. In my view, the words had many positive definitions depending on the person viewing it, which is me, you, or us.

My first vision was of me in space looking down at Mother Earth, being aware of all around me. I could see and feel strands of positive energy, vibrations coming my way as this energy touched my body. I started sending it toward Mother Earth to heal her and all her relatives (which includes human beings) in the name of LOVE.

The next time I looked at Vibration of Love, I looked for the words within my feelings that exemplify or personified them to me. Words like **Respect, Bravery, Truth, Honesty, Humility, Intuition, Trust, Respite, Integrity, Honor, Healing, Peace, Harmony. Let us not forget either about Faith, Balance, Serenity, Pride, Purpose, Compassion.** I think you can think of more, I thought of Source/God Energy.

Grandmother Christine McBeth got five other grandmothers to start looking at Love Vibrations, as she knew she had only a few weeks to live. She asked us to do something to emphasize or call attention to the Vibrations of Love, how it exists in our world and serves us. I have learned the feelings of Love, Joy, and Happiness when I recognize its presents in my life experiences.

Here are words about Goodness I have carried with me over the years from the book *The Secret Teachings of All Ages* by Manly P. Hall: "*In the theology of the Egyptians Goodness takes precedence and All things partake of nature to a higher or lower degree. Goodness is sought by All. It is the Prime Cause of Causes. Goodness is self-diffused and hence exists in All things; for nothing can produce that which it does not have in itself...That All is in God (The Source Energy), God (The Source Energy is in All; All is in All, and Each is in Each.*"

Today, I Look for the Goodness in All!

LOOKING FOR WORK, FINDING INSPIRATION
by Karen Porter Sorensen

First, I was laid off. Trying to claim state benefits from the NY Department of Labor could only be described as a Kafkaesque nightmare. The websites and phone systems broke down regularly as the sea of jobless New Yorkers swelled. It took me over three days on the 'help line,' to get through to another living, breathing human being. Next, I received a threatening letter calling me in for obligatory 'career counseling.' If I didn't attend this crucial session my benefits would be terminated.

At the office in downtown Brooklyn, I came face-to-face with a frowning woman sitting at the front desk. It was clear she didn't like her job or human interaction of any kind. Without eye contact, she thrust a form in my hand saying vaguely, "Take a seat." I had no idea what I was waiting for or how long it would be. The cloud of dust in the air was probably responsible for the foul moods and general malaise. With the unprecedented crash of newly jobless New Yorkers, the offices badly needed an upgrade and an infusion of positive energy. The latest numbers now show 15.4 million Americans collecting unemployment benefits, a 25-year high—400,000 of them from New York State. I figured the least they could do was give the office a fresh coat of paint to offer some small semblance of hope.

As I daydreamed painting the walls red, a woman appeared. She was a vibrant Black woman with a head of tightly-rolled curls radiating around her smiling face. She wore a vermillion sweater with a draping cowl neck and enormous gold earrings. *This woman is in charge*, I thought to myself. At that moment, I decided I wanted to be in her workshop. She instructed all of us to stand up. I was told to report to classroom number 3.

Like all the others, Room 3 was dreary and comfortless. It didn't take long for the small space to crowd with people; a sporty young man with a backpack, a polished lady with a briefcase, and a middle-aged matron passed by. We were a wildly diverse mix, but we all had the same expression plastered on our faces—a mixture of fear and dread.

The vibrant woman reappeared like a magic trick. Her electric presence crackled, filling the deadened room with life. She spoke intimately, almost conspiratorially, telling us her name, Melony. Melony closed the door, saying she needed her privacy to speak freely. She continued, "I have my own way of doing things that are a little different than other people in the NY Department of Labor offices. At 52, I've had countless jobs over the years. I know what you are going through. I've sat where you are sitting now. And I know how difficult it can be when you lose your employment: especially in these trying economic times. But I just want you all to know that at this moment you have an opportunity to redefine yourself. Please, use this time to clarify your dreams."

She had our attention. "I also want to offer you all a little advice; Treat everyone you meet as positively as you can, and magic things will happen."

"Every day," she said, "I go to the same convenience store to get a coffee. The owner of the shop and I have become friends. Just before the holidays, I stopped by his store. He reached behind the counter and said, 'I have something for you, don't open it until Christmas.' I took his mysterious package, thanked him, and wished him 'Happy Holidays.' Both of us were spending the holidays alone, far from our families. His were thousands of miles away in the Middle East, while mine were in Pittsburgh."

"I headed over to the post office to get the mail that I had been looking forward to receiving all week. When I arrived, I found that it was closed. I returned home sad that, not only would I not see my family, I would also not have any of their presents to open. When I got home, I remembered the shop owner and his mysterious gift. Inside, I found an elegant box. On Christmas, I opened the lid, and found a sparkling silver bracelet with a pendant that said 'Mom.' Recently, the homesick shop owner had started calling me that. I was so touched by this gift because I have never been able to have any children of my own. His gift was also the only one I received that Christmas, and for that reason it was all the more special." She smiled, held up her wrist, jangling the silver bracelet.

Touched by her story, an embarrassing trickle started streaming down my face. She noticed it and looked at me with motherly concern. Sitting in classroom number 3, I was simply overwhelmed by the unexpected warmth of her spirit. It radiated through the bleak room and penetrated the souls of all us weary people.

On the way out, she mentioned she was a writer, and that one of her essays was about to be published. I helped myself to a photocopy she made available to whoever was interested. She gave me a hug and wished me luck. On the subway home, I retrieved her essay and noticed she used a pen name; Miss Mellie Rainbow. I laughed and thought how fitting it was. **Amidst the hopeless doom of the unemployment offices, she had emerged from the darkness, and dust like a walking ray of light.**

A BURNING FLAME
by Joy Southers

I was a little girl from a small town, and I had a burning desire to tell stories. I loved the theatrical and had a vivid imagination for storytelling. I participated in musicals, danced, and went to a performing arts school for theater. I knew by 12 years old that I wanted to work in entertainment. I majored in Media in college because I loved photography, journalism, and film. I believed that you could change the world through these stories and images. I thought I could be anything I wanted to be. Somewhere along the way, I grew up and became cynical, and no longer had the courageousness of my childhood or young adulthood. I had lost my self-confidence.

Life—with its many challenges and disappointments, from heartbreak, fear of failure, fear of abandonment, and childhood trauma of losing a parent plagued me. But the burning desire never left me. It would take hold of me as I worked jobs over the years that I absolutely loathed. The resentment began to build inside of me. I had given up on my dreams and become haunted by them. It wasn't until I was 32, and relocated to the Nation's Capital, that I accepted my calling whole-heartedly, not knowing where the path would lead. I still don't. I pursued my passion against all odds. I even lost my job in the process and struggled to make ends meet. There were many nights I begged God to show me a sign and He gave me many. I trusted that what was put inside of me to do, was leading me toward my destiny and I didn't look back.

I believe every person comes here with a burning flame inside them, and preordained with a purpose in their lifetime. Raising a future president or becoming a movie director—we all have a dream—a purpose, an idea, waiting to be uncovered deep within us. It is not until we are brave enough to accept that challenge and pursue it, against all odds, that we reach self-actualization, experience true joy ,and begin to feel at one with the Universe.

Paulo Coelho referred to this oneness as the "Soul of the Universe" in *The Alchemist*, and that our purpose is a lost treasure waiting to be discovered. Elizabeth Gilbert called it "Big Magic"—the idea that we are all interconnected, and that ideas come from the universe, that they choose us to manifest them. If we don't act on the idea bestowed upon us from the universe, they are passed along to someone else until that idea is actualized. No matter what we choose to call it—purpose or magic—we are co-creators with the source of all things. We are the microcosm of God in Heaven and there is nothing we can't do, with preparation, perseverance and opportunity.

I challenge you to walk by faith, trust yourself, and let go of the fear. Let go of the imposter syndrome that you aren't enough. Know that what is already burning inside you to do, or to become, is already yours.

AN AFRICAN IN AMERICA
by Yoro Sow

I slowly opened the door; Demario still had his sleepy eyes on the last pages of the book.

"Do you know what time it is?" I asked.

"I just want to finish this book before going to bed," he replied. "Cheikh Anta Diop seemed to be a very smart guy! Is this the only book he wrote?"

"No, he is the author of many other great books. He wrote a lot about Africans and their civilizations. The biggest university in Senegal is named after him." I said.

"Then, how come we never heard about him here in America?"

"Maybe that's because you don't want to know much about Africa! We do have good stuff and people; including smart people – and also good food!" I joked, which brought a small smile on my roommate's face and encouraged me to keep on going. "Africa is not just about slavery, civil wars, Ebola, famine, poverty, wild animals, and so on."

He remained silence for a few seconds, staring at me. Then he said "I know! And you are absolutely right...When I was a freshman, one of our professors said his biggest surprise when he first went to Africa was that most of the high school students he met knew about Marcus Garvey, Martin Luther King, Malcom X, Michael Jackson, Whitney Houston, Tupac, Mohamed Ali, Michael Jordan, Oprah, or about Michele Obama more than most of our kids in America do, while the only famous African that he knew was Nelson Mandela."

We both smiled.

"Mandela was a chance not only for Africa, but for humanity in general; his life and his philosophy should be taught in all the universities of the world...But we have other great men and women who marked the history of our continent that you guys should know about, like Bakari II, Haile Selassie, Aline Sitoe Diatta, Patrice Lumumba, Kwame Krumah, Thomas Sankara, Miriam Makeba, Wole Soyinka, George Weah, Dr. Thierno Thiam, Pr Souleymane Bachir Diagne, and the list goes on," I said.

"Yeah, and I agree with you. As African Americans, we have to learn more about the history of Africa because that's our continent too," he replied.

"Well, we Africans will always regard African Americans as blood brothers and sisters, and that explains why we are so happy when we see one of you guys excel in politics, sports, music, etc. At the same time, we feel a lot of compassion when any of you faces troubles...I will let you finish your book and will see you tomorrow."

"Ok! We will continue our discussion tomorrow. Thank you and have a good night, Brother!" he said, before opening his book again.

RIGHT TIMING
by Mario E. Sprouse

Back in the 1970s, I was the Assistant Director of the Upward Bound Program at Columbia University. One weekend, we held a winter retreat for our students. The bus was packed, so I decided to take one student and drive upstate New York. On the way it began snowing, but I wasn't worried because I had a nimble sporty Volkswagen station wagon that could handle any weather. The student and I were chatting up a storm as the snow started falling at a pretty good rate. Eventually, the road was getting more difficult to navigate. I slid a couple of times, but I still wasn't worried. I knew we'd make it to our destination.

Soon, up ahead I saw some yellow blinking lights in the right hand lane. "That vehicle is moving too slow," I thought, so I pulled into the left lane to pass.

While I was in the process of making my move, the student said, "Why are you doing that?"

"Doing what?" I replied.

"Why are you trying to pass the plow?"

Then it hit me. This was a metaphor of my life. Struggling to get ahead through all kinds of obstacles by myself, pushing the envelope to the limits of my own strength, when all I have to do is get behind the plow and let it do the work. Humbled by the student's question, I meekly slowed down and got behind the slow-but-steady moving plow. 45 minutes later we arrived at the retreat center on time and safe. Of course, I had to endure the laughter when the student told everyone what happened. It was a small price to pay for a lifetime lesson. **My timing is not God's timing. When things get rough and the going gets tough, don't try to force the issue. Slow down, get behind the Divine plow and enjoy the ride!**

BEE NEST

by Thupten Tendhar

Once on a Sunday afternoon in South India, I went outside to play with two friends named Tsering and Jampa. It was a school holiday, and the weather outside was hot. We were around nine years old then. Tsering saw a small bee nest on a young tree branch in the village field.

Although we all were scared, we tested the bee's nest by gently pushing a bush straw into the hives. Our faces cheered up as we saw pure honey dripping down the straw. We all wanted to eat the sweet honey. After some discussion, Jampa broke the small branch and ran away with the honeycomb.

Tsering and I also ran far away to escape from the upset bees and, of course, to eat the honey. We all shared and enjoyed the small, yummy, honeycomb. In the evening, I told my father about what we had done.

My father was known as a kind and humble man in the village.

"Son, we all like honey, but it is unfair to break the nest and take away the entire honey from the bees," he said. "You know, bees work very hard flying many miles a day collecting nectar to produce honey. They make it to survive and to feed their offspring. Remember, all bees will be gone one day if we continue to take away all their honey."

That was an awakening lesson for me. I remembered my father's lesson as I grew up from a child into a teenager and then an adult. I have never disturbed a bee nest after that. I have realized that bees are important but a small part of the world. So, there is a more significant implication. This lesson applies to everything from the environment to the energy we utilize or consume in our daily lives. We humans have an insatiable desire for comfort, taste, wealth, fame, etc. Therefore, it is important to apply our critical thinking and logical analysis to see whether or not our demands or consumptions are compatible with ethics and sustainability. The reason is that, just like we love our rights and safety, others too love and deserve respect and happiness. We all can and should coexist!

KINGIAN NONVIOLENCE AND DIVERSITY
by Thupten Tendhar

I was a young Buddhist monk when I studied the *I Have a Dream* speech of Dr. Martin Luther King, Jr. I was a delegate of a major Tibetan Buddhist monastery, selected to attend a workshop on "Nonviolence as a Political Strategy for Tibetan Issue." The Office of Chief Tibetan Representative, Bangalore, Karnataka State, India, coordinated the workshop in 2001.

Dr. Mary Gendler and Rabbi Everett Gendler from the U.S. kindly facilitated the week-long workshop. Delegates from each monastery and Tibetan village in the Karnataka State attended the seminar. For me, it was both enriching and eye-opening. I was fascinated to learn deeper about Dr. King's principle of nonviolence and the highlights of the Civil Rights movements in the USA.

After moving to the USA, some close friends provided the financial support I needed to attend the International Nonviolence Summer Institute here at the Center for Nonviolence and Peace Studies at the University of Rhode Island (URI). I participated in the 2008 International Nonviolence Summer Institute along with a diverse group of people from different states and international countries.

Once completing the two-week intensive training at URI, I received my certificate as a Level I Trainer in Kingian Nonviolence and Conflicts Reconciliation. Dr. Bernard LaFayette Jr., a legendary Civil Rights activist and a close associate of Dr. Martin Luther King, Jr., served as the lead trainer of the institute. It was a fantastic learning experience. I felt terrific that I received my second major training in Kingian Nonviolence from Dr. LaFayette, a colleague of Dr. King and an ordained Christian minister.

After two years, I returned to the URI Center for Nonviolence and Peace Studies for the Level II Advanced Nonviolence Leadership Training in 2010. By the time Dr. LaFayette had moved from URI to Emory University, he came to lead the Level II Training during the annual Summer Institute. After his move, the university appointed Dr. Paul Bueno de Mesquita to direct the URI Center for Nonviolence and Peace Studies.

In 2011, I returned to URI and started to help the Center coordinate its International Nonviolence Summer Institute. While working at the Center, I traveled to other campuses in the U.S. and internationally, co-teaching the principle and strategies of Kingian Nonviolence. It is always encouraging to see how many people apply the framework of Kingian Nonviolence to address the specific issues faced in their societies.

Over the years, the Center has broadened its focus to include Gandhian Nonviolence, Inner

Peace, Environmental Peace, and Human Rights, besides the Kingian Nonviolence. In the meantime, I completed my M.A. and Ph.D. in Education in 2014 and 2019, respectively. I received my Level III Nonviolence Certification for Institutionalizing and Globalizing Peacebuilding.

I feel fortunate for the opportunity to coordinate the International Nonviolence Summer Institute and to direct the Inner Peace program. Besides URI students, the Center has trained hundreds of courageous people, including activists, educators, spiritual practitioners, students, and other peacebuilders from over fifty-five countries across the globe. But the Center's mission remains the same: to *'foster mutual understanding among people'* and *'promote a beloved global community'* to reduce suffering in the world.

In his book *Stride Toward Freedom*, Dr. King mentioned how much he learned from reading Gandhi. He was an eclectic thinker who drew from many sources to address national and international challenges. He did not forsake people or their wisdom because of differences in race or religion. As a practicing Buddhist, I am humbled to learn Dr. King's philosophy and wisdom from Rabbi Gendler, Rev. Dr. LaFayette, and cohorts of many believers and nonbelievers.

In brief, the Center for Nonviolence and Peace Studies at the University of Rhode Island is an internationally recognized academic gathering place. As Dr. Martin Luther King inspired; many students, scholars, educators, and change-makers stand together to promote mutual understanding, conflict reconciliation, peacebuilding, environmental protection, and inclusive communities. I feel lucky to have met my friend Rev. Melony McGant here at URI as well.

TAKING A STAND FOR FREEDOM, JUSTICE, AND EQUALITY

By Dr. William Tiga Tita

I was born in Jos, Nigeria, but spent my childhood and formative years as a young adult in Bali, Sasse, and Cameroon. I immigrated to the United States when I was admitted to Duke University in 1966, where I earned a Bachelor of Science in mechanical engineering in 1969. While at Duke, I played a role in the seizure and occupancy of Duke's Administration Building, an action that also propelled the University of North Carolina, like others during that era, into the diversity orbit.

In the fall of 1969, I was one of six Black students admitted to the University of Pittsburgh Graduate School of Business. At that time, it was the largest cohort of African Americans to enter the graduate business school at once, and the pioneering action was a negotiated outcome of the Black Action Society's 1968 takeover of the University's Computer Center.

In the few short months I entered, in October 1969, about a year after the Computer Center takeover, I pioneered the Student Consulting Project, which sent business students and faculty into the predominantly Black communities of the Hill District, East Liberty, and Homewood, tutoring accounting, taxation, and networking. We helped one store owner create an employee interview form, and held several seminars for Black entrepreneurs. A report, written in 1973, noted that the project was designed "to bring technical assistance from the University of Pittsburgh to ghetto businessmen." That language today seems archaic and harsh, but the project was a working model of student involvement with social action.(1) More than 33 business students, Black and White, became involved with the project, which was nurtured by the ideas of the Black Action Society—that the University of Pittsburgh could– and should– do more to improve conditions and alleviate the social problems plaguing the African American community, locally and nationally.

We started in a small office in the Business School, located in the University's "Cathedral of Learning," with a part-time secretary, and a typewriter. However, after we organized, we got right to work talking to business organizations such as the Business and Professional Men's Association, Homewood Board of Trade, the Business League in Manchester, the (Federal) Small Business Administration, Community Action Pittsburgh and others. I saw the segregated world in which small Black businessmen had to operate. It was important to teach individuals certain technical skills, but I wanted to change the environment too. I wanted Black businessmen to form better relationships with banks, major corporations, and the University. I knew such collaborations could provide financial and professional resources. A collaborative effort that linked the University as a customer, a major corporation as a manufacturer, and a community-based business person as a supplier resulted in a multi-million-dollar transaction that was a win for all parties!

We launched a citywide credit union for Black businessmen, a University "Buy Black" campaign, and a series of seminars that educated the larger community on the challenges facing Black businesses. One capstone of these efforts was the first Annual Small Business Men's Night held in the summer of 1970, just nine months after the program began. More than 200 people attended, with representation from city and county agencies, colleges, social, and business groups. The seeds were planted and began to grow. Of the 18 Black students entering the Graduate School of Business in 1970, 17 joined our efforts. We began to address issues regarding insurance, bonding, and how to secure contracts from the University. We were also given a $400,000 Federal grant from the Department of Education's Fund for the Improvement of Post Secondary School Education (FIPSE), to formalize and embed the value of "experiential" learning into the MBA curriculum.

For many years, I provided key guidance on the project. I nurtured a university-community partnership through a Board of Directors chaired by Taylor Thompson, a Hill District Electrical Contractor. Businesspeople and the community at large appreciated this kind of engagement and leadership, which I believe became the key factor in helping to sustain the project. We had as our untiring mentor, Ms. Betty Tilman, who believed in the power of intercultural exchanges and encouraged our engagements in communities local and abroad, notably, in Ghana and Afghanistan.

I was at Pitt for a decade, studying and teaching, and primarily serving as a change agent, working toward building collaborations between the community and the University. But I will not forget that racial division frayed the American fabric both inside and outside of the University's walls. Housing proved to be a formidable barrier at the time, but as someone familiar with challenging and uprooting the status quo, I found a way to turn my personal battle into a community victory.

An 11th hour discovery of a Pittsburgh Courier ad listing an "apartment for colored couple only," enabled me to stay in Pittsburgh and eventually to connect with the InterCultural House, a project supported by the Gertrude Stein Foundation and backed by Pitt's African-American leadership. There were 24 students—10 White, 10 Black, and four international students—who lived in shared rooms and engaged in community services nationally and abroad. It was founded in 1968, in the wake of the assassination of Dr. Martin Luther King Jr. and was created to embrace the legacy of peace and equality left by the slain civil rights leader. I served as founding Resident Director at the InterCultural House with my wife, Bernice. I stayed there until we started our family and I earned a doctorate in business from Pitt. I then completed postdoctoral studies in social ethics as a Kent Fellow at the University of Southern California.

Until retirement, I served on the faculty of D'Amore-Kim School of Business at Northeastern University. I was a visiting faculty member at the Graduate School of Business, Stellenbosch University in South Africa, served as a program manager and chief technical adviser in the United Nations Development Program until 2002. I also founded IOCS-African Informatics, S.A., a Cameroonian software-engineering firm and software reseller.

Much of my career is owed to people, like the members of the BAS, Ms. Betty J. Tilman at the International Student Center who made the call for society to change. When my cohort of six Black students entered the Pitt Graduate School of Business, I vividly recall Dean H. Jerome Zoffer's voice bellowing out, "Give me one year of your life and I will give you the rest of your life." It was a chorus that resonated with the critical mass of African-American University of Pittsburgh students who understood that it was time for us to take a stand for freedom, justice, and equality at Pitt. And we did.

TALE OF A SMILING DRAGON
by George Teroy

I walked through the forest trail in the early morning, lighted only by the stars above. The path felt native, untouched by man. As the dawn light peered through the mountaintops, the gentle clouds swirled overhead. The dew beneath my bare feet felt rejuvenating.

A native Wiseman dressed in earth tones suddenly appeared along the path under the shade of an ancient tree. His wrinkled face possessed an aura of both strength of a warrior's past, and he wore tiger eye stone beads around his neck. As I approached the Wiseman, his wrinkles became more pronounced.

"My name is Whole Water. I am here to help you search for Love," he whispered. The Wiseman quietly gestured towards the tree and handed me an ancient dream catcher made of vibrant feathers and cotton twine. "Close your eyes and imagine your heart smiling with sunflowers. Then ask yourself, are you truly at peace?"

"How do I know if I am in Love?" I asked.

"Love opens doors just as fear closes them. Learn how inner peace will enlighten your soul. Take these magical seeds of inspiration and plant them in the soul of your heart to nourish the growth of self-love."

The Wiseman gave me a bag full of magical seeds. "Someone will soon appear from your dream catcher, and you will experience sunflowers in your quest. Go forth to the shore and take a sailboat to the Islands of Wands. There you will meet your spiritual guide, Keoja."

I swung the canvas bag of seeds over my shoulder, which was tied to the end of a cherry wood branch, and started my journey. I glanced over my shoulder to see him one more time, only to find that he was gone. I was pondering on what just happened, as the wind echoed his voice, *"I will always be in your thoughts."*

I continued my journey along a sandy road, with polished seashells reflecting the bright sunshine overhead. A salty breeze splashed against my face. As I came up to a wooden sailboat sitting on the golden beach, I remembered what the Wiseman said:

"Raise your sails high against the stormy sky, and aim your bow towards the horizon, as you venture forward to face the uncharted sea of uncertainty. When the winds calm down, I will be there to catch you."

I felt at peace going with the flow of the undertow. I launched the boat into the water, hoisting the sails to catch the wind, and the boat sailed beyond the breaking waves, onto open water. Navigating by the stars, I arrived at a tropical island. I was greeted by a heavy-set islander dressed in a colorful cloth wrapped around wide hips. His dark hair was tied into a bun, holding up a giant conch seashell with both hands. I reached into my sack, taking out a magical seed, and tossed it into the waves as an offering to the ocean, thanking them for a safe passage.

The hefty islander had a huge grin and shouted, "Namaste Hermit! Welcome to the Island of Wands. I have been waiting for you. I am Keoja, and you are probably asking yourself how I know you. You have taken the steps to travel beyond your fears by boarding that wooden sailboat. Love opens doors, whereas fear shuts them closed. Follow me!"

Keoja walked into the tropical forest, blowing the conch shell horn with a heartbeat rhythm.

"Where are we going?" I asked.

"Close your eyes and listen to your inner voice," Keoja replied.

With my eyes shut, I followed him into the forest, guided only by the sounds from his conch horn.

"Trust in yourself and listen to the rustling winds around you which ring out your peaceful song," the islander said. "You have given out love vibrations during your travels. Doors will now open in your dreams."

We soon arrive at a forest clearing, covered with woven bamboo mats. "We'll stop here. Now open your eyes," he said, "trust in yourself as you would trust in another, for we are simply a mirror image of one other. The way that you treat others is how you should treat yourself."

Keoja left, retiring into his grass hut for the night.

As the morning sun rose over the mountains, he returned, and gave me a rose quartz crystal wand for my journey.

"Take this wand in your right hand and point it towards your heart. Rotate the crystal clockwise while visualizing how you would love the ones around you without expectations or judgment," he instructed.

I thanked him for the gift. "Will the power of this wand give me love?" I asked.

"You must love and forgive yourself first," he replied, throwing the conch shell back into the ocean. "Attachment to fear-based emotions like possession, ego, jealousy, or disrespect toward others will close doors around you. You create your own fear, and no one else can do this except you. Love opens doors for Love to enter."

I felt at peace packing the wand into my travel sack, removing a magical seed to give to Keoja for his wisdom.

"I offer this seed with magical love," I said.

He smiled back with arms wide open.

"You are beginning to understand the meaning of love, because soon love will appear before you. Now, take the path towards the mountains, where the Smiling Dragon awaits," he said, pointing the way. "Go with Love and Self-Love will open."

I tossed the cherry branch over my shoulder and set off towards the mountains.

As I climbed towards the mountaintop, the path turned jagged and rocky. Each step was more challenging than the last. The base of the mountain appeared to shrink as I ascended upward. I sensed yellow smiles of doubt and apprehension in the distance. I reached into my pocket of mementos from my journey, pulling out a polished shell representing strength and courage. As I viewed my reflection in the seashell mirror, I heard a voice of wisdom, *I am not an image of the past, rather a bright reflection of this beautiful moment.* This inspired me to continue the climb full of confidence and without fear of failure.

As I neared the peak, I saw dancing sunflowers swaying in the wind, each petal flickering an array of light from the sky above. The magic seeds in my bag resembled these sunflowers. I started to plant them into the ground, using the rose quartz wand to cover each hole. I gave a blessing to the field.

"I cultivate you with inspirational seeds of love, nourish you with gratefulness and gratitude for soon sunflowers will display a beautiful dance for all who see them," I said.

I returned the rose quartz wand back into my travel sack remembering the voice of wisdom saying, *Possession is a fear that closes doors. Love opens doors to Self-Love.* Passing through the sunflower fields, I arrived at a golden castle with a large crystal door. I heard the chants from eastern mantras, and sweet incense filling the air. As I closed my eyes, I felt energized.

I took in a cleansing breath, releasing all fears, and the crystal door swung open. The chants from inside grew louder. I heard a voice emanating from behind flowing orange silk curtains.

"Welcome, my traveling Hermit...your journey to find love has always been inside you."

"It was indeed a difficult journey to get here," I whispered, staring with amazement at the hanging crystals & chimes overhead.

"Challenges do spark the soul to seek out self-actualization as long as you love and give that love without judgment or expectations in return. Love opens doors, as fear will close them."

An elderly man dressed in a silk robe with red corral facets appeared from behind the flowing curtains, holding a cherry wood walking stick.

"I am Smiling Dragon. You have planted seeds of inspiration along your journey as others did before you," he said. "Follow me. Take the crystal wand from your carry sack and hold it in your right hand."

We arrived at an ancient tree with a wide trunk and deep twisting branches of wisdom like another I saw before.

"Ancient trees do have ears. But people only see its bark," Smiling Dragon said. "Take a deep breath and say to yourself, 'I love you.'"

I pointed the rose quartz wand towards my heart and rotated it in a clockwise motion. Suddenly, I was overwhelmed with love and peace for the first time. A door at the base of the ancient tree door swung open.

"Walk through its outer bark," he instructed, "and see the grain of life for which you will find your Fortune Wheel to complete your journey."

I thanked the Wiseman by giving him my rose quartz wand as a sign of gratitude.

"You have found your Love to give and forgive," replied the Wiseman. He took and mounted the rose quartz wand onto his cherry wood walking stick. It was a perfect fit. "I thank you for returning the energy back to the crystal staff, for it will be yours to turn the Fortune Wheel at the end of your journey and find the answer of love."

"I am aware of my life's purpose to love without expectation and to forgive those who failed your joy of love. Knowing that I will attract the same love as I give myself, I will be with the spiritual love as I see myself," I replied, accepting his generous gift.

I pulled out a polished seashell from my pocket and placed it in the tree bark along with other mirrors from seekers before me. The colorful rainbow reflected by these shells shot across the blue sky.

"Go forth, and meet your love who is waiting at the end of the Fortune Wheel rainbow. Collect sunflowers to embed seeds of inspiring love along the way."

As I headed back down the mountain and away from the golden castle, the Smiling Dragon's chants got softer in the distance. This time I need not look back over my shoulder, knowing that the wisdom I attained during the journey will always be there to guide me.

HEART RECIPE
by Sebastian Teroy

My favorite recipe comes from the heart like my dad taught me.

I want to feed the world around me with love and awareness so no people will go hungry.

All you need is a portable kitchen to prepare this special dish.

The cooking ingredients are free like breathing air but better.

Take a big bowl of your inner thoughts and mix in a scoop of kindness.

Blend in a smile and a dance to shake up the body.

Grab a handful of hugs and pour it into the mixture of laughter.

Sprinkle unlimited amounts of sweet kisses and blessings until the feeling becomes warmer.

Stir the big bowl with a bamboo spoon,

turning in a clockwise direction like Earth circling the Sun.

When all ingredients become one, the dish is ready to be served in the palm of your hands

and given to the next person.

If we feed the world by giving, no people will go hungry.

I love to cook in my kitchen.

CHILDISH TALES OF TWO CITIES
by Micheal Vann

"When I was a child, I spoke as a child, I understood as a child: but when I became a man, I put away childish things." 1 CORINTHIANS 13:11

And he said: Verily I say unto you, except ye be converted, and become as little children, ye shall not enter the kingdom of heaven. MATHEW 18:3

On June 18, 2022, (God willing) I celebrated my 65th birthday. Like everyone else during the Pandemic, there was plenty of time to reflect on one's life. The two scriptures I draw from to paint the canvas of my soul's journey are contrarian in nature, but reflect the holistic circle of one's life. That season of your life is when arthritis is the first thing that taps you on your elbow or knees, and you smile. As a child growing up in Gary, Indiana, the most important image outside of my parents, and extended family was the omnipotent image of Jesus Christ. Moreover, there was no other book that influenced my life more than the Bible and the stories of Jesus, Moses, and Samson, in that order. But really it was Jesus with whom I wanted to mirror. And just like Jesus, I made the grown-up decision to get baptized as an adult at 12 years old. I thought I was a man. Heck, I had my first job at 12, and as a teenager I was able to buy my own Chuck Taylor gym shoes with multi-colored shoelaces, sporting my collection of Italian knit tops, and spending my own money to go bowling, concerts, and eating at Lee's Chicken Shack whenever I wanted. This adult stuff was a piece of cake.

I must confess though, letting go of childish things, the ever-present ego has been a lifetime process. Every 10-years I hit a different milestone of getting out of God's way, eventually understanding that I have no control over anything that is meaningful, purposeful and all important in my life. Fast forward, August 1979, fresh out of college, I was bound for New York City. The city provided me the playground to explore all my adult ambitions, I set my own rules, and submerged my adult self into my personal Gotham quagmire. How do I maintain my spiritual consciousness, and navigate through these minefields? Driven by the eye of the Tiger, but grounded in the heart of the Lamb.

I have now been in New York City for over 42 years. Approximately 40 years had passed from the time I came and when COVID-19 shut everything down. I have come to believe that these 40 years equated to the 40 days of wilderness Jesus experienced in the desert. I'm not saying there weren't wonderful times here; I became one of the first African Americans to become a menswear buyer at Lord & Taylor, I opened my first restaurant at 34 and co-owned over 6 restaurants in 10 years, and even had modest success as a commercial actor. However, I never felt my soul was ever grounded in my purpose. Everything I manifested as an entrepreneur was transient. I could never build the foundation that would sustain my personal vision, my company mantra, "building brands that build communities." It took the pandemic to cultivate my efforts to dig deeper in my soul for the answer.

As I now journey into the 4th quarter of life and reflect, it is the humble life of Jesus Christ I still truly aspire to live. As a child, my life was effortless; I was a dreamer and essentially lived from my inner most thoughts to manifestation. My parents and the homelife they created were extremely nurturing. I knew I was loved and never had any doubt on what I could achieve. God provided the pathway. Ego never came into play until in my 30's, when I began to have modest success in my entrepreneurial ambitions. The minute I began to step in, God could make a way, and I experienced a new reality. Yes, God still loved you, but you need to get out of the way. Low and behold, after some 42 years and a global pandemic, I have decided it was time to go back to where it all started; unconditional love, family, dreamscapes, childhood memories of God cradling me like baby, opening doors and lighting my path effortlessly. **I am going home; the prodigal son returns to finish the good work left undone. Thank you, Lord, for loving me unconditionally.**

am no one, yet I am everyone: living a life defined by the purpose I must fulfill in order to remain a part of this world. Yet, it is not my own purpose. To whom or for what end do we serve? This question has been with me since childhood when I watched a butterfly slowly emerge from its cocoon.

It was an amazing transformation; I watched as the colors emerged and wings began to push through the sticky fibers. Despite my yearning to help, I could only watch. It seemed so cruel: to witness something beautiful struggle so much just to fly free.

After these long days spent emerging and pushing against the confines of its prison, something miraculous happened—the butterfly finally flew away! At that moment, I understood: sometimes we must endure pain and suffering in order to truly understand our own strength and potentiality. It's only in this moment that we can soar above all else and into freedom.

My struggles are similar. Although I've faced circumstances that have felt unbearable or too much for me to handle on my own, I've learned that if I stay true to myself, my soul will eventually find liberation from whatever binds it down here on Earth. Perhaps that's why we're here. Without experiencing our own unique pains and struggles, we would never know how strong we truly are inside; nor would we ever appreciate our power or transcendence over any obstacle placed before us.

When I became a single parent, I had no idea what I was getting myself into. It seemed like in one moment, my life was orderly and predictable. In the next, pages were ripped from my storybook, as if to say fate would write this chapter of my life instead.

As time passed and I looked into the faces of the children placed on my journey, I began to understand that perhaps more than just random luck was at play here. Maybe there really is a grand plan at work in our lives, guiding us toward something greater than we could have ever imagined.

The moments are fleeting. They are often forgotten or overlooked completely, but these are actually markers on our timeline that define who we are set to become. We experience love and pain, birth and death, gain and loss: contrasts that summon an understanding of ourselves that we can only experience through extreme emotion.

Like butterflies emerging from their cocoons after a time of struggle and transformation, we must sometimes be pushed to our limits to realize our true purpose in life. Though it may feel like chaos or confusion now, each piece will eventually come together perfectly; as if a part of something far greater than any individual component could ever fulfill alone.

What was revealed to me—and I now share with you, my dearest reader—was a philosophy of existence. With this, I contend that if applied to your own daily life, your true nature and meaning will be presented to you as shared so many times before with those who've experienced the blush of death and breath of life. The words are not spoken and can only be heard, with the true limits of your existence tallied into five life statements:

1. How we've LIVED
2. How we've LOVED
3. What we've LEARNED
4. When we've LET GO
5. What we've LEFT BEHIND for others

Please take a moment and repeat these statements in your mind a few times. Allow them to resonate with you, evoking an introspection as you recall those moments in your life when choices were made.

It was a crisp Autumn day, the kind that brought out the best in people. The sun shone brightly, and everyone seemed to be filled with joy and hope. Though beneath this outward show of cheerfulness, a deep longing for something more existed.

I had been on a journey for some time now, seeking something I could not put my finger on, but I knew it would bring me closer to true fulfillment. That is when I stumbled across the stories of people who've encountered near-death experiences: the contents of which beget the

Five L's Philosophy: ***Live, Love, Learn, Let Go, Leave Behind.***

The words resonated deeply within me, as if written just for myself at this precise moment in time. It spoke about how one should live life today as if no other days lie ahead, expressing our talents and skills towards others with kindness and compassion, so we can look back one day without regret or remorse. To love fully and unconditionally despite any setbacks or heartbreaks along the way—as love is at the core of our existence—while learning from each experience no matter how painful or rewarding. Then, letting go of anything negative that holds us back from living up to our full potential, and leaving behind rewarding contributions to society and people we successfully influence.

I felt inspired to apply these teachings to everyday life and make them part of my very being, embracing every moment with intentionality, so that nothing falls through the cracks from now until eternity!

Remarkable legacies are not always those of bronze statues and stoic men in paintings. The truly remarkable memories are someone you held hands or embraced with when he or she needed you the most. Maybe it's the sacrifice you made to bring joy—if only for a moment—in another person's life, or your remembrance by either a few or many for your good acts. Perhaps it was the words you shared as a beacon of light in the darkest of times. In the end, your life is defined and measured by these sums.

This life needs you. Clearly, you agree, as you exist to read this now. We need you, as you and I are the fabric of the exponential existence of collaboration. Remain perfectly you as you reveal yourself along this journey we share, a beautiful purpose for a blessed soul. Light and love to you.

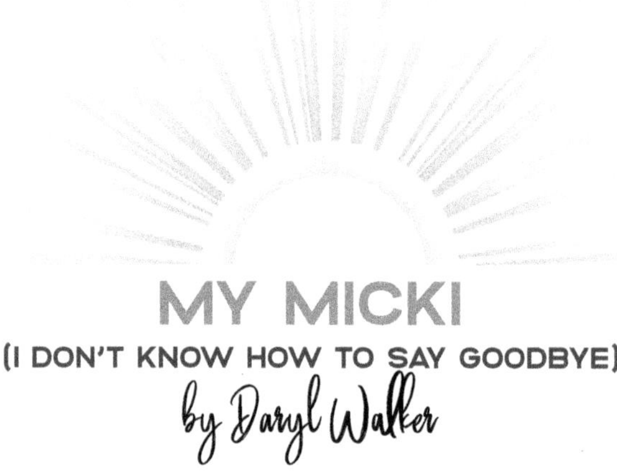

MY MICKI
(I DON'T KNOW HOW TO SAY GOODBYE)
by Daryl Walker

Micki Grant is renowned as a multi-award-winning lyricist, composer, writer, director, actress, and singer who has been revered as a trailblazer for African Americans in theater, television, and music for over six decades, many of whom credit her for giving them their career start through working in one or more of her many theatrical productions.

She garnered several "firsts" as a woman and an African American. A few of her most notable firsts include: first African American to go beyond the silent roles Blacks played in commercials to the principal performer; first African American to write commercial jingles, garnering her the coveted Clio Award; first African American to garner a contract role on a Soap Opera as Peggy Nolan in *Another World*; first woman to write the book, music, and lyrics to a Broadway Musical with *Don't Bother Me, I Can't Cope*, in which she also starred; and the first woman to win a Grammy Award for Best Score From An Original Cast Show Album with *Don't Bother Me, I Can't Cope*.

Some of her most prominent awards and nominations are:

- Drama Desk Awards - 1972 – WINNER, Most Promising Lyricist Gold Star – *Don't Bother Me, I Can't Cope*
- Drama Desk Awards - 1972 – WINNER, Outstanding Performance Gold Star – *Don't Bother Me, I Can't Cope*
- Obie Awards - 1972 – WINNER, Music and Lyrics Gold Star – *Don't Bother Me, I Can't Cope*
- Grammy Awards – 1973 – WINNER, Best Score from An Original Cast Show Album – *Don't Bother Me, I Can't Cope*
- Tony Awards - 1973 – NOMINATED, Best Book of a Musical – *Don't Bother Me, I Can't Cope*
- Tony Awards - 1973 – NOMINATED, Best Original Score (Music and/or Lyrics) Written for the Theatre – *Don't Bother Me, I Can't Cope*
- Grammy Awards – 1977 – NOMINATED, Best Show Cast Album - *Your Arms Too Short to Box with God*
- Tony Awards - 1978 – NOMINATED, Best Original Score (Music and/or Lyrics) Written for the Theatre - *Working*
- Helen Hayes Awards - 1997 – WINNER, Outstanding Lead Actress, Non-Resident Production Gold Star - *Having Our Say*

- A multitude of additional awards includes the NAACP Image Award, the Outer Critics Circle Award, Audelco's Outstanding Pioneer, and Vivian Robinson Legacy Awards, the AEA's Paul Robeson Award, the National Black Theatre Festival's Living Legend and Sidney Poitier Lifelong Achievement Awards, and the 2012 Dramatists Guild of America Lifetime Achievement Award. In 2003, the NY City Council issued a Proclamation extolling her "outstanding contribution to culture". Proclamations she received from other major cities include Los Angeles, Dallas, Newark, and Mobile.

Some of her other theatrical works include:

- *Croesus and the Witch* (1971), musical – music and lyrics
- *Step Lively, Boy* (1973), musical – music and lyrics
- *The Prodigal Sister* (1974), musical – music and lyrics
- *The Ups and Downs of Theophilis Maitland* (1976), musical – music and lyrics
- *I'm Laughing but I Ain't Tickled* (1976), musical – music and lyrics
- *Alice* (1978), musical – music and lyrics
- *Eubie!* (1978), musical revue – additional lyrics
- *It's So Nice to Be Civilized* (1980), musical – book, music, and lyrics
- *Phillis* (1986), musical – music and lyrics
- *Step into My World* (1989), revue – music and lyrics
- *Carver (Don't Underestimate A Nut)* (1996) – music, lyrics, & book

Some of her additional writing credits include many of the popular commercial jingles of the '50s and '60s, as well as the pop song *Pink Shoe Laces* (1959) recorded by Dodie Stevens, which reached number 3 on the US singles chart.

She did so much for, and meant so much to, so many. Of all her accomplishments, she was most proud of the doors she opened for others. With the biggest and brightest smile, she would always say, "the thing that was so wonderful for me was that I put all these wonderful, talented actors to work . . . that was the most gratifying thing for me."

With all her creative genius and success, she was always gracious, approachable, and willing to help anyone who asked for or needed it. In fact, she had over fifty charities and organizations that she diligently and cheerfully gave to annually. She truly adored people, and people, in turn, truly adored her.

But for me, Micki Grant was so much more than all these things. For as long as I can remember, she has always been just MY MICKI, who was also the source of many personal firsts for me. My first memory of anyone outside my immediate household was MY MICKI. In fact, the first meltdown I can remember having was because of MY MICKI. I was no older than three or four when she stopped by our house one night, came into my room with my parents, and woke me up to say goodbye as she was leaving Los Angeles for New York. My dad literally had to pry my hands from around her as I just couldn't let her go and say goodbye. Before she left, she gave me my first instrument--a toy bongo, which I'm a bit embarrassed to admit I slept with for too many years because she, MY MICKI, gave it to me. Upon learning to write, the first letter I ever penned to anyone was to her, MY MICKI. My first long-distance call, my first time seeing snowfall, my first time throwing a snowball, and my first time seeing the Time's Square New Year Eve's Apple fall were all with her, MY MICKI.

I was always quite possessive of MY MICKI too. She'd often laugh at how I would let my family and friends only get so close to her before boldly declaring, "she's MY MICKI, not yours!" In photos that both she and I are in, you'd most likely find us right next to each other no matter who else was in the picture (parents, siblings, grandparents). You would only need to locate one of us, and the other is bound to be right there next to them.

MY MICKI was like another mother, sister, aunt, and best friend, all wrapped into one to me, and I guess I filled a void for her as the child, the son, she never had. In one of my last conversations with her, we discussed our unique relationship, contemplating why God had given us such a strong bond. I remember her saying, "It's really unexplainable...but just maybe it was because He knew how much I would need you to take care of all my needs during these latter years."

It has truly been my privilege, honor, and joy to have loved and cared for MY MICKI all my life. And still now, as it was when I was that little boy, I'm constantly finding myself trying to avoid the inevitable meltdown associated with saying "goodbye". But MY MICKI actually penned the perfect words years ago in a song for one of her yet to be published works, and these words have helped me immensely since her physical departure from us:

I DON'T KNOW HOW TO SAY GOODBYE © 2022
From Phyllis, by Micki Grant

If I seem somewhat awkward and at a loss for words
It's not because I'm reticent or shy
In fact, I've often tended to be a bit long-winded
But I don't know how to say goodbye
Were I to write a poem on what I think of you
The verses would pour out in great supply
Whatever else has ailed me, words have never failed me
But I can't find the words to say goodbye

Finding you I found the rarest of treasures
Knowing you I've known my greatest joy
Is it any wonder I have no words to say
How it feels to stand here and let you go away

I don't know how to say it, I don't want to say it
What's more, let's not even try
Let's just say "til then", MY MICKI
"Til we meet again," MY MICKI
But never ever say goodbye

And so now, I'll wrap-up as was my tradition with her by saying, "I LOVE YOU MADLY, MY MICKI." And I look forward to that glorious day when I'll once again hear that special new word she coined and would affectionately reply, "MADLIER!"

MOLLIE GUSTINE: SHE WAS MY MOM AND A NYPD OFFICER IN THE TURBULENT 60'S

by Bonnie Weaver

Detective Mollie Gustine was my mom. I will discuss her journey as a New York City police officer, but first I want to introduce her. My mother has always been a constant figure in my life and was always there. When my mother informed the family that she was going to become a police officer, it really didn't resonate with me. I was 10 years old, my world was school and outside. We weren't allowed to sit in on adult conversations, unbeknownst to me her job as a police officer would have a lasting impression on a 10 year old Black girl.

It was during "Parents Career Day." This classroom event was a " shaming" for the Black students. Our white classmates proudly describe their fathers' jobs; Lawyers, doctors, professionals, while the Black students bent our heads down describing our fathers' jobs; post office, construction, and working on highways (paving roads), or janitorial. Among us in the Black community, those mentioned jobs are honorable. When it was my turn to describe my mom's job (I mentioned my dad built apartments, worked on the Ohio Turnpike. There were no special ooo's or ahh's." But when I told them my mom was a cop, the teacher said "you mean she's a Metermaid." I said "no, she's like a man, only she's a woman." Then the teacher said "She must be a crossing guard." Again, I said no. I mentioned she had a gun. That teacher was trying to convince me that my mother lied to me. I told my mom what happened. Nothing more was said.

I went to school the next day, and my mom came up to my class in her full uniform, and her gun. I didn't know she was coming. Every Black student's chest and head rose up tall and strong. That teacher was shocked. It was the talk of the school. This was my mom.

My mother was an industrious member of the NYPD. Through her perseverance, faith, and work ethics, she broke several "class ceilings" (see statement of her being elected to PBA, NYPD Guardians Association, and citation for her undercover work in the FBI).

In February 1982, Detective Gustine was shot during an attempted robbery. Unbeknownst to the robbers she also had a gun. Shot in her left breast, she was able to enter into her house and reloaded. That's my mom. On August 20th, 2023, Detective Gustine was given the ultimate honor of having the street where she resides co-named after her.

This street co-naming was lit with several elected officials, community leaders, lifelong neighbors, family and friends. But the presence of former NYPD Commissioner Keechant Sewell (NYPD first Black female commissioner) was proof validated that my mom's tenacity, determination, and confidence was a catalyst for future NYPD women Police Officers.

My mother joined the NYPD in 1963. During that time women were relegated to duties as matrons or working in Juvenile Courts. The challenges she had to endure would have broken some, but my mom was determined to provide for her family. There were times when some of her fellow officers didn't want to ride with her. Racial slurs were used, but she stayed focused. She fought hard to prove herself "one of the boys."

Her greatest accomplishment while working for NYPD was becoming the first African American woman in the history of the NYPD elected Delegate to the Patrolmen Benevolent Association, representing over 36,000 police officers. She also served as a DEA delegate.

At a ceremony honoring present and fallen NYPD officers, the former Police Commissioner James P. O'Neill stated, "for a select few, public service is truly a life's calling. Your career with the NYPD spanned seven police Commissioners, four mayors, and six US Presidents through a time of international war, domestic civil unrest, and cultural change. Through it all , you chose to serve, and I want to personally thank you for your long-standing commitment to the people of New York City. You were a true pioneer and every cop who continues your legacy owes you a tremendous debt."

Detective Mollie Gustine Was Called Many Names, but She Was Always My Mom.

WHY DID ROSA PARKS HUG ME?
By Nita Wiggins

Excerpted from 2021's *Civil Rights Baby: My Story of Race, Sports, and Breaking Barriers in American Journalism*

I met world-history icon Rosa Parks on February 4, 1988, at her seventy-fifth birthday celebration given by the city of her birth, Tuskegee, Alabama. On that memorable day, I had been a TV news reporter less than two years and was enjoying my new status as bureau chief for Columbus, Georgia's WTVM Channel 9.

I took pride in being professional, polished, and prepared.

I spied Mrs. Parks alone before the event. How that could be! How could the woman to whom the event was dedicated be waiting in silence when, all around her, men and women in business clothes and teenagers in school uniforms buzzed with activity?

I walked toward her, recalling the crisp black-and-white pictures I had seen in school books. Her police mugshot—with the inmate number *7053*. On December 1, 1955, she had refused to obey a direct order from an armed bus driver give up her seat. This triggered her arrest by Montgomery police. The city's black population responded with a crippling bus boycott.

Mrs. Parks became the spark, most people believe, that ignited the blaze in the organized rebellion. And now, I was moving toward her.

I need her to remember me!

I reached her and realized we stood at nearly identical heights. I was five-foot-three, so she must have been, too. Her signature dark hair was mostly gray and pulled into an updated French twist. Modified cat-eye glasses with light-pink frames had replaced the wire frames on historical record. Her lilac-colored rain slicker and baby-blue flapper's hat beautifully set off her honey-colored skin. The overall vision of her stirred a familiarity in me—as if my paternal grandmother were present.

I'm standing here with Mrs. Parks!

My mind raced to find something enduring to say to leave an impression on this woman who had done so much.

I formally extended my hand to shake hers. I stated my first and last names clearly.

Then something changed.

Her eyes had settled on me as she listened to my name. I looked beyond the frames of her glasses, gently meeting her gaze. *These eyes, the eyes of Rosa Parks, have seen so many changes.* I became aware of how petite and thin she was. Death threats, insomnia, ulcers, and extended financial stress had ravaged her body, her life, and the lives of her loved ones.

I knew that I needed to pay something back to her, but there was nothing I could give to repay her for what she had done for black people and for society beyond the American borders. Nothing—except my physical self.

I shed my professional demeanor as if I were slipping out of clothing and said, "Excuse me, Mrs. Parks—I never do this—but is it OK for me to hug you?"

She replied, "Sure, baby," and sounded just like my beloved Georgia-born maternal grandmother.

I leaned in to embrace her, shoulder-to-shoulder, the skin of our cheeks touching. She offered a surprisingly firm hold, like a mother might wrap her arms around her child. I contracted the muscles in my forearms to pull her close. I closed my eyes and lost myself in her arms.

My world became silent.

Our hearts rested in proximity in our quiet cocoon. We breathed slow and unhurried breaths.

With my eyes still closed, I again heard street sounds and nearby conversations. Stirred from my state of intoxication, I suffered a jolt of embarrassment. What happened to my signature professionalism? Had I stepped over a boundary? Yet, she still held me, and I still held her.

I was hugging her in gratitude, thanking her for what she had done for my life. But I had done nothing for her—had given her no reason to embrace me. *Do not impose on this precious woman, this treasure. I don't have the right.*

We embraced so long that I felt I should signal the release.

I let go first. Regretfully.

But for a second or two more, Rosa Parks hugged me longer than I had hugged her.

More than thirty years after that 1988 embrace, I do not know her reason. Did she see herself in me? If she had been born not in 1913, but in 1963, we might have been trendsetters together in television journalism. Was that her thought? Was my barrier-breaking career a stone of triumph in a road of opportunity she had helped to pave?

I will never know the answers, for Rosa Louise McCauley Parks died on October 24, 2005, at the age of ninety-two.

If I had been fortunate enough to meet her a second time, I could have asked many questions about her intense desire for worldwide human rights and her seventy years in the struggles. She was not an accidental participant.

Even as she and I held each other, I knew that what Rosa Parks wanted from me was not a *thank you* but *action*—a continuation of her fight against injustice.

I am convinced that with our heart-infusing embrace, I had become a child of the movement she personified.

It took nearly thirty years to germinate, but I now know how to grow the seeds of her incalculable gift. I focus on social-justice concerns as a classroom instructor, public speaker, storyteller, and television, podcast, and radio guest. I provide a perspective that brings out empathy in a way my students and other audiences have not heard. They inform me of this; they welcome it, they say.

I feel good about this. That good is powerful beyond measure.

The city center's clock tower struck midnight, gongs of the bell echoing throughout the streets of Halo. Despite how late it was, people roamed about. They hung at the open bars and pubs, drinking cheerfully, laughing loudly, and the clinking of gambling coins being added to another pile could be heard. A single white-cloaked figure silently passed through the night scenes, a hand on their hood, and was hurriedly heading to a certain destination. She made a turn into a dark alleyway and paused for a moment. Looking behind once, as if to make sure no one had followed her, she set her eyes ahead again.

Cupping her hands together, a single orb of golden light appeared in her palms. It floated upwards, lighting up the dark alleyway just enough so that she could continue her journey. The orb of light followed alongside her as she walked forward.

She entered where those who were struggling resided; people in makeshift tents, sleeping on newspapers or cardboard against the hard cement ground were seen. A strong odor filled the air, but it didn't seem to bother the figure in the cloak. She silently weaved through them, careful not to disturb anyone.

After making a few turns within the alleyways, she stops in front of a wooden door attached to a crudely built, yet sturdy, stone house. The orb of light returned to one of her palms. She raised her free hand to knock lightly on the door. Footsteps were heard before the door opened a crack. A woman, in her early 30's, dressed in simple linen clothing emerged. Their eyes were lined with dark circles but brightened upon seeing the cloaked figure.

"Healer Thea! You're...really here. Please come in," the woman exclaimed quietly, opening the door further for the other.

The cloaked figure nodded, stepping into the stone house, and the door was shut again. Warmth reached her hands from the flames in the small stone fireplace against the center of the back wall. The orb of light disappeared from her hands. She took off her hood, face now visible. Strands of light brown hair reached past her shoulders. A single braid was pinned across the back of her head.

"Of course. I promised you that I would be here, no matter what," Thea responded, smiling kindly. "Now, bring me to your child."

The woman quickly led Thea over to one corner of the room where a wooden baby crib sat. Within it was none other than an infant, nearly one-year-old, swaddled in blankets, and silently asleep.

"This is my sick child...they've been constantly running fevers and I'm not quite sure what's wrong," the woman explained.

"Is it alright if I hold them?"

"Yes...please do as you need, Healer."

Thea reached forward to gently hold the infant in her arms. She felt the child's energy then, and there was definitely something bothering them. The infant was a brave soul, she could feel it, as they continued to sleep soundly despite being in a stranger's arms. She placed them back down in the crib.

"Your child...they're going to be alright. It is nothing serious. Most likely due to the weather changes...but also, are they getting enough to eat and drink? The fevers they are running may be the cause of that," Thea asked the mother.

"Healer Thea, I really do spare everything I have for them. Yet sometimes, I am ashamed to admit, there is not enough," the woman said, tears filling her eyes, and cast them down onto the floor.

Thea already knew that would be the answer. With a wave of a hand, a large pouch appeared at the wooden table in front of the fire.

"Here, I brought this for you. It should last you both for a month or longer. Consider it as a gift from me. The other Healers and I have been doing our best to provide food for the ones in need. Please take it," Thea informed. "There's also medicine in there for your child or in case you ever get sick."

The woman got on her knees then and began to thank the Healer. Thea was quite alarmed by this action.

"Thank you, Healer, thank you so much...how can I ever repay you?" she said, beginning to sob, grabbing the edges of Thea's cloak.

"Please don't– come on now," Thea said, holding the woman's arms gently to help her stand. "The Healers promised to dedicate their lives to aiding others. We are only doing what we are supposed to with our gifts, and no repayment is expected from anyone. Live on happily, and be there for your child. That is all I ask of you."

The woman nodded then, wiping the tears from her face. With that, Thea pulled up her hood again and bid the mother farewell. Stepping out of the stone house, weaving through the alleyway slums, she soon became a single figure in the streets of Halo again.

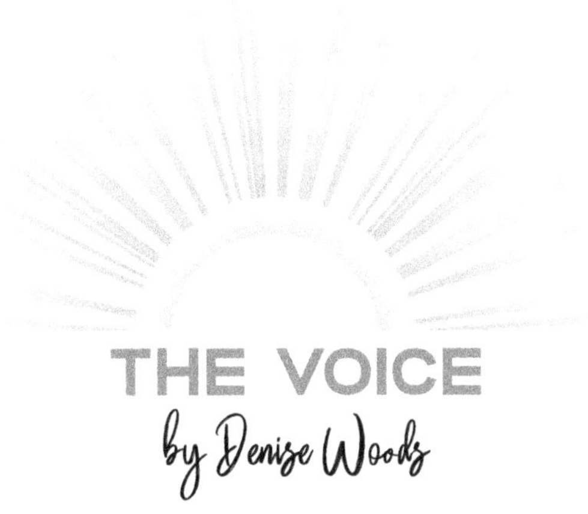

THE VOICE
by Denise Woods

If eyes are the windows to the soul, then VOICE is the portal to the spirit.

When I was a baby, the Mothers of the Metropolitan Baptist Church in Harlem declared to my Mom that I was a special one, that I had "been here before." Interestingly enough, I can't remember a time that I didn't feel special, not better, just different. This special "difference" was, at times, a source of great pain or euphoric triumph, depending on the stage of my life. What marked the standout difference throughout the years was my voice; strangers would remember me upon a second meeting because of my voice. After a quiet and painfully shy childhood, I developed a confident voice that served me quite well in every aspect of my life. I grew to know that my voice was my secret sauce. However, as I matured as an artist, a mother and as the woman I was put on the planet to be, it became increasingly clear that my "inner" voice was my most powerful gift. That small voice within was not so small after all, it was clearly what those Mothers of my childhood church saw in me when I was an infant.

One late summer California afternoon, as I drove alone, westward, to my sleepy coastal community, I heard a vaguely familiar voice come from the empty passenger seat of my car. It was as plain as day, it spoke, "I love you! I'm going to bless you beyond your wildest dreams." I typically drive this stretch of the freeway without music because the mountain views and orange groves are so majestic; I want to take it all in without disruption. In fact, it was the silence in the car that amplified this Voice, it startled me. I can vividly remember grabbing the steering wheel tightly, looking over at the passenger seat and loudly exclaiming, "Who ARE you?" I wasn't scared or angry, I just needed to know what this presence was that I had been hearing and feeling my entire life. But on this particular day, the Voice was louder and more pronounced than it had ever been. My past experiences with it had been quiet and uneventful. I hardly remembered them at all until that moment. It was then that I sensorially recalled decades of dialogues with my ancestors, with Spirit, with God. I desperately needed to know more deeply who "they" were, so I asked again, "WHO ARE YOU?" The response I received to my question calmed me, it comforted me. The response was simply, "You know who I am…" And for the first time in my life I actually knew… I knew that there was a Divinity that spoke to my heart and this time spoke directly into my ear. That Divine now speaks to me in the voice of my deceased father, and sometimes appears in the form of my dear dog that transitioned a decade ago, it even teaches me in the form of my higher self, my higher knowing. Over the years I had been reminded by a handful of noted spiritualists that I had "a gift" of discernment, but life's challenges sometimes make us forget our divine power. I am forever grateful that an ordinary California drive revealed something extraordinary, that my true secret sauce is my divine voice.

A large part of my shyness as a child was due to my vivid imaginary world. I was completely comfortable in my own space, which made it less desirable for me to explore outside of it. I remember drifting off to different worlds as I stared out of the window of my first grade classroom. I imagined life as a bird or a tree. I can recall peering into the window of the Lower East Side tenement building directly across from my school and creating entire scenarios for the families that lived inside. My teacher, Miss Millendorf, put a stop to my outdoor gazing by strategically moving me to the other side of the room. I later found out that my mother was in on "the move" conspiracy, and according to their plan, it made my grades skyrocket. Great grades were wonderful, but my ability to drift off and create imaginary people, places and things at such a young age informed my deep emotional work as an artist. I had a visceral connection to images and experiences that was far more than déjà vu; it was as if I was reliving them. Truthfully, that deep "knowing" has been a resource for my work as a Voice Coach in Hollywood. That afternoon car ride released a deluge of spiritual gifts that were just waiting to be tapped. There have been several memorable Divine conversations since then, but two remain most significant.

The first was the voice of my father, who passed away when I was five-years-old. He told me very definitively to "take care of your mother." I asked this soft voice if my Mom was going to die soon and his reply was joyful, almost funny. He said, "oh nooo... She has a lot more work to do before she's ready." I immediately knew what he meant and chuckled. I was comforted by his words. The second was a question that I've been wondering for years and now I had a conscious space to address it. I asked, "Why do MY life lessons have to be so harsh?" And again, the almost funny reply was, "subtlety doesn't work well with you!" I responded, "I need the sledgehammer approach to really get it, huh? I remember laughing and saying, "ya' got THAT right!"

The Voice guides me, it comforts me and directs me to a high spiritual frequency when it seems as though the world is going to hell in a handbasket. This is how this loving Voice shows up in my life. Are you ready for it to show up in yours? Then, I encourage you to turn down the volume and tune in to your internal GPS. It will guide your triumphs and challenges, but most of all, it will guide you back to YOU.

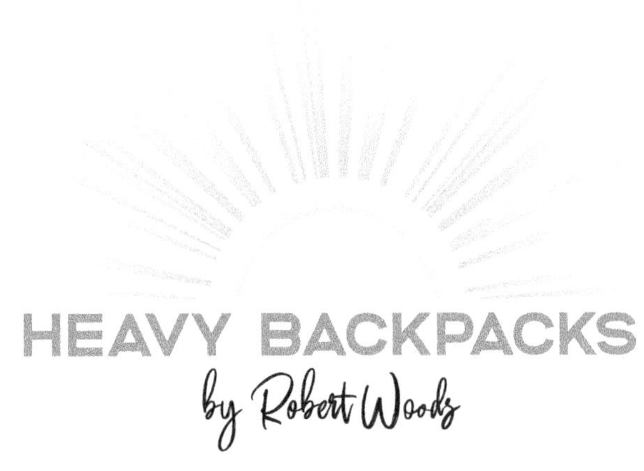

HEAVY BACKPACKS
by Robert Woods

It is hard to imagine the weighted worries a Brown boy stuffs into his backpack before hurrying off to school each day. His heaviest is that of fear. He always fears his safety because he believes America does not like him. America does not know him. While out, he worries that people will harm him because of who he is – a Brown boy. He prays a lot, especially mornings before leaving the house:

"Lord, let me journey safely through today. Keep all evil away from me and let me come back home. Amen."

When outside the home, be the Native American, African American, or Hispanic American, the Brown boy has learned to privatize his fears via the falsities of braveness. He has mastered the skill of controlling himself when in the company of those deemed likely to harm him. By default, he understands that the added melanin in his skin poses a threat to persons who do not have any. They are the ones who are most likely to call him a "thug" before they learn his name, and they are the ones who are most likely to stop him from returning home.

The Brown boy also "play-acts" a lot. He is proficient at posturing his outer self so that others may feel safe around him – he is aware that most feel threatened in his presence. However, if you are not a close friend or family member of the Brown boy, you will not sense that he is play-acting, and therefore you will rarely get to see the *real* him. He is not a Dr. Jekyll or Mr. Hyde, mind you, but he does understand that if you do not look like him, you are probably somewhat afraid of him. Because he knows your fear, plus his fear of knowing himself to be a human target, he knows that you are apt to spiral into a falsehood of how he lives life and thus cause him harm. His days are timid ones, and he rarely gets to be himself.

When in school, he knows that teachers and administrators have the authority to alter his day and school career drastically. They can change his life in what is known to be the fastest minute on earth – a "New York "minute. They can embarrass him, punish him, call the police on him, suspend him, fail him, or place him in a special needs class, all because he may be having a "bad" day. For this reason, he knows to keep his "guards" up; watch the tone of his voice, gestures, his temper, and above all – he must be mindful of lessons he's learned from the *"The Talk."*

All Brown boys know of the *"The Talk"* – a legendary scripted lecture given to them by their parents on the dos and don'ts of behaviors they must use when outside the home. How well he listens, adapts, and maneuvers the lessons he's learned from *"the talk"* will ultimately determine his success in getting through the day, completing grades K-12, or returning home for dinner that evening. If he adheres to the talk's script, the teacher or school leaders will never detect that he is afraid and play-acting. However, other Brown boys around him will – but you, the teacher, may not. For example, suppose a teacher routinely singles him out for lousy behavior when others in the class are acting just like him. In that case, all Brown boys will feel as if the teacher is harassing them individually. Or, when the teacher sees his raised hand but intentionally overlooks it, other Brown boys understand what is happening; they will each then empathize and inwardly share the victim's feelings of inadequacy, rejection, and embarrassment.

For a Brown boy, his only source of self-preservation is to daily strap on a breastplate of armor. The breastplate shields his emotions and deflects negativity heading towards him. Like an action hero from the pages of a Marvel comic book, his breastplate is a daily reminder that he matters. He knows that the school has become a dangerous place to go and learn. A slight disagreement with a teacher, administrator, or classmate can be life-altering for him. A trip to the principal's office can result in being suspended, held back at a grade level, handcuffed, riding in a police car, or even worse, getting introduced to the criminal justice system. The fears and insecurities Brown boys' tote in their backpacks are real and alarming. Some who pack this fear are mere "babies," preschoolers who have been on this planet for less than five years. They, too, quickly observe that when in pre-school, where suspension rates are highest amongst boys of color, they can be mistreated and disciplined differently than boys who don't look like them.

It is disturbing that schools are the major contributors to the Brown boy's crisis. They must overcome so many hurdles to be relevant and graduate from their classes. And, as if that were not enough for them to worry about, their concentrated effort to avoid being introduced to the penal system via their school is even more threatening. Being separated from their families, deported, prevented from supporting their children, becoming jobless, or feeling less than a man, are equally frightening hurdles that no male child should have to fear consistently. As former Education Secretary Arne Duncan once noted, "The undeniable truth is that the everyday educational experience for many students of color violates the principle of equity at the heart of the American promise. It is our collective duty to change that."

For reasons often beyond their control, more and more African, Hispanic, and Native American school-age-males between the years of 4 to 23 are failing to graduate our schools. Their failure to do so destroys lives, costing American taxpayers billions of dollars in increased health care, incarceration, and social services. *As we agreed to call them, Brown Boys* are the most vilified and targeted learners in our school systems. They are confused, worried, self-conscious, hesitant, depressed, and fearful of tomorrow every single day. Most believe the schools they attend mirror the same biases, stereotypes, brutalities, and unfairness shown to them via the media, judicial system, and the streets and neighborhoods from which most come.

In an education system that has for decades perceived them as meaningless contributors to the goals and ideals of the country, Brown boys feel destitute. Traumatized by a system that does not nurture, protect, support, serve, or view them as a source of hope, Brown boys are searching for a better tomorrow. They hope for a tomorrow where no one judges them as severely, and they do not blame them for all the wrong in America.

America has been down this path before. The academic crisis of brown boys to graduate from our schools is not new, and it comes as a surprise to no one. Their problem in the last decade has been incensed by white nationalism and a heightened racial climate. Their crisis has metastasized to become a social virus that racially divides our schools and one that is ripping apart the very foundations of our learning institutions. To keep our status as having the world's best education system, our Nation must address the rising dropout rates of Black and Brown boys and young men. One need only look at school achievement stats to realize that we as a nation are failing this group of male student learners. We are educating them with a "backward" mentality instead of a "forward" mentality. Backward to a time when history did not speak well of our schools because they reaped Jim Crow laws that dehumanized men of color and forbid them to learn to read or write. Schools have returned to historical times, whereas the same set of factors prompting the 1960s Civil Rights movement is being re-enacted and fought for once again. Virtually the same laws, policies, and practices that previously separated brown and black students from the mainstreams of White learners in our classrooms continue to separate them today.

Given all the progress America has made since 1619, it is troubling that Black and Brown U.S. citizens are still demanding that they have equal access to the best schools, qualified teachers, financial resources, books, and advanced education opportunities. It is troubling that brown boys – as young as four – consider themselves largely unnoticed, irrelevant in classrooms, and a burden to society. It is disturbing that they attend schools that model social themes that Black and Brown's lives do not matter; they are unteachable, problematic, and a nuisance. Many do not feel "liked" or "tolerated" by those whose job is to teach and accept them.

Scholars who study academic differences between ethnicities agree that the same set of factors used to define justice, punishment, and equality in our society's political, economic, and social realms also elevates the crisis destroying minority males in our schools. And while current literature readily admits that all boys generally struggle in their academic pursuits – especially when compared to girls – all agree that minority boys work the most. They continue to be at the bottom of the totem poles in reading, math, and science. Scholars note that the root(s) of their struggle is likely also to be found in the political, economic, and social constructs of the schools they attend.

There is hope for ending the crisis of Brown boys in our classrooms. Educators and school leaders can start by giving their stories newer narratives: narratives that deem *all* students, worthy learners. Colleges and Universities must begin training their graduates on teaching diverse students and hiring more teachers of color to instruct them. Moreover, the learning materials in their backpacks – and school curriculums – must become better inclusive of the cultures, learning styles, and contributions of Native, African, and Hispanic Americans. When considered and treated as worthy learners, Brown boys do the work and graduate from their schools. They are psychologically more robust than most think.

Understanding that they are not asking for special treatment or a hand-out is crucial to better educating and graduating these valuable groups of male learners. They want school leaders to see them, think of them, and treat them equally. They do not have to *love* or *pamper* them, but schools do need to *respect* them. No matter how young, they can handle the rest. After all, a brighter future for them means a brighter future for us all.

Excerpt from: The Brown Boy Crisis: Educators Must Step Up to
Meet the Challenges of Educating Non-White Males

THE GIFT WITHIN THE PRESENT . . . SIMPLY BE

by Esshe Zampaldus

A soft ray of honeydew sunshine beamed through the cracks between Bea's velvet curtains, gently highlighting the right side of her face. Savouring every moment, she quietly saluted the sun.

"Same dream again huh? How interesting!" she mumbled to herself as she slowly walked to the bathroom. "I wonder what it all means?"

Quickly tying her locs into a bun, Bea smiled in the mirror and said out loud "I am a Grateful Powerful Co-Creator." Synchronistically, her iPhone alarm went off just as she had finished her affirmation.

Walking into the cold office, her peaceful mood instantly disappeared. It was replaced with her manager's, Rose, screeching voice.

"Nice of you to arrive on time for once," she said sarcastically to Bea.

A heightened sense of anxiety permeated the office, rumours of redundancies being made in other departments. As Bea quickly sat down, the phone on her desk rang straight away. She picked it up on the third ring.

"Hello you're through to British Utility Services and you're speaking to Bea Samuel. How may I help you today?"

A lovely soft voice responded. "Hello, my name is Sue. I'm a beekeeper with 60 properties all due for renewal in May. I have this letter here, offering me cheaper prices–can you help me please?"

"Oooh, a beekeeper, how lovely! Yes, of course I can help you!" Bea replied. They spoke on the phone for over an hour, exchanging meter details, emails, prices, gestures of appreciation, and their love of bees.

Rose hurriedly approached Bea's desk as soon as she put the phone down. "Was that a deal? "

"No, it's a call back, for tomorrow."

"Why is it a call back, you know you're supposed to close a deal on every call!"

"That's not possible Rose, some customers like to build a rapport before they agree to anything."

"That's not your job Bea!" Rose said in an angry tone. "Your job is to get customers to agree to utility contracts on one call. We don't pay you to talk for hours on the phone about bees!"

Bea did her best to stop herself from replying back in a rude manner. "Stay in the present," she whispered. Taking three deep breaths, she stood up and cautiously walked out of the office. Passing Malachi's desk, he gave her a reassuring look. She loved how he always had a calming effect on her.

As Rose started shouting in her direction, Malachi carefully interrupted her, verbally signalling that he had an angry customer on the phone, requesting to speak to a manager. He passed the phone over and nervously headed towards the door. Rose always made him feel a bit nervous.

"Let me take you to lunch," he said softly, while holding the door open for Bea.

It was still breezy outside–the gigantic white clouds cloaked most of the blue sky. The tender caress of the wind swayed Bea as she stared into Malachi's eyes. It felt like he could easily read her thoughts, their synergy felt so magnetic. They both sat down on a newly fitted black park bench, which had a gold engraved message on it. "In Loving Memory of Gigi, May You Always Reside in Mother Nature's Beauty." They sat in silence for a while, taking in all the vibrancy surrounding them. In a way, it felt like a mini rejuvenating recharge.

Bea heard her iPhone ping–Rose had messaged her. Just as she was about to read it, a gigantic bumblebee glided by purposely, as if it said, "look at me!" Mesmerised, they both curiously stared as it brazenly made its way to a beautiful yellow tulip, tenderly removing the pollen with a profound accuracy. Circling the flower twice, it swiftly disappeared towards some oak trees and into the warm light of the sun.

"Look, a rainbow!" It startled Bea. "For three days, I've had this recurring rainbow dream, and you're in it Malachi. So was that bee!"

Suddenly, Malachi felt a huge surge of energy shoot up his spine and go straight into his heart. He intuitively knew this was the right time to say something. Leaning in, he gently fondled Bea's hair, lightly kissed her forehead and softly on the lips. The sweet sensation filled their bodies with waves of electricity that could have lit up the whole park. It felt like time paused. Everything looked brand new when they opened their eyes, the sun seemed to be shining brighter. Malachi smiled satisfyingly. He began to speak from his heart,

"We've worked together for 5 years and somehow, I knew you'd be an important person in my life. Sometimes I'd sit at my desk and see you beaming like the sun, with positivity, kindness and so much joy. You float around our office like a little cute busy bee, helping everyone, enhancing their day with your light, vibrant energy. We've all been feeling fed up and frustrated hearing about the redundancies, the uncertainty and fear of losing our jobs, but to be honest I would be more devastated if I lost you! I love you for everything you are!"

Bea let out a quiet sigh of relief, releasing all her worry, anxiety, fear, and frustration. She finally realised the importance of enjoying the sweetness of life, by simply 'BEEING' because she knew everything manifests in divine timing.

"I Love this present moment," she excitedly affirmed. Malachi affectionately hugged her–no words could describe the tides of emotion, surging around within them, no more hiding or denying it.

Walking slowly back towards work, Bea told Malachi that Rose had texted her apologising. Sue emailed her too, confirming she'd like to proceed with the gas & electricity contracts for all 60 properties. Omg! 120 deals in one day.

"I've won that sales incentive, the trip for two, to Antigua," Bea said, grinning.

Holding hands, they both recited Proverbs 16:24: Gracious words are a honeycomb, sweet to the soul and healing to the bones.

SECTION FOUR

MS. BETTY J. TILMAN LEGACY TRIBUTES

For each child that's born
a morning star rises and sings
to the universe who we are

For each child that's born
a morning star rises and sings
to the universe who we are

For each child that's born
a morning star rises and sings
to the universe who we are

We are our grandmothers prayers
we are our grandfathers dreamings
we are the breath of the ancestors
we are the spirit of God

"We Are," Song Lyrics by Dr. Ysaye Barnwell

CITY OF PITTSBURGH

OFFICE OF THE MAYOR

A Proclamation

Ms. Betty J. Tilman

*Celebrating a Life Full of Milestone Achievements
With Love*

Friday, October Seventh, Two Thousand & Twenty-Two

WHEREAS, Ms. Betty J. Tilman, Founder of the Good Neighbor Project in partnership with the POISE Foundation was born in Washington, DC on December 20, 1933. Ms. Betty left this Earth Realm on June 29th, 2022, at 9:15pm. She strongly believed that "Service Is the Rent We Pay for Our Space on Earth"; and

WHEREAS, Ms. Betty J. Tilman traveled to more than 40 countries around the world and was passionate about our collective responsibility to use our personal resources to honor the legacies of those whose contributions to opened doors for others; and

WHEREAS, Ms. Betty, was well known for her activism not only in the Pittsburgh Community but also for her contributions to lives of many thousands of people in various parts of the world. She worked for 28 years at the University of Pittsburgh assisting thousands of International Students as they negotiated learning and adjusting to life in the United States,; and

WHEREAS, Ms. Betty J. Tilman worked tirelessly for civil rights in the United States and was a mentor and friend to people of many cultures, religions and social economic backgrounds; and

WHEREAS, The University of Pittsburgh's Nationalities Rooms/African Heritage Classroom Committee created a scholarship in honor of Ms. Betty J. Tilman, and that scholarship now continues in her Memory.

WHEREAS, Ms. Betty J. Tilman was a Heritage Lifetime Member of the NAACP and a founding member of the African Heritage Classroom Committee. Ms. Betty, previously served as the Vice Moderator for the Pittsburgh Presbytery and the Chair of the Social and Racial Justice Committee. Ms. Betty has been recognized by the United States Congress and received a plethora of awards for her activism. Ms. Betty is an extraordinary example of courage, perseverance, conviction and established a legacy of excellence and dedication for generations of her loving family and caring friends.

THEREFORE, I Ed Gainey, Mayor of the City of Pittsburgh, do hereby proclaim **Friday, October 7, 2022,** as **Ms. Betty J. Tilman Day** in the City of Pittsburgh.

*Given under my hand and the **Great Seal of the City of Pittsburgh** at the City County Building in the First Ward of the City of Pittsburgh 414 Grant Street, Pittsburgh, PA. 15219 on this Seventh day of October in the year Two Thousand & Twenty-Two*

Ed Gainey
MAYOR OF PITTSBURGH

BETTY J. TILMAN: A UNIVERSE-FOCUSED VISIONARY

by Rev. Dr. Ronald E. Peters

A Mother, Griot, Mentor, Counselor, Activist, Leader, Mystic, Friend, Gift of God, Teacher: all these laudatory titles, although accurate, only show a part of the story that is Betty J. Tilman's life and contribution to the betterment of our national and global society. Her dreams before, during, and following her 28 years at the University of Pittsburgh, her leadership in the Community of Reconciliation Church, as Moderator of Pittsburgh Presbytery (PCUSA) and Chair of its Racial/Social Justice Committee led her to inspire others in ways that systematically changed lives and institutions for the better. How did she do it? While the laudatory titles above give key insights to the Great Spirit she was among us, there is another characteristic that also sheds light on the gift of God her life proved to be, for countless people were touched by her love; Betty J. Tillman truly was a *Visionary*.

Vision, in this context, *describes the power of sight as well as perceiving by clear thinking to imagine positive realities*. Betty Tilman's unique *powers of sight* as well as *perceiving by clear thinking to imagine positive realities* reflected her awareness and confidence in her oneness with the universe and its *Ultimate Source*, variously understood as *God*. Sadly, for too many people, our human reality is often shaped by tribe-focused, hierarchically divisive, greed-oriented, and spiritually confused realities. Against this backdrop, fear and doubt withers perception of any affinities or oneness with those immediately around us, much less a sense of oneness with a wider universe. This is true regardless of ethnicity/tribe, culture, geographic setting, socio-economic, or ideological context. Like all visionaries who inspire positive and uplifting outcomes, Ms. Tilman's genuine love for people near or far was infectious. Her capacity to perceive/dream of possibilities and actions that would improve the quality of life for other people enabled many to move beyond life-limiting barriers; to achieve life-enhancing realities or what Martin Luther King, Jr. called *"beloved community"*—contexts where love, justice, mutual respect and affirmation are the norm.

Visionary personalities are documented in sacred writings: *Moses* atop Mount Sinai perceiving possibilities that would move doubt and fear-filled people toward new possibilities of better life; a post-Calvary *Mary of Magdalene* in a graveyard, perceiving new realities that would inform doubt and fear-filled disciples of Resurrected hopes and possibilities previously unthinkable; *the Prophet Muhammad* in a cave perceiving teachings that would allow doubtful and fear-filled people seek right-living through submission to God. Beyond sacred writings, other visionaries like Harriet Tubman, Howard Thurman, Mary McLeod Bethune, Mahatma Gandhi, Ella Baker, Nelson Mandela, Angela Davis, or John Lewis—to name a few—inspired others to move beyond boundaries toward life-enhancing perspectives framed by love, justice, and hope. **Betty J. Tilman's legacy stands among these visionaries. Her *visionary perception, clear thinking, and actions* enabled others to see their oneness with the universe and move beyond life-limiting situations to help change society for the better. Her legacy of hope and possibility is our spiritual inheritance. Now, it's our turn.**

MS. BETTY J. TILMAN
TRIBUTE OBITUARY

International & intercultural bridgebuilder and community activist, Ms. Betty J. Tilman (b. 12/20/1933 - d. 6/29/2022) took her last breath on Earth at 9:15 pm on the 29th of June 2022. It has been recorded that Angels surrounded her and sang BREATHS, a Sweet Honey in the Rock song she loved. As they all ascended into the Heaven Realm, Angelic drummers and whisperers shared the news across the continents.

The brother of Betty J. Tilman, **Alexander McGant** was shocked with the painful news that the family matriarch had left the Earth realm and said "I so Loved my sister and will miss her. I will always Love Her. She was a beautiful, kind woman who taught me to have courage from the time I was a child. She also loved my cooking and had a wonderful sense of humor!

Sister-In-Law **Virginia McGant Jones** wrote "Betty, you are my Sister in Christ. A sister with so much love, joy, happiness and more. We will always remember your loving ways; you warm our hearts in those precious days. You will always have a place in our hearts that will never keep us apart. You reached out and traveled around the world. You gave so many your love and care. Even though God took you to his home. There is no place better than near his throne. We are glad we got to know you before God called you to his marvelous light.

In Riyad, Saudi Arabia, upon hearing the news, there were many tears in the heart of **Dr. Khadeeja Ghozhee** but she, **Dr. Abdullah Al Nifay** and their children rejoiced in believing that because it was 1st Dhul Hijjah in Mecca at the time of the transition, MOMBetty had gone on to Paradise.

"I know that MOMBetty is in the Heaven Realm, and that she and my Beloved Mother (Dr. Vernell Audrey Watson Lillie) are soaring and spreading their collective wisdom and love along with other Sheroes of ours.) said **Charisse Lillie, Esq**. in speaking to Rev. Melony McGant, daughter of Betty. J. Tilman.

WHO IS BETTY J. TILMAN? Mother to Rev. Melony McGant as well as Sister, Friend, Aunt and Godmother to a Large Multicultural Tribe!

"Her leadership and significant contributions to the African Heritage Room Committee and to the Nationality Rooms and Intercultural Exchange Programs is a legacy on which the future of the program can rest. With love and appreciation to be a part of this special celebration of Ms. Betty J. Tilman" said **Kati R. Csoman**, Director, Nationality Rooms and Intercultural Exchange Programs, University of Pittsburgh

Retired PNC Executive **John Brown, Jr.** and his sons Jay and Ernie wrote... "A special person, a kindred spirit, a kind soul, and a great friend, who on this earth served others with kindness and compassion. She leaves a legacy of love and devotion, and now begins a new journey in the heavenly estate with her God and creator. Thank you. We love you. We will miss you!."

"I've met a lot of people in my life, and there have been very few that I would say that "knowing them made me a better person". Betty J Tilman was one of the few. I am proud to have had a long friendship with Ms. Tilman. Her kindness, her generosity, her quick wit, and unselfish nature was just part of this phenomenal woman. She was thoughtful, funny, well informed, and current on most issues. Betty J. Tilman was one of the most decent human beings I have ever met. She will be missed terribly." said **Bruce Blakey** with wife **Patricia Backers Blakey**.

"Betty Tilman, you were all of these things to me and more: a friend and a mentor who was always special, giving, sharing, caring, including, encouraging, loving, praising, supporting, inspiring, involving, remembering, and real. You were truly a blessing in my life and while I will miss your presence here on earth, your love and energetic spirit will live within me forever." **Shirley M Scott**

OMG, A beautiful soul has left a crater amongst the many lives she touched. I Loved her. She was one of my favorite friends. I'll miss her. May she rest in peace. **Regina Chow McPhie**

Said Fine Artist **Brandon Jennings**, "Ms. Betty is an important mentor who inspired me to collect African art. After seeing her collection, I became intrigued with art from Africa. I have a few pieces that remind me of Ms. Betty, I feel good knowing that she will always be in my Home. I love you Ms. Betty!".

Mark Lewis, President of the Poise Foundation wrote Betty Tilman was truly a woman of the community. I was deeply impressed by her connections to young and old. If you had any concern for our community, Ms. Betty knew who you were and would let you know how you were going to help her, help us. We thank you for being a guiding light, beautiful spirit, and example for us all.

 Mashaiel Al Nifay, who graduated from Pitt with a MS in civil engineering wrote "Whenever I needed a mother, a cool friend and even a partner in crime; she was always there. Wherever she went, Mom Betty brought joy, love and her kindness was so contagious and for that her memory will live on forever with us. I must say Mom Betty believed in my dreams more than I did sometimes. She inspired me to become the woman that I am today and for that I and my family will be always in her debt!."

Said renown retired sound engineer **John Butler**, "I will miss my friend Betty Tilman. She is a lady who would never stop helping others. May God keep his blessings upon her daughter and all the people she has helped in the past. I shall never forget her.'

"I trust she had a peaceful homegoing. Her time with us here on this plane was positive and those of us that had the honor of knowing her have benefited greatly. **James Aloway**

Betty Tilman touched so many lives and was a source of inspiration to everyone who was blessed to know her." **Valerie and Saihou Njie**

For around 28 years Ms. Betty J. Tilman, worked at the University of Pittsburgh in Pennsylvania where she assisted thousands of International Students on both the undergraduate and graduate level as they negotiated learning and adjusting to life in the United States. She is a Founding Member of the African Heritage Classroom Committee at the University of Pittsburgh and with Jackie Mullins, she assisted in the founding of the Homer S. Brown Association for African-American Law students at Pitt and Duquesne Universities. She has also served as Vice Chair of the Pittsburgh Presbytery, Elder and Chair of the Community of Reconciliation and for many years was Chair of the Racial and Social Justice Committee for the Pittsburgh Presbytery. For more than 30 years she served on the boards of the Pittsburgh NAACP and the African American Music Institute and was an avid fundraiser for both organizations.

Ms. Tilman was well known for her activism not only in the Pittsburgh Community but also for her contributions to the lives of many thousands of people in various parts of the World. Before it was popular and at personal risk, she worked tirelessly for civil rights in the United States, and actively raised funds for Nelson Mandela and the Free South Africa Movement Against Apartheid. She has been and is a mentor and friend to people of many cultures, religions and socioeconomic backgrounds. She has traveled to many more than 40 countries around the world and is passionate about our collective responsibility to use our personal resources to honor the legacies of those whose contributions have opened doors for others.

A Heritage Lifetime Member of the NAACP , over the years Ms. Betty J. TIlman has received a plethora of awards for her activism, including the Pittsburgh YWCA Women In Social Justice Award, the Maharishi Award for Community Service and the Venezuelan Grande Mariscale Award.

Upon hearing the news **Ludwick "Luddy" Hayden** (University of Pittsburgh A&S '66, EDUC '68) wrote "I was quite saddened to learn of Betty's passing but was immediately buoyed by the thought that we might find a way to celebrate her life and work at The University of Pittsburgh.

I first met Betty not long after entering Pitt as an undergraduate. I was fairly naïve then about international affairs, even as included in an academic environment. Betty was sort of my informal connection to the world of foreign students at Pitt and the true significance of the Nationality Rooms.

After spending several years as an undergraduate, graduate student, and staffer in the College of Arts and Sciences, I ultimately joined the private sector. I was working in Public Affairs at the then Pittsburgh headquartered, Gulf Oil Corporation, when Betty approached me with the idea of sponsoring a Pittsburgh speaking tour for *Roots* **author, Alex Haley**. We were successful in mounting this effort and ultimately raising the first major tranche of funding to establish the African Heritage Classroom as part of the Nationality Rooms Program. My work with Betty during this period was confirming of her long-standing passion for the Intercultural Exchange Programs, the Nationality Rooms, and the work of the African Heritage Classroom Committee. Betty was well known in Pittsburgh for her support to a number of groups and organizations. However, this work at the University was at the core of her passion. It is most fitting that her work with the Nationality Rooms, Intercultural Exchange Programs, and African Heritage classroom be at the core of any celebration of her life and legacy.

Dr. William Tiga Tita, Northeastern University Professor, (Retired) wrote "I am a humble and cheerful adorer of BJ! "Betty J" was always pursuing one unifying theme (Intercultural Exchange -appreciation) from several angles!! She was a pillar of our "Intercultural House" project (ICH), assisting us to meet and surpass the 20% international students quota! She worked tirelessly with us to identify and arrange destinations, notably, Ghana, Afghanistan et al. for the travel/work program of the ICH project. The Nationality Rooms/ African Heritage Classroom initiative was the sweetener from my perspective! She was also my cheer-leader as I sought to integrate the Pittsburgh Black Business Community into the fabric of PITT's Business School and the University as a whole- the SCP! As you can see, it matters less the angle from which we choose to honor and celebrate her life and legacy! We will all end up at the core, a champion of Intercultural Exchange!!!I am pleased to be an aspect of this movement!

For me Ms. Betty was my guiding authority on the history of the African Heritage Classroom Committee and was very supportive of me when I began AHCC Chair. She was the first scholarship director. I watched and took notes on how Ms. Tilman made personal contacts with the faculty, staff, and students regarding scholars' presentations, becoming new members and adding funding to the endowment. Ms. Tilman was the ultimate organizer and worked on numerous committees, one event was to bring in Alex Haley, the author of Roots to the University of Pittsburgh. This event showed Ms. Tilman visionary skills. This was also my first introduction to the AHCC wrote **Donna Alexander**, AHCC Secretary.

Dr. Sandra Murray, President-elect of the American Society for Cell Biology and Professor of Cell biology at the University of Pittsburgh wrote "Betty, the queen mother of Pittsburgh, shared her wisdom and gifts for organizing and bringing about change with those all over the world. Her global impact on our lives will be missed. In her position as an international liaison she worked with students that arrived from many different countries to teach, mentor, guide, and advise them on the culture of academia in the USA. They learned from Betty how to survive and thrive while away from home. She opened her home and heart to friends as well as strangers and taught them great lessons on living. She was a community organizer, and she brought the momentum needed to get a project started. She was an organizer and producer who brought many groups to perform in Pittsburgh thus increasing the communities' awareness of different venues. Her concern for others was boundless and she cared for and helped so many.

Now she has gone to be with the ancestors, the words of a song that Betty liked are brought to mind and I picture Betty softly singing the words of the song "BREATHS" performed and composed by Betty's friend, **Dr. Ysaye M. Barnwell** and the group that she brought to Pittsburgh several times, **"Sweet Honey In The Rock."** The words in the song are, *"listen more often to things and not beings . . . the ancestor's voice is in the sound of water . . . in the sound of the wind . . . in the sound of rustling trees . . . tis the ancestor's breath when the fire's voice is heard . . ."*

Betty, before joining the ancestors, let her light shine for others and raised her voice to help the next generations achieve their goals and now that she is with the ancestors we need to listen because as the words of the song suggest, tis the ancestors voice that can be heard, if we listen!

In Honor of Ms. Betty Tilman, donations to the African Heritage Room Committee Scholarship can be made online by visiting www.nationalityrooms.pitt.edu
Select the About button at the top left and then select Donate to the Nationality Rooms!

To donate by check, make the check payable to the University of Pittsburgh and mail to: University of Pittsburgh, PO Box 640093, Pittsburgh, PA 15264-0093.

 Donations online and in the check memo line can be noted as: African Heritage Room Committee Scholarship in memory of Ms. Betty J. Tilman.

EXPRESSIONS OF CARE AND COMPASSION FOR BETTY J. TILMAN

"The heavens are in awe ..as MomBetty J; Tilman entered the pearly gates, she was smiling as angels circulated around her head," **– Patricia Portis Blakey**

"Miss Betty was a very caring person who as I always remember had deep spirituality. She had a worldly perspective that was felt by all. It was as if she had many lives and ways of worldy loving that she shared unselfishly. She cared for people of this earth and wanted their walk to be fulfilled," **– Ernie Brown**

"Melony, Sorry to hear of your Mother's passing! Sometimes hard for me to digest how fast time passes, as the amount of. "past-time" continues to accumulate. With that said, I know that your Mom (Aunt Betty) lived a long and fulfilling time in this world whilst touching and sharing aspects of herself and others with all of us, throughout her journeys! I am truly happy to have had opportunities of such encounters, and through God Almighty we have been blessed with her being and spirit! With an embracing hug to you, we will miss her!" **– In love and prayers, Monte Chandler.**

"Betty was a kind, compassionate dear friend. She loved me and embraced me for my efforts to promote Caribbean Culture in Pittsburgh," **– Verna Crichlow**

"Thank you. Miss Betty J. Tilman. May her memory be a blessing. I did not have the opportunity to meet Miss Tilman, the blessings I received from her are through continuing the work and the legacy of her work with the African Heritage Room Committee.I'm the director of the Nationality Rooms and intercultural exchange programs at the University of Pittsburgh, I know that, and Miss Tilman, was a founding member of the African Heritage Room. And the committee along with Dr. Buba Misawa and others who began their work in long before t 1991 the African H eritage Room Committee has supported 52 scholarships for scholarly and experiential endeavors in Africa. The countries in which students and scholars have conducted research and participated in study abroad and internships include Congo, Ethiopia, the Gambia, Ghana, Kenya, Madagascar, Mali, Morocco, Namibia, Nigeria, Senegal, South Africa, Tanzania, Uganda, and Zimbabwe. Miss Tilman's legacy has profound impact not just beyond Pittsburgh, but really beyond the United States and into the world," **– Kati Csoman**

"I would like to think I sent accolades to Miss Betty long before she passed. Whenever Melony had a celebration for her mom, I was always in attendance, and Mother's Day comes to mind. Having lost my mom many years ago, I naturally wanted to talk to Betty Tilman. Little did I know it would be her last Mother's Day on Earth. After speaking with Melony, I called the nurse's station at Shadyside Hospital and left a message from me, her adopted daughter living in Atlanta. Ms. Betty Tilman was also the inspiration for my insatiable desire to live in South Africa. I recall she had planned a trip to South Africa with Dr. Venell Lillie and the KUNTU Repertory Theatre at the University of Pittsburgh. My thought was "There is no way Miss Betty is going to South Africa without me." She later became ill and could not go, but I went without her and had a wonderful, insightful journey. I will miss Ms. Betty J. Tilman and her supportive, encouraging words; I will always hold her wisdom in my heart." **– Gayle Hodnett Dobbs**

"Betty J. Tilman, a sweet, sweet spirit, walked this earth in the beautiful light of faith. As a believer, she endeavored to put her spirituality into daily practice, mindful of the collective fruit of the Spirit—love, joy, peace, forbearance, kindness, goodness, faithfulness, gentleness and self-control (Galatians 5:22-23 NIV). My dear friend personified these attributes while doing whatever she could to honor the requirements of the word of God: to act justly, to love mercy, and to walk humbly with her God. She valued, encouraged and supported the efforts of others and now that she has joined the ancestors, those she touched may choose various creative ways to memorialize her many contributions. I am honored to have called her friend. I am grateful for our friendship. I give thanks for her earthly presence and for her heavenly ascension. Betty J. Tilman, I speak your name with reverence and love," **– June Pickett Dowdy**

"Betty J. Tilman touched my life by coming to my plays and by supporting me as an artist,,, by saying to me, "you can do this" and by allowing me to feel my African heritage. We are joyful of the spirit of Mama Betty J. Tilman and the celebration of her life and legacy in our hometown of Pittsburgh, PA where she lived and worked and gave her life to many," **– Kim El**

"Betty was such a light for all of us and I know how you must be missing her. When we have a single parent, they are like our sun, our moon and our stars. I am going out to a sacred Washoe site in the woods this afternoon where I have been blessed with a vision of the White Buffalo Heaven. I will be holding space and sending Reiki and love to you here on Earth and your Mom as she journeys," **– Libby Evans**

"I believe when you have a labor of love, you plant seeds that change everything that you touch. You enhance everything that you touch. You empower everything that you touch. And out of this labor of love; We Give. Ms. Betty J. Tilman gave. She helped a lot of people. She informed people about important community issues and encouraged people to vote. More importantly, Ms. Betty poured into people. She poured into people the empowerment and love that they needed," **– Pittsburgh Mayor Ed Gainey**

"One incident, I think, was very revealing of Betty Tilman. When designing the **African Heritage Classroom**, I was chair of the Design committee, and we'd gone through a lot of iteration, a lot of ideas, a lot of controversy over what that room was going to look like, what it was going to consist of, contain, what it was going to represent. Finally, we came up with what we thought was a good design. And one evening, Betty called and said she wanted to come over to my house to see this design, to see the drawings. **I knew this was like an audition for whether this thing was going to fly.** Betty came in and very serious, she came up in our sunroom, my wife was there we pulled out the designs and Betty looked them over and she didn't say much. But that was the sign that Betty was approving. So once we had our next committee meeting, the design passed. So I know Betty had been on the phone and talking to the members. Betty, I think, was the turning point. She's the one who sold the designs to the members of the African Heritage Classroom Committee. I'm Always Grateful For That!" – **Dr. Larry Glasco**

"Betty was a motivator. Her mind was always stirring and coming up with projects to help to fix the community, or to work on a problem or to support the development or growth of some institution. Often it involved preserving the legacy of our people, teaching our children and helping to push forward a progressive political agenda. Betty was a dear friend and a mentor. She had ceaseless energy, with a mind as sharp as a hunter's knife. Her vision was insight. She looked into problems and the needs of so many people of different races and ethnicities. She was a champion of her culture and people making history while trying to preserve it. She was a person who cared about others and helped them overcome the harshness of racism while understanding the dignity, culture and intellectual contributions of Africans and African Americans. She was an extraordinary, good neighbor," – **Walt Hales**

"I met Ms. Betty Tilman in the winter of 2014 when I moved back home to Pittsburgh Pa to help take care of my mother who had Alzheimer's. Betty and another neighbor were very helpful with bringing me up to date about our apartment building we lived in which was important when you are a caregiver and the living conditions must be safe and comfortable. Little did Betty and the other neighbor know I had been an advocate for tenants rights and the assistant secretary to the head of New York State tenant and neighborhood coalition in Manhattan New York. We were able to help get fire regulations in the building a well as making sure the tenants received home fire extinguishers for each tenant apartment.

I became aware that Betty Tilman's biggest passion was making sure the children were being taken care of. Betty found out I was a professional singer, musician and music teacher that continued to educate children in voice and piano as well as song writing. She would always advocate for children to always get special programs and to never to be forgotten. I can go on up until Betty Tilman's passing of how she took me under her wing to bring me up to date about Pittsburgh and its culture, politics, education and so many things in the short time I was blessed to know her. I will miss you Ms Betty Tilman and I will continue your mission in making sure our children will not be forgotten!" – **Ednah Holt**

"Mother Betty was everybody's mother. Especially those who were under her age. Before I came to Pittsburgh from Louisiana in 1977, I had heard she was like an ambassador to foreign students from the University of Pittsburgh. She was so much more to so many! Betty found me, my wife Pamela and four children a house to live in. For many, many years she was a board member for the **Afro American Music Institute** and always supported our fundraising efforts. We are grateful for her leadership and Love. I know she's watching us from heaven and will always be looking down on me with that finger that said, Please Listen!" – **Dr. James Johnson**

"My soul weeps! She and Alma Fox were my mothers who immediately took me under their wings when I first moved to Pittsburgh! Mother Betty lives on in my heart and spirit and all of the wisdom

I learned from her. Please know, Melody, that she was the consummate encourager and lifted me out of the depths of disparity many days and restored me to realms of illuminating rays of light! She will always live in my heart! I will lift you before the Throne of God in prayer for enhanced strength, healing, and peace!" – **Rev. Rose Johnson Thompson**

"Aunt Betty has inspired and touched my family, my children, and me in such a positive way. She has taught us in many ways how to love and appreciate the African American, African, and international communities, and family. May she rest in peace and God keeps her. Our prayers and sympathy are with you. We love you much." – **Katie McGant Jordan**

"I will always remember Aunt Betty as a adventurer. I loved hearing her stories about all the places she traveled. I loved her ground nut chicken. It was so exotic and wonderful. Aunt Betty was a leader, a fighter for equality and a very kind person. The heavens are brighter with her in them," – **Christine McGant**

"May God Bless My Aunt Betty. Bless Her Loving and kind Spirit as she enters into God's presence," – **Andre McGant**

"When one speaks I always wanted to say I'm delighted to be here, but I'm really not delighted to be here because we will no longer have the presence of Miss Betty Tilman. Typically, most of us referred to her because she was so informal, as Betty. She made the world a better place to all whose lives she has touched. Betty was never without a smile. She was a good listener, and always with empathy and a willingness to explore options. One of the things but she really adored and liked, was to entertain. I'm sure many of you have been at a place at least once or many times more because she got a great thrill out of seeing people happy. She always had a deep desire to aid and help. I know Betty is looking down on us today with a joyful smile. Knowing that she has done good deeds, so much so that the unmoved mover would bestow the greatest blessing as a reward for having lived a good life. Thank You Betty!"– **Dr. Jerome McKinney**

"Betty was an amazing spirit. I first met her when we worked together at the Indo-Chinese Refugee Camp in Pennsylvania. We traveled the scenic route to the camp. Yes, that means we got lost along the way. We saw many tiny communities we never would have seen in that travel adventure. Betty became a life long friend and adopted mother to Adrienne Bennett and me. When ever I was in the Pittsburgh area I would visit. One time my oldest son and I visited the Church of Reconciliation. I recognized Betty and Dr. Pinky Familoni seated a few rows in front of us. After the service we went up to say hello and Betty recruited us to take a visiting African Ambassador for a tour of Pittsburgh. She was a shining light and motivator. We also have an African art collection. I so enjoyed talking with Betty about our shared joy of intercultural studies. She was loved by many and will be deeply missed," – **Melanie Marshall**

"Oh dear kind friend, Melony, I offer to you my deep sympathies at this time of parting. Heaven gains what we, in mortal flesh, have lost; yet only temporarily for surely, we will be reunited once again!" – **Andrew Nimick**

"Ms. Tilman "Betty", we love you & miss you; your wise counsel, your encouraging words, your active support of our community work, & your willingness to stand against mistreatment of anyone. You always answered our calls & gave us sound advice. We love you "Betty" and we thank God for your legacy of love, care & concern, & strong ladder of support. You are an anchor of love that enabled us to touch & help many lives! Thank you so much! We miss you much! God bless you!"– **Rev. Mark & Vickie Okere**

"I met my dear sister Betty Tilman in 1970. My deceased husband Dr. Amram Onyundo and I moved to Pittsburgh because he had accepted a job at the University of Pittsburgh. Betty selflessly showed us around and assisted us in finding housing. From then our relationship grew. She was always very kind, thoughtful, loving, caring and a truthful person. Such a gem to be in constant contact with. She would always be there at the right times. She would advise my children and she always demonstrated strength and poise. She would have no difficulty in always seeing the good in people. She was always ready to help by giving advice or writing a reference. She was always willing to be a servant of God to lift others,"– **Charlotte Onyundo**

"My wife Sheila and I were pleased to know Betty Tilman. She, Walter Worthington, Nancy Harriet Lee, Kathy Irvis, Dr. Larry Glascoe, Luddy Hayden, my dear mother ascended, **Bertha Petite**, and many others were Founding Members of the **African Heritage Classroom Committee at the University of Pittsburgh**. Great efforts were made in order to make this possible. They had to raise $100,000 back then for this room, and they raised the majority of that money in the black community. But they found out that an additional $50,000 was needed. And they raised that too! We honor their legacy and need your help to maintain it and grow the the impact of the African Heritage Classroom Scholarships that benefits students interested in journeying and studying in Africa!" – **Oscar Petite, Jr. J.D.**

"As a child I grew up three doors down the street from Cousin Betty's Grandparents, Alexander and Eva Brown, whom she often visited. The first thing I came to notice was Betty's attire. The beautiful dresses and shoes she adorned made her a fashion model in my eyes. Later on Cousin Betty moved to the city of Pittsburgh. There Betty began her journey that would lead to many accomplishments, world travel, and civil rights activist. Cousin Betty was Royalty, a true Queen and influencer. Her most important role was her ability to instill all that she had learned into a guide for her beautiful daughter, Rev Melony McGant. Cousin Betty, you lived life to its fullest, you loved, and you made your mark on this world. Fly High Beautiful Queen," – **Cousin Patsy (Phyliss Scott)**

"I met Betty through a mutual friend, Dr. June Dowdy. Upon meeting Betty, it was obvious that her heart was always filled with love for her daughter Melony, extended family, friends and her local and international community. She was an inspiration to the many young people she counseled and supported through their educational journey. Betty was a loyal friend who respected her colleagues with whom she worked to create a more caring and inclusive community. Because of her vision, and social and political activism, she gave hope to those who felt hopeless and fought for racial, gender, ethnic and economic equality by supporting positive social transformation. Her desire was for a better life and future for all by always triumphing over life's challenges. She will be missed. I thank Betty for her treasured friendship," – **Dr. Carol A. Scott**

"Betty Tilman, you were all of these things to me and more: a friend and a mentor who was always special, giving, sharing, caring, including, encouraging, loving, praising, supporting, inspiring, involving, remembering, and real. You were truly a blessing in my life and while I will miss your presence here on earth, your love and energetic spirit will live within me forever," – **Shirley M Scott**

"I met Betty around 1969 through our work with the Pittsburgh Branch NAACP. She introduced me to Dr. Nathan Davis. And because of that, he ended up doing some musical arrangements when I was recording in the early 70s. And he told me sometime later that those are some of the most beautiful arangements he ever did. Betty Tilman was the epitome of what Reverend Dr. Johnny Monroe said. When I considered running for the presidency of the NAACP, he asked the question, Are you a thermometer or a thermostat? Or do you want to tell us the temperature or are you one who sets the temperature. Betty Tilman was a special lady and was a living thermostat for change! She helped everybody. Whatever they needed to do, she helped. Her spirit remains and will always be good. It is my pleasure to call her my friend," – **Tim Stevens**

MASTER WEAVER OF COMMUNITY
by Dr. Stephanie Clintonia Boddie

There are times in our lives when we need earth angels. Ms. Betty J. Tilman showed up at a time when I truly needed her. She infused courage, hope, light, and joy into my life. She announced to me that it was my time to step into my authentic power and to fully display the person God created me to be. She reminded me that I deserved to be happy. The good she brought to my life was beyond what I could ever measure!

Though I met Ms. Tilman at an Edna B. McKenzie Branch of ASAHL meeting almost a decade ago, it felt as if I knew her all of my life. There was an immediate connection. Ms. Tilman and Dr. June Pickett Dowdy were among the first to greet me and welcome me into the McKenzie Branch family. Not a month went by that Ms. Tilman did not call to invite me to a meeting or check in to ask about my well-being and the development of my projects. I did not understand why she was so generous with her time and support. After meeting her daughter Melony, I now know that it was just her nature. She cared deeply for people, especially young people.

Ms. Tilman was also a master weaver of community. Before I knew it, she was connecting me to other young women and inviting me to volunteer and attend events sponsored by Black-led organizations. One of my favorite memories orchestrated by Ms. Tilman was co-leading a workshop to prepare students participating in Gwen's Girls to attend their first opera, The Summer King, a story of baseball legend Josh Gibson. To prepare to deliver this workshop, I attended an event for educators. I got a peek backstage of award-winning mezzo-soprano Denyce Grace and other cast members before the Pittsburgh premiere. Presenting this workshop was likely Ms. Tilman's way of encouraging me to share the good life I had been given with this next generation of Black girls. I had the opportunity to open a new world for them just as she had for so many during her lifetime.

I would not be where I am today without Ms. Tilman. She also confirmed strengths I had not yet seen in myself and helped me to consider new ways to use them. By many measures, I had accumulated several significant achievements before we met. However, when we did meet, I was devoting far more time keeping other people's worlds in order. She minced no words telling me that I was not living up to my potential. She was relentless in getting me to see that I was investing much more in other people's dreams than my own. I was a caregiver for my younger brother and consultant for several local initiatives. It was clear to her that I had allowed my career to drift into a direction I had not anticipated.

Ms. Tilman insisted that I prioritize my scholarship including my musical documentary, *Unfinished Business: From the Great Migration to Black Lives Matter*. She helped me in so many ways to move this project forward. She connected me to people to interview and a filmmaker as well as a fiduciary for project fundraising. She also identified a panelist for the post-screening discussion event and facilitated a co-sponsorship with the McKenzie Branch of ASAHL. She encouraged me to invite Dr. James Johnson and the Afro-American Institute Boys' Choir to participate in the musical documentary. She also helped publicize the event.

Though it was a winter evening, my *Unfinished Business* event drew a standing room crowd of 200+ people. I owe much of the credit for such a successful event to Ms. Tilman's vision to attract an intergenerational, interracial, and ecumenical audience. To date, the documentary has been screened in over 20 venues to diverse audiences. She could imagine this and more.

Though I was still working at University of Pittsburgh during most of the time I spent with Ms. Tilman, I never heard her U-Pitt story until recently. Somehow it seems she was determined to make sure I did not relive those parts of her that would cause me pain and to remain on the margins in Pittsburgh. Without ever recounting her story, she used the wisdom from her journey to call me to shine with confidence, live with integrity, and to love boldly.

When I was invited to take a position in Waco, Texas, at Baylor University, she was among the first to encourage me to close my Pittsburgh chapter and begin a new life in Central Texas. I can say with more assurance now that Ms. Tilman saw in me something that I could not fully see in myself at this time. I appreciated her clarity, boldness, and wisdom. I was inspired by these qualities in her and grateful for her investment in me. She challenged me to examine my life and recommit to a life fulfilling God's divine purpose for me. She insisted that Pittsburgh was not the place for me. She was right! So, I left to take a tenure track position at Baylor. The new chapter opened the kinds of doors she suspected it would.

In just a few years after my appointment at Baylor, I was invited to speak at a conference in China, traveled to Montreal, Kenya, and the United Kingdom for presentations and performances. I was also chosen as mentor of the year in 2020. As I think back, I am sure Ms. Tilman knew that these doors would only open for me if I left Pittsburgh. I will always remember the special afternoon I shared with Mrs. Tilman and Dr. June Pickett Dowdy before leaving for Waco. Ms. Tilman dropped pearls of wisdom as we enjoyed the warmth of a summer day and high tea service with assorted finger sandwiches at The Café at Frick Park. She left all who knew her something good and something to nourish yours and the community's soul.

ODE TO A SAGE: BETTY TILMAN
by John Calvin Brown III

I know a majestic bird. Her name is Betty Tilman. She soared so high. Her flight inspired and impacted me and the lives of hundreds. She encouraged and educated humanity on the Golden Rule, "Do to others as you would have them do to you." (Luke 6:31) and "Do to others whatever you would have them do to you. This is the law and the prophets." (Matthew 7:12)

Betty had many positions in life. She was a mother to all who wanted and needed wisdom and guidance. To those who suffered affliction she administered aid, i.e., an unbounded love. Her first love was to serve the needy. She did it with an everlasting devotion and an unequivocal steadfast determination. Maybe she was not wealthy with the contemporary currency of "gold" and "silver," but she was bountiful in care and concern, the wealth of a golden heart. As a child she began teaching me and other "students" in the art of diplomacy. She introduced us to her international contacts from places like Africa, Venezuela, and Saudi Arabia. She even shared stories of when she met Pablo Picasso. All of these experiences were renowned because they showed that the language of humanity is love.

Pittsburgh and the University of Pittsburgh were so blessed to have been visited by such a kindred spirit. In fact, the world has been blessed to have made her acquaintance. The value she added to the human race is unmeasurable and incalculable in her many positions. Professionally, she had achieved the position of "liaison" at the University of Pittsburgh. This position allowed her to transition to the wise mother sage, kindred to all of our hearts. Given all her "spiritual works of mercy," and all of her "corporal works of mercy" completed in this life, I can only describe her as a person who preceded her era, a person who was before her time. Any person of this caliber has an everlasting account of high magnitude and of infinite value in the heavenly abode. Thus, I dedicate this writing to her "majesty," a friend and kindred spirit whom I miss very much. I dedicate myself to honor her at every forum and to honor her at every venue where appropriate, so that her legacy is indelibly manifested in this finite existence and honored in her eternal estate and beyond.

One definition of Faith is the following: "Faith is the realization of what is hoped for and evidence of things not seen." (Hebrews 11:1) Thus, I have faith, and we should all have faith, that Betty is now in a place of great peace, and from that place of peace she ministers to us, her friends, and the world, spiritually by prayer and petition, because her spirit is infinite. Thus, her spirit is in the position to create harmony in the heavenly abode. Her spirit is working and catering to some of the most renowned sentient beings who have walked the earth and beyond. At this time, I would like to acknowledge and thank the Heavenly Father for the existence Betty J. Tilman:

Dear Heavenly Father, thank you for the example of such a saintly "daughter," Ms.. Betty J. Tilman. I know she is in good company now. I desire to be in her company and yours someday, but in the meantime I pray that you guard and protect her with your majesty, and keep her in the company of the other sentient beings who worship you forever in Heaven, who are creating universal harmony. Please help me follow in the footsteps of your beloved "saints," who seek your will in all things. Amen.

By this prayer, we have faith that Betty is kept safe and that she is in good company, with a plethora of infinite tasks to create eternal harmony in this world and the next. Thus, we have an eternal example of how to conduct ourselves in this life to promote peace and harmony amongst the human family.

We live in an unkind world. A world that is harsh and cruel. A world that is rife with wars, injustice, and racial inequality. We live in a situation that causes a loss of hope. However, the heavenly realm calls us as a human family to, " Rejoice in hope, endure in affliction, persevere in prayer." (Romans 12:12) We can have solace and "rejoice in hope, endure in affliction, [and] persevere in prayer," by looking at Betty J. Tilman as an example of a person who suffered much adversity, but who always focused on "hope" as a positive outcome. Thus, via her example and her counsel we can endure any situation thinking there will be a positive outcome. She is a beacon of hope.

I am very fortunate to have had Ms. Tilman in my life as a "surrogate" mother. There are so many instances and experiences in my life where I have been fortunate to have her friendship, wisdom, and counsel. She has advised and saved me from the onslaught of spiritual destruction at times. In the wake of affliction and despair, she has comforted me with words, actions to promote endurance, and her ethos has been hope.

DON'T CALL HER BETTY, CALL HER BET-TY

by Martha Richards Conley, Esq.

You will have to climb into a time machine to hear about my friend, Betty Tilman. I met Betty in 1968 in my first year of law school at the University of Pittsburgh. I met her on the third day of classes at Pitt Law school; I had been there long enough to know that I was in way over my head. There were only seven women in my class, and I was the only black woman. At that time, Betty was working at the Office of International Student Services where she helped multitudes of international students navigate their way through the University of Pittsburgh. Betty was an internationalist. She has hundreds of friends around the world. She loved to travel and was always going abroad. She was a godsend to me at Pitt because I felt very much alone. I hate to think how I might have fared without Betty to lean on and help me navigate the Pitt Campus and culture.

Betty was always busy, busy, busy. Name a progressive black organization in Pittsburgh and Betty probably belonged to it. She was a staunch member of the **NAACP**, on the board of the **Afro American Music Institute**, and we was both charter members of **Edna B. McKensie branch** of **ASALH, the Association for the Study of African American Life and History**, a national organization founded by **Carter G. Woodson** in 1915. Dedicated to preserving Black History, Betty Tilman was a connector and was always trying to bring like minds together. She was delighted when her connections hit it off. And many of them always did.

Betty Tilman and I had a circle of close mutual friends that included international union activists **Jackie Mullins** and **Maida Springer Kemp. Dr. Vernell Lillie** was also a very close friend of Betty's, and she missed her terribly when she passed.

Sharon Smith and I were good friends of Betty. Sharon and I were college roommates at Waynesburg. We both majored in French. Sharon went on to teach French for many years in the Pittsburgh Public Schools, but she also taught adult classes at CCAC. I decided to take the class as a refresher and Betty decided to take it too. Sharon and I still laugh about it because Betty would come to class listening to Spanish on her earphones. The class started at 5:30 pm. Betty would come in, sit down, and promptly fall asleep. Sharon would wake her up at 8:30 pm and take her home. We teased her about that, but it didn't alter her behavior. Betty may have learned some Spanish, but she didn't learn any French in Sharon's class.

My friendship with Betty enriched my life and the lives of many others. I will not mourn. I will celebrate her. She created a truly wonderful life.

I entered the University of Pittsburgh in 1970. A Minister named Dr. Frank Horton invited me to apply. Dr. Horton spoke at my Church in Memphis, Tennessee. Later in the afternoon, he met with my youth group and extended an invitation for us to all do so. I was accepted, and with my parents' blessings, I took a leap of faith. Once I settled in, Dr. Horton on the ministerial staff invited me to attend worship services at University and City Ministries. Since the church was close to campus, I began attending UACM. Dr. Horton introduced me to members, and that is how I met Ms. Betty J Tilman. Ms. Tilman welcomed me and offered her assistance. One Sunday, she invited me to stop by her office when I was on campus. It was a wonderful visit. I learned about her job as a Counselor to International Students who attended Pitt. I shared with her my recent involvement in the Civil Rights Movement that occurred in Memphis, my hometown. I spoke about my involvement in the Memphis Sanitation Strike and my participation in the marches and mass meetings. My Pastor, the Rev. James M Lawson, invited Dr. King to Memphis in support of the Sanitation Workers who were striking for better working conditions given that two workers had been killed on the job.

I came to enjoy attending services at UACM. The diverse staff and the welcoming congregation made it a perfect fit. A new young minister on the staff started a Gospel Choir. Rev. Stith and his wife, Claudia, had both been soloists at Virginia Union University before coming to Pittsburgh. The choir became very popular at UACM. At some later point, Ms. Tilman approached Rev. Stith about the choir going on a tour to East Africa. We were speechless. Over two years, we raised the money and embarked in August of 1972 on the trip of a lifetime throughout Kenya, Tanzania, and Uganda. This was the handiwork of none other than Ms. Betty J. Tilman.

I left Pittsburgh in 1981. Down through the years I've kept in touch with Ms. Tilman. I always wanted her to know how much I loved and appreciated her. One is very blessed to meet someone who impacts one's life in such a way that one's purview of the world takes a different form. The legacy that Ms. Tilman left us with is the realization that the ways we are similar are far greater than the ways we are different. We serenaded an African Youth group with the backdrop being Mt. Kilimanjaro at dusk, and they sang for us. It was simply electrifying. Though we did not speak their language, and they, not ours, our warm embraces afterwards proved that music truly is a universal language.

Where do the thank yous end when a woman, who is such a visionary, can bring two cultures together the way Betty Tilman did? Clearly, her Christian faith was an impetus that drove her "Purpose Driven Life." God gave Betty to her parents and to all of us. In turn, used her life to Glorify God. It is safe to say that all good works begin with good intentions. We honor Betty Tilman because her good works have followed her in the lives that she touched and ultimately transformed. Betty gave back to God what he had given to her. She mastered the task of loving God so much that her life served as a mosaic of what He meant when he asked us to love our neighbors as ourselves. Ms. Betty Tilman succeeded in doing that par excellence. Each person's life that she touched gained a new purpose for their own, and we are much better for it because our paths crossed with Ms. Betty J. Tilman.

My endearing tribute to Ms. Betty Tilman is best expressed in the following scripture: **"And now, dear brothers and sisters, one final thing. Fix your thoughts on what is true, and honorable, and right, and pure, and lovely, and admirable. Think about things that are excellent and worthy of praise," Philippians 4:8 (NLT)**

THE ENCOURAGER
by Dr. Lucenia Dunn

If Betty J. Tilman had lived in Europe during the time of the Knights of the Roundtable, she would have been known as Betty the Encourager. She identified human potential and went after it with gusto. I am one she encouraged, and I did not invite her to get involved with my education or my life. But she did it anyway and I will be eternally grateful.

I am Dr. Lucenia Williams Dunn and at that time I was a Campbell. Let me tell you about the Encourager:

I was quietly sitting in my mother's house in Tuskegee, Alabama when Mommy came into the room and said: "I just spoke on the telephone with this woman who informed me that she has a place for you to stay when you come back to finish your doctorate. First, who is Betty Tilman, and have I ever met her?"

I was shocked to say the least because I had no idea where Betty Tilman got my mother's telephone number. Secondly, how did she know I was struggling with whether or not I was going to return to the University of Pittsburgh to complete my studies? To make a long story short. I said to my mom, "Betty is a friend of mine and it is safe to talk with her."

As I tossed everything in my mind, and with a place to stay, I informed my mom and dad that I was going to go back to Pittsburgh to finish my doctorate. My parents were elated. I finished my studies and became Dr. Lucenia. Who was happier about that more than me or my parents – Betty J. Tilman – The Encourager. Some years later, I was elected the first woman Mayor of the City of Tuskegee. Who was there to encourage and support me? Betty J. Tilman. Who supported me as I go about my current duties as President/CEO of the Tuskegee Macon County Community Foundation, Inc.? Betty J. Tilman.

I will sorely miss my friend, *The Encourager*.

BETTY: A MENTOR AND DEAR FRIEND
by Marieta Harper

I met Ms, Betty J. Tilman sometime around 1969-70 at the University of Pittsburgh when I was searching for housing near the Oakland campus. I was there to obtain my Master's degree in Library & Information Science (MLIS). She worked with international students from all over the world. Betty was a mentor who became a great friend. As a bonus, I got to meet Betty's daughter Melony, who has also been a great friend for many years.

While at the University of Pittsburgh, Betty introduced me to the secretary, Mrs. Tolbert. Mrs. Tolbert's husband was William Richard Tolbert, Jr., a former President of Liberia. Tolbert served as president from 1971 to 1980. Prior to becoming president, he was the Vice-President for 20 years (1951 to 1971) under President William Tubman.

I had the privilege to attend the presidential inauguration for President Tolbert in Liberia, in January 1972. I had so much fun attending all the private inaugural ceremonies. This would not have happened had it not been for Betty's connections and diplomacy.

As I continued my studies in library science, the Black students had a sit-in and took over the computer center demanding to have Black history studies at the University of Pittsburgh. As such, the Department of Black Studies was founded and created. They needed a librarian and Betty had encouraged me to apply for this position and, of course, gave me a glowing recommendation.

At the time I had just finished my Master's degree and was hired as the first librarian to develop the collection for the Black Studies program. I worked on acquiring more historical publications on and about African American forebearers of this country.

Betty was always encouraging me to grow and expand my horizons. I worked in this position for several years before resigning and moving on to the Library of the Department of Education in Washington D.C where I worked for a few years before joining USAID.

I joined USAID as a traveling librarian going to different countries starting with West Africa (Nigeria, Ghana, and Ivory Coast) to assist local libraries to set up information about U.S education, as the students there had interest in studying in the U.S.

After USAID, I moved to the Library of Congress in the African Section of the African & Middle Eastern Division. There, I worked as an Area Specialist for Anglo & Francophone West & Central Africa, The Sahel.

Though we spoke often by phone until her transition, the last time I saw Betty was in 2009, when she and Melony visited me in Washington D.C. They came in town and stayed with me for President Barack Obama's first inauguration as the 44th and first African-American President of the United States. We also had the opportunity to attend the Congressional Black Caucus Inaugural Ball which was held at the Capital Hilton during that weekend in January of 2009. **Betty was a wonderful friend who will always live in my heart!**

SISTER BETTY J. TILMAN: WORTHY OF GOOD WITH INTEGRITY!

by Melvin Hubbard El

I have known Sister Betty J. Tilman since the 1970s and always she has been a woman of worthy of good with integrity. Though she has left us, her impact is still felt. She was congenial and humble yet extremely forceful. She moved in many circles and was known for getting things done.

As Senior Community Advisor to Mayor Ed Gainey, I was honored to serve on the Committee for the Celebration of the Life and Legacy of Ms. Betty. J. Tilman which was held at Heinz Chapel at the University of Pittsburgh on October 7th, 2022. Mayor Ed Gainey had a Proclamation created and named that day Ms. Betty J. Tilman Day in Pittsburgh.

It was a beautiful program with an African Processional led by Oba Elie Kihonia and Oronde Sheriff and an African Blessing by Oba Elie Kihonia, Dr. Buba Misawa and Dr. Ahmed Sharif. There was a host of speakers and performers that included Martha Conley Esq., Kati Csoman, Kim El, Mayor Ed Gainey, Dr. Larry Glascoe, Walt Hales, Dr. James Johnson, Mrs. Pamela Johnson, Kenneth Love, Dr. Jerome McKinney, Regina Chow McPhie, Carlton Scott, Shirley Scott, Tim Stevens, Rev. Rose Johnson Thompson, Dr. William Tiga Tita, Rev. Charles Timbers and Rev. Deryck Tines.

Sister Betty was affiliated with a large number of organizations and wore several hats. She founded the Good Neighbor Project Committee in association with the Poise Foundation. She had been Consistory Chair and Elder at COR (Community of Reconciliation) and Vice Moderator of the Pittsburgh Presbytery, a long-term board member of the Afro-American Music Institute and the Pittsburgh Branch NAACP. She was also Founding Member of the African Heritage Classroom/Nationality Rooms at the University of Pittsburgh. The African Heritage Classroom Committee/Ms. Betty J. Tilman Scholarship was created in her name while she was living and that scholarship which supports study in Africa continues as a part of her legacy.

Sister Betty J. Tilman was also a staunch community activist who personally knew many legislators on a first name basis and often called on them to assist others. As long as I've known her, she's always been a compassionate person who listened deeply, guided and helped provide solutions on a personal and community level.

Mayor Ed Gainey said that her legacy lives on through others. This truth continues to bring light to her influence. More than 30 years ago Lady Gladys Olebile Masire, (wife of then Botswana President Quett Masiri) visited Pittsburgh. Sister Betty J. Tilman contacted then Pittsburgh City Councilman, Bishop Duane Darkins and Lady Masire was welcomed in Pittsburgh City Council Chambers.

The City of Pittsburgh recently hosted the Botswana Ambassador to the European Union, H.E. Mrs. Mmasekgoa Masire-Mwamba. It was if Sister Betty was still advising and guiding us. This time we welcomed the next generation. Ambassador Masire-Mwamba was literally walking in her mother's, Lady Gladys Olebile Masire footsteps. We came to know about the Ambassador because of the friendship and relationships cultivated long ago by Sister Betty J Tilman. Ambassador Masire-Mwamba's visit has opened a door for potential partnership with the African country of Botswana and the City of Pittsburgh. **For me the lesson that Sister Betty J. Tilman leaves us with is this...**

Compassion, kindness and legacy manifests in beautiful ways and can continue over many generations! May We All Aspire to Be Worthy of Good with Integrity!

WORDS ABOUT MY BUDDY
by Brandon Jennings

When I was asked to write a few words about Ms. Betty J. Tilman, it took a few days to figure out what I would say about her. I began to reminisce about the many enjoyable interactions that I have shared with Ms. Betty. I met Ms. Betty in 1991 when I worked at McGant Broadus Inc. Ms. Betty was a strong part of the McGant Broadus Team. We instantly became buddies. In fact Ms. Betty became my mentor. I considered her family because, just like my parents, she embraced and supplied me with lots of wisdom and love as if I was her son. Whenever I came into the office, I enjoyed the way her face lit up when she saw me. Because of my personality, I could make her laugh a lot.

Ms. Betty obtained a wealth of wisdom and information and I often thought to myself, how does she retain all this information? Ms. Betty was very active in the African American community in Pittsburgh PA, and I'm sure she was involved in other cities and countries. She was well educated and well-traveled, I was most impressed with the many countries that she has visited in Africa. During her travels to Africa she collected several artifacts from various countries which she proudly displayed in the office of McGant Broadus, Inc. Ms. Betty had a story and background for every piece of African art in the office in which she shared with me. One piece of art that she spoke of with me was a rare and very old photograph of several members of the Zulu Tribe, which was the largest ethnic group in South Africa. This photo intrigued me because it was slightly blurred as if the photographer was moving in a vehicle. Judging from the expressions on the Zulu's faces, they were not happy with whomever it was taking the photograph. It seems they were trespassing and my guess, it was a white photographer. Another piece was a huge African drum from Kenya made of beautiful cow hide and wood, in fact she had a set of three. Ms. Betty inspired me to collect African art. I have a large collection of African artifacts today and I give thanks to Ms. Betty for opening the eyes of a young 26-year-old to this beautiful art form. A lot of my paintings are influenced by the African Diaspora and I give thanks to Ms. Betty for sharing her stories and wisdom with me.

I spent a lot of time with Ms. Betty because I would take her home. I would say "You ready to roll Ms. Betty?" She would say, "I sure am" and then I would say, "Let's roll baby!" She would crack up because I called her baby! It was in the car where we would have our most profound conversations about Africa, African Culture, African Americans, art, fashion, politics, racism, inequality, my career path, family, work, and many more topics.

We would have a lot of conversations in the office as well, but then Melony would come and spoil it by saying "Mom, Brandon has work to do and you are distracting him." LOL!

Ms. Betty was never a distraction, in fact she was a beautiful walking encyclopedia, and she was my buddy. It didn't matter that she and I were generations apart in age, the fact was we were tight. Once I stopped working at McGant Broadus, Inc. Ms. Betty and I lost contact for several years, however I ran into my buddy in a restaurant and we reconnected, exchanged telephone numbers, and chatted on the phone a few times. It was like old times. One conversation that I wished that I had with my friend would've been me expressing to her how much I appreciate her for spending time with me, sharing her knowledge. How much African art is a huge part of my life and that it was because of her. How every time I see a beautiful piece of African art that it reminds me of her. I will miss my buddy; however, **I have rejoiced in knowing that she, along with my parents and other ancestors, are now in my home protecting me and my family. I love you Ms. Betty, when I make it to heaven, be ready to roll baby!**

AUNT BETTY MCGANT TILMAN FROM OUR EYES

by Martha K. Jordan (Katie)

Recalling our father, Arthur Houston McGant, Jr., the brother of Betty McGant Tilman, he often spoke of his siblings when we were noticeably young and told us stories about his childhood, growing up in Washington, D.C., trips to Pennsylvania he took with family where he explained to us that he was originally from there but was born in Washington D.C. Nevertheless, it was not until after moving from Lompoc, CA to Houston, PA, the east coast was where we got to know our wonderful and amazing Aunt Betty, our father's sister, more intimately.

Our family had moved to the West Coast from Washington D.C. in the early 1970s to escape the aftermath, tension, and fallout from the riots of the 1950s and 1960s from the civil rights movements, assassination of President John F. Kennedy and Dr. Martin Luther King Jr. I was about 5 or 6 years old then when we left the city. The riots had left the city of Washington D.C. in distress, and crime was becoming a big problem, especially within the African American community. Our parents found it incredibly challenging raising 7 young children during that time in the inner city. At the time, me and my siblings, Andre, the oldest, Crystal, Ozzie, Carl, Victor, and Patrick. In addition, the doctor suggested that the west, specifically Arizona, would be better for my father since he suffered from bronchitis and pneumonia while living in D.C. during the winter time.

In the late 1970s, our mom and dad decided to move back to the East, in Pennsylvania, to be closer to family. By this time there were 8 of us, which included our youngest brother Zachariah. This decision was influenced by the passing of our grandfather, Arthur Houston McGant Sr. Our father felt a desire to be closer to his mother, Katherine McGant, who had moved back to Canonsburg, PA after retiring from the Naval Medical Center in Washington D.C., and siblings (Gloria, Betty, and Butch) who were living near or in Pittsburgh, Pennsylvania as well. His sister Barbra was still living in Texas. Our father was most close to his brother, however, he and our mother encouraged us to keep a fruitful good relationship with our aunts, uncles, cousins.

The first time I recall visiting with Aunt Betty in Pittsburgh, PA, I remember her infectious smile and how welcoming she was. When she saw us, her smile would light up the room. In her place, she shared with us all sorts of artifacts and gifts from West Africa and other countries. Her place was filled with all kinds of genuinely nice international items (painting, sculptures, instruments). We were not very exposed to the international communities at this time and knew truly little about traveling abroad. She told us about her journeys to the Ivory Coast and parts of west Africa and how intrigued she was with some of the people she met on her Journeys in Africa and the Middle East. She also told us about her connections to the University of Pittsburgh and her support of the international students who attended Pitt University. Since I was noticeably young at the time around 10 or 11 years old and had never traveled abroad, the stories and items she showed and shared with us were remarkably interesting and exciting. We could only imagine how much fun and exciting it was to her. She was very dedicated, involved, and took a lot of pride in what she was doing with the school of international studies at Pitt University. She was always happy to see us with a huge smile.

Around mid-year 1979 my mother decided to move back to her hometown of Washington D.C. where her parents and sibling resided. Our dad stayed in Pennsylvania however, when opportunities arose during the holidays, we would visit Pennsylvania and our Aunt Betty. Our Aunt Betty and mother would stay in close contact with one another and provide updates on how we were doing. Our Aunt Betty was also involved in the NAACP and she would travel to Washington D.C. for various conferences and galas and we would meet up with her. As we all grew and started our own families, we made sure to keep in touch with our Aunt Betty and the rest of our aunts, uncle, and cousins on the McGant side of the family.

Our Aunt Betty was there in times of joy and in times of sorrow. When our father passed away in September 1987 around his birthday, Aunt Betty with her infectious smile along with his other siblings were there for the funeral to comfort us in our loss and somehow managed to put a smile on our faces. As we began our own lives, started our families, and ventured off to other parts of the country, Aunt Betty stayed in communication with our family by phone, email, and periodically sent us cards to let us know that she was thinking of and cared about us.

After not seeing Aunt Betty for an extended period, we caught up with her and her extended Family for her 75th Birthday celebration party in Pittsburgh, PA. By the grace of God, all my kids had the opportunity to meet their Great Aunt Betty, all 7 of them. I was working on a contract in Rockville, MD when we also met up with Aunt Betty, and her daughter, my cousin Miss Melony McGant, to celebrate the Presidential inauguration and Election of the American's First Black President, Barak Obama. We all went down to the Capitol building the night before the inauguration and walked around where President Obama was going to take the oath of office and do his speech. It was such a fitting time for a person like my Aunt Betty, who was so motivated to support and serve the African American and International communities.

Our last visit to Pennsylvania was particularly for visiting Aunt Betty around June 26, 2020. My daughters, Iman, and Diannah, traveled along with me. In her true self, Aunty Betty insisted that we eat together at her place and that we visit the African American Baseball Field in Pittsburgh. We drove to the top of the mountain so that we could see all round Pittsburgh, PA. Lastly, she insisted that we have ice cream at the Italian Ice cream shop, Rita's, before taking her back home. **I have learned much from my Aunt Betty, who opened my eyes to seeing another perspective on life and communities of people beyond where I was from. She truly gave more than just being an "Aunt." She expressed and presented a reason and sense of being and a reason and sense of Family which is truly a blessing to be treasured. This is a story about Aunt Betty from our eyes.**

MEETING AN HONORED GUEST
by Mark Randelle King

Memories of Ms. Betty J. Tilman and her doting daughter, Melony McGant

Long ago in Pittsburgh, PA, "Sugar Top" was considered by some to be the exclusive Black middle-class district in the Hill District community. I had grown here and was grateful to know many of the wonderful residents. One day I got a call from Melony McGant, my dear friend and doting daughter of Ms. Betty J. Tilman. Both of them are one of a kind and have broken the mold of what is expected. Everyone sees they attract others with their spiritual energy of sunshine and laughter of celebration of life! It's as if you have never heard or seen anyone like this in all your lifetime before, it's very unique.

She says "Mark! What are you doing right now? Stop and come down to 262 North Dithridge Street. We have a very, special and surprise guest here, waiting to meet you when you arrive. Please and thank you!" All with her famous signature laughter. In much haste, I jumped in my classic 1968 Volkswagen Beetle, and thundered up and down the famous street of historical Sugar Top residences where the mothers and fathers of artists', musicians including jazz drummer Art Blakey, and sax player Stanley Turrentine lived. They all lived in close proximity of one another.

Once on North Dithridge, I parked my car in front of the Intercultural House. It was the first place in the country where black, international and white university students all lived together. I don't remember exactly what but it seemed like Betty Tilman had some influence over what went on at the Intercultural House. Ms. Betty's apt building was next door. I went up the elevator to the apartment. Arriving at the door, I rang the bell, and sunshine Melony appeared with that smiling laughter and youthful spiritual energy. Talking with her secret, special guest from another room; I know it's a woman with a beautiful accent. I had the honor of entering this grand room of art, books, and rare artifacts from all over the world. Food was cooking in the kitchen, and the aromas were seducing as you walked into the apartment. Upon entering the living room and gathering space, you know you're in an extraordinary place, about to have a rare historical lifetime experience. As Melony greeted me, I saw a beautiful African woman, exquisitely dressed, elegantly sitting on the couch. She looked like royalty. I knew Melony had planned something and you could feel it in the air!

Melony says, "Come meet our honored guest, Ms. Mmasekgoa Masire. She is from Botswana; Africa and her father is President Quett Masire! Her Mother is First Lady Gladys Masire."

I was so honored to meet such a prestigious royal family member; this was around the time Eddie Murphy made *Coming to America* popular at the movies. Melony gave me all the respect to meet her and the experience was something I always cherished in my lifetime! When do you get to meet the African royalty of any country? It was mind-blowing, then and now! I couldn't stop looking at her. We had a great conversation.

Then, the princess of Botswana says, "Would you like to see an image of my dad, the president?" She went into her purse and pulled out a currency bill with lots of zeros. It was a happy and blessed day for us and our ancestors to experience the real Coming to America. What a day! Okay. I know that Botswana is a democracy and the title of princess is not used but wow it was amazing to see a Black Man on the currency of the country of Botswana more than 30 years ago.

This is what I mean when I say Ms. Betty was a special, knowledgeable, ambassador of her own in Pittsburgh. She was the Angelical spirit-president ambassador of the communications of countries, oceans beyond oceans, and people of all colors for Pittsburgh's rooms.

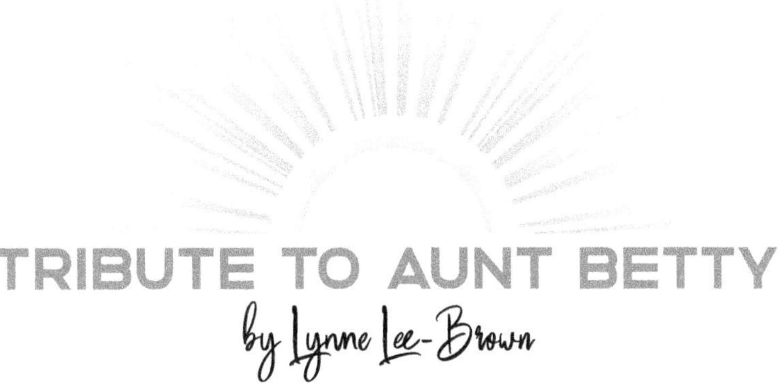

TRIBUTE TO AUNT BETTY
by Lynne Lee-Brown

remember Aunt Betty fondly through the eyes of a child and later as a mature wiser adult with the capability of understanding "truth."

As a child, Aunt Betty exposed me to a world very different than I experienced on a daily basis. I was and was not familiar with the Pittsburgh Hill District. You see, I lived my formative years in a "*majority*" semi-rural neighborhood in Pittsburgh. This neighborhood was void of educated Black families. As a young black child, I excelled in grammar school but had no knowledge of the world beyond. Aunt Betty welcomed me to her world and the wonders of the Hill District's Anna B. Heldman Center. Summers spent at the Center allowed me to escape constant babysitting duties. The Center allowed me to mingle among environments very different from mine. It was at this Center where I was first exposed to educated and worldly African and Caucasian folks. There, I learned and enjoyed constructive play, in a park-like environment on equipment created and specifically built for children. Because of Aunt Betty, I attended ballet performances. True, my attendance at such events were more often viewed as "*required*," but in time I learned to appreciate the skill and commitment such art demanded. My attempts to learn the violin helped me understand the deep commitment mastering such feats required.

Aunt Betty provided me a safe haven during the most turbulent family times. It was during a family separation that I first began to understand the "*sting*" of racism. In May 1961, I arrived after school to our temporary home at Aunt Betty's to find my mother and Aunt Betty tearful. They were studying the newspaper account of the incredibly courageous Freedom Riders.

The Freedom Riders were groups of African American and Caucasian civil rights activists that rode buses through the American South and protested segregated bus terminals. Their goal was to challenge state laws that enforced segregation in transportation and demanded the federal government enforce the Supreme Court Boynton v. Virginia ruling, prohibiting the segregation of interstate travel. Despite the numerous incidents of documented and televised extreme violence resulting in the death and maiming of many, the Freedom Riders were successful in convincing the federal government to enforce integration of interstate travel.

As a seven year old, I could not fully comprehend either the importance and dangerous work of the Freedom Riders or the many tragedies of that era. Finding my mother and Aunt Betty in such a woeful state that day caused me to begin to wonder what fate awaited me as a Black girl in the United States.

As an adult in my forties, I reconnected with Aunt Betty and began to learn so much more about her life in a community that simultaneously respected and disrespected her. She overcame so much as evidenced by her many challenges and *"firsts"* such as…

- Family dynamics where she was occasionally ostracized;
- The negative perception that she was *"bourgeois"*;
- The unpopular desire to explore our African ancestral roots;
- The importance of travel outside these United States, particularly to African countries;
- Embracing the creative arts viewed as unnecessary to many of African descent;
- Her association with of *"all"* people of color to include mid-Eastern cultures;
- The value of higher learning considered unnecessary to those interested only in daily survival;
- Her indifference toward material wealth;
- The importance of consistently mentoring without any promise of payback;
- Her steadfast commitment to positive change through politics evidenced by her incessant writing to political leaders and encouraging me and others to do likewise;
- Her encouragement of youth to explore unfamiliar and sometimes scary paths to self-actualization.

I am certain there were many more challenges and "firsts" others could identify!

As I visited with Aunt Betty for hours during her extended hospital stay in the early 2000s, we shared previously untold life stories. She expressed pride in the life I built with my husband and others. Aunt Betty assured me time and time again, that my life was so special that documenting it was required. And because of my dear Aunt Betty, I have embarked on the journey. When I write, I constantly hear her encouraging words and for that, I will forever be grateful for what one day will become *"a book!"*

CARRIE MCCRAY'S MEMORIES OF BETTY TILMAN

Written by Steven McCray as told by Carrie McCray

My name is Carrie McCray, and at age 92 I am so humbled and honored to be able, upon the request of my Daughter in Spirit Melony, to reflect and share just a few of the many fond and lasting memories that I have, of her mother and my friend of over 55 years, Betty J. Tilman.

Betty and I met under somewhat precarious circumstances. This was during the post-volatile 1960s, entering the more promising 1970s of which Pittsburgh was in a transitional phase and was attempting to rebrand its image in every way possible be it racially, economically, politically, and spiritually. Not necessarily in that order, and not out of guilt. It was because the times and many like us, in the community at large, demanded a more inclusive cultural shift within the dynamics of everyday living in Pittsburgh, and its surrounding communities.

If my memory serves me correctly, it was in 1969 when the Pittsburgh Presbytery made a bold move and decided to create an inter-denominational and interracial church located at Bellefield and 5th Avenue, which at the time was Bellefield Presbyterian Church. Betty worked in an office space that the church rented to the University of Pittsburgh. As one of the founders of this new, original experiment, Betty and I crossed paths often and became good acquaintances.

Soon the church had "evolved" into two entities--The Community of Reconciliation (COR), and the University and City Ministries (UACM). We worked in tandem with the University of Pittsburgh and the Oakland community, with various concerns focused on the foreign students' needs, especially in the area of student living, as well as being a safe haven for fellowship.

Another fun and creative addition to this grand experiment of UACM, was the formation of a gospel choir. Betty and I used to be tickled at the fact that there was a **Presbyterian gospel choir** within the city of Pittsburgh. Another first! The choir "Soup" consisted of church and community members, as well as some university students. UACM Choir became well known, beginning to perform all around Pittsburgh. This was a springboard for the summer of 1972. There was an opportunity for the choir to visit East Africa—Kenya, Uganda, and Tanzania, in particular. **It was Betty, who drew from her exceptional coordinating and diplomatic skills through the University of Pittsburgh and various international embassies that helped to make that trip possible.**

As Betty and I were landing in Kenya, we were super excited but also cautious. We were aware of our dual roles as tourists and chaperones for these 26 young choir members, who were so excited and eager to explore the "Motherland," without taking into full account that this was still a foreign land.

As the days wore on, Betty and I depended on one another more, developing an even better perspective as to what our role actually was while visiting the Motherland.

And as we were leaving Tanzania to return back to the United States, the entire group realized that we were leaving a country that was part of a vast continent that, in reality, was only 10 to 12 years removed from gaining their independence from colonial rule. It was truly an eye opening moment. **The journey was absolutely one of the highlights of both of our lives.**

Soon afterwards, with inspiration from the journey to the Motherland, "**Show Me The Way,**" UACM's Gospel Choir first and only album was produced and released as a joyful Love offering. As the months and years moved on, Betty and I became close friends. We talked a lot about the politics of the day. The seventies Apartheid South Africa. Nelson Mandela was still being imprisoned. The United States and Israel still supported South Africa. And then there were The Watergate Tapes. I remember Shirley Chisholm running for president and becoming the first Black female to be placed on a Democratic Presidential ticket!

Other hot topics of discussion in 1973 included Roe v. Wade became law (boy did that come full circle), the Apollo moon landing, and in 1975 the Vietnam war ended. We appreciated the lighter as well. **Fred Rogers** (yes, that Mr. Rogers, who would eventually become a national and an international celebrity, who at one time, was also part of the children's ministry at COR), on any given day, would walk from his office in the WQED building just to say hello to Betty and me. He would strike up a conversation and then leave with his trademark, "**I love you just the way you are.**"

Yes, Betty and I were knee deep in the conversation and activities of creating a better world, operating as foot soldiers when necessary. **And this was just the seventies!** It was also around this time when I had decided to make use of my entrepreneurial skills and opened an African clothing and jewelry store called the Knot Shop on 5th Avenue in downtown Pittsburgh, where Betty was a frequent visitor and customer. She had also generously given me referrals of Nigerian vendors from whom I could buy items from. We also had a little secret. The rear of the store also served as a meeting space for Duquesne University Black students who often felt that they were being "watched" by the campus police.

It also was a time for us to explore the many new things happening in our environment. We worked along with many others in helping to bring into existence the **African Heritage Classroom** in the University of Pittsburgh's Cathedral of Learning. We enjoyed attending plays written by local, but nationally known, playwrights Rob Penny and Dr. Vernell Lillie. We attended the numerous community events and festivals that occurred year round. **These were happy and proud moments to be in "the skin we're in."**

Although I did not know specifically what Betty's job was at the University of Pittsburgh, I did observe that she always had around her an eclectic array of International visitors. They ranged from heads of state, dignitaries, educators, their families, and students. It became much more apparent that Betty's role, far as her involvement as a liaison, to concierge and host many of these people was an important position at the University of Pittsburgh. Betty J. Tilman was the perfect person for it. She was a renaissance woman, well-known, and respected 'people person' within the community.

It was in this atmosphere that our friendship flourished even more. Betty was aware that in the years that followed our 1972 trip, my husband Leon and myself had traveled back to the African continent at least twice to re-acquaint ourselves, not only with our heritage, but with the people who We Were and are undeniably, a part of it. So, at times when Betty would be hosting a foreign visitor, primarily of African descent, she would call and say in her matter of fact way, "Carrie I have something going on, guess who?" We would have meet and greets, and sometimes host in our home, enjoying the most spiritually enlightening conversations and cultural exchanges as ever.

One of my most memorable moments with Betty came when she called to tell me that the First **Lady of Botswana, Gladys Olebile Masire**, was visiting the University of Pittsburgh. She had come to give a speech about a boy's school that she was building in Botswana, Africa, and after she spoke, she wanted to spend time with an African American family.

I was both flattered, excited, and instantly agreed. Later that evening, Betty brought the First Lady, along with her "lady in waiting" and her bodyguard, to my home. Of course, I told my two children who were still living in Pittsburgh, Steven and Jeffrey (and daughter, Charia), about this chance encounter, so they hurried over to meet the group. Everything seemed surreal at first, but after a short period of time, it became apparent that we were just having a conversation with everyday people with the same issues in life, and that living an ocean away does not change the humanity of the spirit.

After a few photo ops and the First Lady Masire loving on my granddaughter Charia, (she had no idea as to her part in this historical event), my sons were about to say their farewells when my son Steven turned to everyone and said that this was definitely no chance encounter, but now a significant part of our family history. Now, as I reflect on this story, I can pull out some pictures to show my granddaughter Charia, that **Michelle Obama** was not the only Black First Lady that she's ever known! **Thank you, Betty!**

Lastly, I would like to share with you an event that fell short of a miracle. In 1993 there was a decision made, as part of a fundraiser for the 25th anniversary of the **Community of Reconciliation's** existence, to have a concert at Carnegie Music Hall in Pittsburgh, featuring the internationally acclaimed acapella singing group, **Sweet Honey In The Rock**. The congregation, though small, was very excited for this event to happen! **The one major concern upon signing the contract was the performance date which was scheduled for January 9th!** Winter concerts were not the best sell out for venues in Pittsburgh. Murmurs of a concert bust were being whispered throughout the involved membership. To make a long story short, January 9th, 1993, came and the concert had to be delayed only because the ticket lines were so long that the concert started late to accommodate the unexpected sales. It was Betty's persistent public relations campaign that caused this to happen. It was a wonderful winter sold out concert.

So again, I say thank you Betty J. Tilman for allowing your energy to flow through me so that I can share your story as only Sisters In the Spirit Can. Peace & Love.

A LOVE LETTER TO MY MOTHER, MOMBETTY J. TILMAN IN HEAVEN!

by Melony McGant

MOM, I feel so privileged to have you as a Mother and to have journeyed with you in this lifetime.

Looking back on this time on Earth, my life has been one of learning, adventure, and more Joy than I thought imaginable.

You Exposed Me to the Best Life Had to Offer!

Sometimes I was fearful. You pushed and pushed and told me that I had a right to walk any path I choose in the World.

So often I felt that I was not good enough and unworthy of these great gifts. People whispered behind your back and made fun of me when I articulated using my extensive vocabulary. They said I was born with a silver spoon in my mouth.

Looking back, it was funny how some of the relatives and community associates or so-called friends looked for ways to undermine your authority and convince me to go right when I should have gone left.

What I thought I wanted was to be "normal." I didn't understand that being different and unique was a Great Gift.

Though I tried to run away from all you had taught me, it was so imprinted in my mind and my heart and my Soul that the further I ran, the closer I came to it.

I Thank You for a first-class education, for swimming at the YWCA, ballet and drama at the Pittsburgh Playhouse, camp in Tenants Harbor, Maine at Blueberry Cove, and studying musical instruments like the violin and recorder. I never did master either but at least I love music!

I've become a person who loves people of different cultures. Travel is like eating chocolate and I honor all Faith traditions and continue to explore the Divine Essence of MotherFatherG-D through Love.

I look at myself now and know that I am a product of your magnificent efforts! Thank you for all you have done for me. Your Goodness inspires me. Your toughness helped me learn how to survive in a World that would say "Who do you think You Are?" Instead of "How Can I Help?"

You Taught Me that GOOD IS POWERFUL BEYOND MEASURE!

My Queen and Precious MOM Betty J Tilman, I Love YOU Into Eternity and Send All My Love to You in the Heaven Realm.

THE DESEGREGATION OF TOWN PARK POOL IN CANONSBURG, PA

by Allante McGant, National Guard Sgt

My Grandfather Alexander "Butchie" McGant lives in the house his grandfather built in Canonsburg. He's retired from the U.S. Army. Most people don't know that he was for a time, a weapons instructor at West Point. He used to love fishing and hunting but now that he's in his 80's, he tells stories.

He has told me many stories about when he and his sister (my Great Aunt Betty) were younger. It was mostly good times and some of their adventures. I think one of the most interesting and admirable ones on Aunt Betty's part was hearing about her role in the desegregation of the Canonsburg, PA Town Park Pool around1951 or 1952.

Aunt Betty was only 18 when she pushed, organized, and helped lead the movement for the desegregation for Town Park Pool in Canonsburg. My Grandfather said that she argued...

"The black community pays municipal taxes just like the white community. Why should we not have the privilege of something that is being funded by our hard-earned money?"

My Grandfather Butchie was around age 9 but he and his friends and many older kids met Aunt Betty at the pool. It seemed like attending the "talk of the town". He told me how the black supporters of all ages, whispered about it at school. On the appointed day, they showed up as planned at the Canonsburg, PA Town Park Pool and joined to swim with the whites.

The whites refused to swim with the blacks and left the pool. The whites got out of the pool and then went up the hill that overlooked the pool. They threw rocks at the black supporters but eventually left because the supporters were unphased by their actions.

Because this brazen act of desegregation Canonsburg, PA Town Park Pool had taken place on a weekend, the following Monday at school there were many fights. However, after that weekend there was no more segregation at the pool. After that, slowly desegregation began to become a norm in the Canonsburg community.

I think if not for Aunt Betty's bravery and leadership to push and organize the desegregation of the Canonsburg Town Park Pool, it would been much later before that desegregation would have come. My Grandfather Alexander "Butchie" McGant has told me countless stories of him and her when they were younger but this one is definitely one of my favorites!

THE INTERNATIONAL GLUE AND MOTHER AFRICA: A TRIBUTE TO MS. BETTY TILMAN

by Dr. Buba Misawa

As we gather here today, the words of recognition and tribute to Ms. Betty Tilman is much easier than bearing her passing away. Ms. Betty, you left us, but your life endures. We remain in deep pain, yet you showed us how to be tough and exemplary through the years. Since my first contact with you in 1982 as a young student applying to graduate school at Pitt from Nigeria, you made things sound and look normal, and indeed, very reassuring always, including in your own last few months alive. You built futures for many young minds and bridges across the world, and especially the African diaspora bridge.

While many people gave flowery speeches about African Americans and Africa, you simply exemplified the relationship by nurturing African students, scholars, and professionals in Pittsburgh. You never lost any hope, even with the clear lack of understanding of the essence in unity and African identity among the two groups. Your love for humanity brought people from around the globe to you; thus, making you the international glue without the great fanfare and notoriety that you so deserved. Most people would have claimed popularity and fame in helping others, but you chose grace and kindness from your heart with full joy and happiness. I wished I, and hopefully the world too, had your great determination and desire to help others, as well as offer friendship, understanding, guidance, loving care, and true humanity to every person we come across, like you did. We lost you, even with a life fully lived and acknowledged by hundreds of others. However, you laid enough foundation in endurance, family ties, care, love, encouragement, support, unity, courage, and bravery.

The Rev. Melony McGant, your daughter, has inherited great values to carry on with your work. Your great sense of history attracted the African diaspora to so many events that you initiated and successfully organized in the Pittsburgh area. Ms. Betty, your inspiration is profound and enduring. Your positive thoughts, encouragements, laughs, and comforting smiles even in difficult situations, kept many international students reassured and hopeful in navigating the American cultural landscape. You always found ways and means of addressing critical issues and questions for everyone, most times, with your hilarious sense of humor! I will fondly remember you and miss you dearly. Our condolences to the whole family.

A NEVER FORGOTTEN CONNECTION

by Ambassador Mmasekgoa Masire-Mwamba

Betty Tilman! However brief the encounter was originally intended to be, from the minute she met up with Lady Olebile Masire, then first Lady of Botswana on what was to be a short visit to Pittsburgh, they smiled at each other, and they clicked. It was clear to both of them that their spirits connected. They instantly bedded down the seeds of friendship that developed and expanded well beyond the official programs and continents, a solid friendship that transcended time, distances, and endured throughout the ages. Indeed, shortly after that first meeting, they had an opportunity to collaborate on a project that could have been named 'taking care of Mmasekgoa in Pittsburgh.'

As they had foreshadowed, I arrived in Pittsburgh to pursue my graduate studies at KGSB. I quickly realised that though I left my mother's home all the way back in Botswana, here I was standing in front of Betty. I was meeting Betty for the first time and I too found in Betty that I instantly had a friend, had family, had my own mothers proxy, a kind and welcoming home, right here in this far place called America. Betty opened her heart to me, and to all my peers from the continent of Africa, everyone felt welcome.

Africa always had a special part in her life. She went out of her way for so many of us as students and professionals coming into the State. Hers was an open and welcoming heart. She was always there looking out for us. The warmth of her love and support has never left me. I welcomed this opportunity to pay tribute to such a gracious and embracing soul. She gave herself fully; she loved, laughed, lived. A lively soul indeed!

In recent years, I have travelled to London, Japan, Germany, and spent many an hour on zoom, reaching out to Pittsburgh students, sharing my experience. My journey continued to honour the first spark that ignited these two formidable ladies, my own mother and Bettey Tillman. I have stayed connected with Pittsburgh and have always understood, it was way bigger than me just getting an education, standing on the shoulders of these two ladies whose spirits are now intertwined in the heavens. Their powerful memory still lives on, continuing to guide, inspire us to do more, to be better, reach out, help however and wherever we can! With a warm and loving memory of Betty Tilman.

AUNT BETTY HAD A DREAM—FOR ME
by Donna Baxter Porcher

Ms. Betty J. Tilman was a true gem in the Pittsburgh community. As soon as I met Ms. Betty, or Aunt Betty, as I was told to call her, I knew she was unique. Her tales of the successes of African-Americans in Pittsburgh captivated me every time we spoke, and I felt as though I were listening to a walking Black history textbook. Not only was she knowledgeable about the city's rich Black history, but she also actively worked to preserve and promote it. She organized events and outings that brought together people from all walks of life, fostering a sense of unity and community. Her passion for Black culture was contagious, and it was impossible not to be inspired by her.

In addition to being a historian, Aunt Betty was a mentor and a leader. She gave me a lot of insight into Black Pittsburgh and its people. She even schooled me in places at my own university. Because she was a founding member of the University of Pittsburgh's African Heritage Classroom Committee, I learned more about Pitt's African Heritage Room from her after I graduated than I did while I was a student there.

She supported me after I was elected president of the National Association of Women Business Owners (NAWBO). I remember bringing her to some of the seminars and workshops. I'd look out into the audience and she would be smiling and attentive. Being originally from Johnstown and having few relatives that live near Pittsburgh, I always felt like I had family there to support me when Aunt Betty was around.

She was also proud of what The Soul Pitt, my own business, had accomplished. She became one of my biggest cheerleaders for the media company that I had started as a hobby and that served as a resource for the African-American community through a website and a free quarterly print publication. I would take copies of the *Soul Pitt Quarterly* to her apartment building lobby, so she could make sure the residents got issues to read and share with people she knew. I would talk to her about my future plans for Soul Pitt and my love of technology. She would enjoy giving me advice, story ideas, encouragement, and I graciously welcomed it all. I must admit, Aunt Betty believed in me more than I believed in myself. She had lofty goals for me, and after talking with her, I felt a little overwhelmed sometimes, but was always left inspired to dream bigger, because Aunt Betty dreamed BIG!

It's truly remarkable when someone comes into your life and sees your potential in a way that you don't see it. They believe in you more than you believe in yourself, and their faith in you can inspire you to dream bigger and reach higher. These people are invaluable and can have a profound impact on your life, helping you to unlock your full potential and achieve things you never thought were possible. Aunt Betty was that person for me.

In July 2014, I received an email from Aunt Betty that I'll always cherish. It remains in my inbox today:

Subject Line: My Dream of the Grand Opening of the Soul Pitt Neighborhood Techmobile
From: Betty J. Tilman <bettyjtilman@yahoo.com>
To: "soulpitt@gmail.com" <soulpitt@gmail.com>
Date: Jul 14, 2014, 9:11 PM
On the morning of 7/2/14, I awakened at 4 am, recalling my last night's dream of the invitation to the above subject on July 1, 2018 at the Kingsley House parking lot. Malia and Sasha Obama served as honorary hosts for the red-carpet luncheon, in the lavishly decorated gymnasium. This project was founded and initiated by Ms. Donna Baxter, with major funding from Bill and Melinda Gates. Most of my dreams are in technicolor, as this one was and seemed very real that I started taking notes for a feasibility study, which I will share with you. Let us begin working on this. I would be a member of the team that puts this together. I know it is in the works. God has many plans for you. Donna, I am so very proud of you, Love Aunt Betty

"Wow, that was a big dream!" I thought as I finished reading. After that, I wondered, "Did she really begin drafting a feasibility study?" I giggled to myself, thinking that only Aunty Betty would have such a dream. I called her, and we talked about her dream. We even discussed the concept of having a "techmobile" that would deliver technology to the Black community as a means to help shrink the digital divide and bring tech to the people. While I haven't heard from Bill and Melinda yet, and Malia and Sasha Obama might be busy, I have started the process of creating a non-profit, and I will undoubtedly keep Aunt Betty's idea in mind and utilize it as motivation.

The impact that Aunt Betty had on me and the Pittsburgh community is immeasurable. She will always be remembered as a true trailblazer and an inspiration to all who had the privilege of knowing her. Her legacy continues to live on through the many people she touched and the memories she created. Though it was only for a little over 10 years, I am so thankful that God put Aunt Betty in my life and so blessed that she had a dream for me!

CELEBRATING MS. BETTY J. TILMAN AND THE AFRICAN HERITAGE CLASSROOM COMMITTEE
by Carlton Scott

I want to thank Reverend Melony McGant for affording me the opportunity to say a few words about what it means to support the African Heritage Classroom.

The African Heritage Classroom/Nationality Room at the University of Pittsburgh symbolizes the creation of great African civilizations that many are unaware even existed. It symbolizes the struggle and perseverance of African descendants on all fronts, the importance of cultural memory, the power of knowing who you are, and the influence your ancestral culture has had on the world. It is also a symbol of potential, the seemingly limitless ways we can, in a word, remember, which can mean to never forget and also to make whole.

Scholars have spoken and written about the thousands of years of African history that existed before the trans-Atlantic slave trade and why it is important for enslaved African descendants to understand and share that history. The African Heritage classroom endeavors to do that.

As Chair of the African Heritage Classroom Committee and Executive Director of the Intercultural House, I am honored to be part of two significant parts of Ms. Betty Tilman's legacy and to see and hear the profound impact she had on so many lives. Elders like Ms. Betty Tilman and others fiercely advocated and raised money for the establishment. Their passion, pride, perseverance, and vision live in all of us who continue to advocate for and support the room.

I recently spoke with Ludwick "Luddy" Hayden about the room and he made reference to the wooden door that was made in Nigeria. He also talked about the times he visited Africa, the impact of seeing the slave castles and the "door of no return," which referred to the opening that led to the sea. Once the enslaved went through that door they never returned home. I found Mr. Hayden's experience particularly moving because the African Heritage Classroom Committee sees the door of the classroom as the **"door of opportunity"** whether one is walking into or out of the classroom. We see it as our opportunity to have our elders pass down their knowledge, wisdom, work ethic, and other practices to the next generations as theirs did with them. It is the spirit of this transaction that we are celebrating today.

We are hoping this celebration of Ms. Betty J. Tilman brings a renewed energy to seek out those who we can support, motivate, mentor, and watch them achieve excellence as Ms. Tilman did so many times. Thank you!

A LETTER TO MELONY IN CELEBRATION OF MY FRIEND BETTY!

by Delores Southers

Dearest Melony,

Betty joyfully connected with God and others. She was love in action; sharing our History and Culture from generation to generation, seen through you, her loving daughter Melony.

Melony, I was so blessed to have known your Mom Betty and to be in that number to witness "Celebrating the Life & Legacy of Ms. Betty J. Tilman." It was a joyous experience with the Word; Music, Dance, Art and fellowship!!! You did a superb, beyond anyone's expectations, honoring God, your mother, our ancestors and those in the room from the White House to the out house; representing those who have traveled in life's journey in your mother's love shown...in action!!!

Every one that spoke shared so much history of your mother's involvement in their personal lives as well as their professional lives. They shared social justice issues that were addressed through her efforts of informing, connecting, organizing and working with them in communities at large; home & abroad... globally; to reconcile divisions and make our world a better place.

Betty showed her faith, by her work, with love and compassion. I felt that everyone there must have been touched by her in some way and experienced her genuine love for God and people. I'm convinced that those who spoke from the podium, shared the sentiments in the hearts; of many of us, in the audience, from different cultures; that were there; to revere God and Betty Tilman's Legacy! "To God Be The Glory!"

Pam Johnson and her husband from Afro American Music Institute in Homewood. told their story. Dr. Johnson said when they came to Pittsburgh, from Louisiana; that Betty got a house for them and helped them get established here, in Pittsburgh, within three months. Wow!

Afterwards, Pam sang "Let the Work I've done speak for Me." It was so touching!!! I'm sure others felt the same.

Ministers, Mayor Ed Gainey, representatives from the community, University of Pittsburgh students, whom Betty served and worked with; who are now lawyers, professors, artists, musicians, dancers, friends, neighbors, others, family; especially you, Rev. Melony McGant, Your Mom Betty's beloved daughter; who is continually carrying out the plan and purpose that God gave them, to love

Him and others, from generation to generations for His Glory! Yes, Love in Action!"

What an inspiring **Celebration of the Life & Legacy of Betty Tilman** that will continue from generation to generation!

May God perfect all He has begun in you and others; In serving Him and others, for His plan, and for His purpose, and for His Glory! Keep hope alive! Keep making history! Jesus Loves you and so do I. *"Whoever believes in my Father, above in heaven, is my brother, sister and mother," Matthew 12:50.*

WHAT BETTY TILMAN MEANT TO ME
by Charles (Chuck) Timbers

For countless numbers of years Betty J. Tilman mentored, embraced, and encouraged those who crossed her path, including me, Charles E. Timbers Jr . I was not as fortunate as many who were students at the University of Pittsburgh in the Africana studies program to witness the genuine love and caring of this woman. Betty Tilman knew who I was when we first met because she was actively involved in the theater program and Kuntu Theater with Rob Penny and Dr. Vernell Lilli.

In late December 2016, I received a call that I did not expect from Ms. Betty Tilman; she informed me of an upcoming event at the Benedum Center in Pittsburgh. Ironically, I had been cast in the ensemble with Pittsburgh Opera. This encounter was the beginning of a great friendship. She embraced me as though I was one of her family because that was the type of woman she was, and welcomed me into her home. We had long talks on the telephone just about life and she would discuss some of her future plans which always seemed to be humanitarian in nature, uplifting people.

This relationship helped me to see my self-worth and to be proud of who God made me to be. She entrusted and honored me with the task of taking a token to the one and only Dr. Vernell Lillie in Washington D.C. It was a baseball bat from The Summer King honoring Josh Gibson. I had issues with self-esteem and never thought I was good enough, that I did not fit in for a long time, but Betty Tilman helped change that. I will forever be grateful to her. **There are angels who walk among us, and Ms. Bettty Tilman was one of those beautiful kindred souls, one of those angels. Thank you, Betty Tilman. Take your rest. Job well done.**

Afterword
Acknowlegements
Author Bios

AFTERWORD
FROM MELONY, BELOVED DAUGHTER OF MS. BETTY J. TILMAN

Beautiful People,

I was nurtured in the womb with compassion and birthed by a Woman of Courage in times of Great Change.

As a child I made mudpies filled with hope; picked blueberries with joy, learned to swim in the ocean and climbed apple and acorn trees in search of wisdom.

When I fell, the Woman of Courage hugged me and nurtured my cuts and bruises. I was a wild child dancing through fields of grass and flowers, chasing butterflies in the morning.

As a child in the early 60's I met Pete Seeger when I was at the Blueberry Cove Camp (Maine). I will always remember his warmth, his laughter and his beautiful, Generous Spirit! I am still singing a song he taught us---"This Land Is Your Land, This Land Is My Land!"

Looking back, I realize that as a child, I learned to read and travel the World through books! At night I imagined what life would be like if I could ride on the moon and share my toys with other children in the sparkling stars.

The Woman of Courage laughed and taught me to write stories and use my imagination. She told me I was a special gift and would help make the World better. She taught me to Pray and say Thank You for my good life.

As I grew, the World kept Changing. The Woman of Courage, My Mother, Betty J Tilman taught me to use my voice and speak out for Justice and to Serve All with Love. She taught me to respect others and shared her dreams for Peace in the World. We marched and sang and prayed that all children could be free to grow in Love.

The truth is, most of my life I've had to share My Mother, who lived in Pittsburgh, PA. I shared her with great grandparents and grandparents, aunts and uncles and cousins and so many, many other people. Often, they were people of different races, religions, and cultures; with languages I didn't (and still don't) understand.

People from Africa, Asia, Europe, South America and yes, even North America took to Her Love Like brown or white on rice, red on apples, yellow on bananas, and green on tree leaves.

Over the years that I have known her, I have discovered that countless numbers throughout the World called her a dear friend and named her Godmother or Aunt to their Children.

There were many times I felt left behind. I often was. When she marched for Civil Rights in the segregated states, she left her young, willful, outspoken daughter in the safety of family friends.

When she bicycled miles and miles with the Peace and Freedom Movement or went off to study Transcendental Meditation, my thought was "What About Me?"

Today I can answer "What About Me?" My Mother used her energy, her voice and resources for equal rights for Me and All People of all cultures, race and religions.

There is Miss Betty, Aunt Betty, Lady Betty, and MOMBetty but in the Castle of My Heart, she will always be the ONE who gave ME, her daughter the opportunity to Grow with Wisdom, to Shine with Confidence and Learn to Love beyond my imagination. My Mother Will Always Be My Queen!

Looking back, I now know that I was so very Blessed to grow up in a household where learning my history, having an imagination, believing I was special and participation in the Civil Rights Movement was essential.

Sojourner Truth, Harriet Tubman, John Brown, Mary McLeod Bethune, Ralph Bunche, W.E. B. DuBois, Kwame Nkruma, Gwendolyn Brooks, Charles Drew, Katherine Dunham, Romare Bearden, Franz Fanon, Franklin Frazier, Langston Hughes, Countee Cullen, Howard Thurman, Martin Luther King, Jr., Malcolm X, Harry Belafonte, Fannie Lou Hammer, Shirley Chisolm and Barbara Jordan, James Baldwin and Paul Laurence Dunbar, Gordon Parks, Randall Robinson, SelmaBurke, and Richard Wright were just a few of the many names discussed at our dinner table.

My mother, Betty J. Tilman was the Founder of the Good Neighbor Project Committee (in partnership with the POISE Foundation), worked for 28 years at the University of Pittsburgh as a Foreign Student Advisor/Liason, etc., was a founding member of the Nationality Rooms/African Heritage Classroom Committee, a Golden Heritage Member of the NAACP, and also sat on the Pittsburgh Branch NAACP board of directors for 30 years and the Afro American Music Institute. She has been Vice-Moderator and an Elder in the Pittsburgh Presbytery. She was an activist in the Civil Rights, Peace and Freedom and the Free South Africa Movements.

Because of her involvement with the Friend's Meeting House (Quakers), in 1970, I spent the summer traveling through Ghana and came back with a real appreciation and respect for "Mother Africa!"

As a teen, I worked in the office of Pennsylvania Legislator, the Honorable K. Leroy Irvis and in the offices of a political consulting firm. As a young adult, and professional in Pittsburgh, I often volunteered on local, state and national political campaigns. I believed, and still do believe that the Right to VOTE and live in a democratic society is a great gift!

In 1974 when I was 19, I joined the Navy. While stationed at the Norfolk Naval Air Station I wrote for the base newspaper and later was stationed in Puerto Rico.

In 1978, I returned to Pittsburgh at the age of 23 and became involved with community advocacy. I was appointed as an NAACP board member, served on the NAACP Human Rights Dinner Committee, was editor of the NAACP News, and briefly hosted a weekly NAACP radio talk show. My poetry was published by the Pittsburgh Courier. One piece was titled "The Unworthy, Worthy Politician". Even then as I do now, I questioned the unfair system and the integrity of some of our leaders.

In 1980 I relocated to West Virginia to complete my undergraduate studies at Marshall University, and later to Washington where I was awarded an internship and hired as assistant to the fundraiser (Gary Rivers) for the Congressional Black Caucus Foundation.

In 1990, after several years in NYC, I relocated back to Pittsburgh, owned my own business, and found myself involved in both a local & national movement in support of MBE/WBE programs. One of my most memorable marketing projects was a campaign for the Minority Business Enterprise Legal Defense and Education Fund (MBELDEF). I have been a feature writer for the New Pittsburgh Courier, been featured in MBE Magazine, and have written for several other publications.

It is interesting to note that I now believe that one of the greatest errors of the Civil Rights Movement was for People of Color to refer to ourselves as minorities. The definition of minority according to Random House Webster's College Dictionary is "the smaller part or number part or amount forming less than half of the whole." People of Color Are the Majority People in the World. We Are Not Less Than. I believe that we should teach our Children that they are brilliant, unique and special!

In life I work to be patient, sincere, kind, and responsible. I believe in listening, and in providing support or encouragement to every individual. I enjoy people of all cultures. They inspire me, and I enjoy sharing my knowledge with them. Most importantly I have a passion to serve, and to assist in the healing of hearts, so that more individuals can grow and flourish as productive members of our society.

And yet, often I pray and sit in silence asking for guidance and direction. If you were to ask to have, we failed, I would say that I don't know the answer. Racism, sexism, classism, colorism and many other negative "isms" still exist throughout the World.

Certainly, the lack of focus on our youth, inequitable education, as well as violence, guns and drugs circulated in many communities are symptomatic of society's values and lack of moral compass. These facts cause me great despair.

In our society today, there is too much emphasis on the acquisition of "things" and not enough emphasis on compassion, Love and respect for each other.

Sometimes I feel as If I have failed, and that my miniscule actions leave no footprints in the sands of time. Still, there is a place deep in my heart that tells me that I am wrong.

It is only my disappointment that causes this pain in my heart to move through my body as my nerve endings become filled with acute anxiety.

What I am feeling is what many of you may be feeling. The question some of us may be asking in this time of painful transformation is "Will Hope Be Enough for All to Re-Connect to Our Divine Source of Love?" The Truth Is that All Sincere Unselfish Actions of Love Make this World Better!

There are moments when I daydream. I close my eyes, trust and allow time to pass. I breathe and exhale. In Hope. Out Love. I follow the Light through the darkness. Each step I take into my heart fills me with Grace and gives me Hope.

I Vision Good Change on Earth. Good Change is not always comfortable or easy. Sometimes Change brings confusion and chaos. I Breathe. The World Is Changing. I Am Changing.

I hold on to Faith and ask for more Courage. I keep moving towards the Light. I Breathe. In Hope. Out Love. I thank Our Blessed Creator. I honor Our Ancestors, Angels and Saints.

As I step into Good Change, I imagine that I become the Light. All around me are other Lights. We are those Spirits Awakening with Respect and Integrity. Together We Are Breathing. In Hope. Out Love.

My Dream of Equanimity and Peace for the United States and Our World continues. I imagine that Collectively we honor our Elders and our Children.

Together, We Vision a World of Loving Peace where there is economic equity, good education and housing; as well as a blossoming sustenance and Good Possibility for All. We share Lovingly. We Forgive. We smile and decide to work together to help heal our broken hearts and our EarthHeart.

Somewhere buttercups, tulips and magnolia trees blossom. Robins and hummingbirds sing. The powerful voice of blue jays is heard even by dolphins and whales. The oceans roar and the wind calls on us to Love. And Love vibrates and spins new melodies.

Yes, even with all of our difficulties, hate, inequity, injustices and wars; if we are to survive and prosper, we must embrace Good Change. We must commit to work together to allow Hope, Love and New Possibility to fill the air. It is time to continue our individual and Collective Journeys with Courage, Integrity, Purpose and Respect for Each Other.

I invite YOU to take a moment to still yourself and bow in Gratitude for your Life of Good Purpose.

Though we have made progress, there is much we must do.

Right Now, let us offer prayers for those who are lost, suffering and in need of our Compassion.

May Integrity Awaken our Humanity and allow Love to Lead so that our Children thrive and grow in prosperity.

May Good Dreams flow everywhere throughout the World.

Breathe and Exhale Deeply 10 Times.

In Courage with Good Purpose Healing, Integrity and Love.

Out Disappointment, Fear and Hurt...

I pray that We All continue to learn to take greater steps on the path of Love.

With Joy, Humility and Gratitude...

With this thought, let us All open our hearts and Breathe Deeply....

GOOD IS POWERFUL BEYOND MEASURE!

ACKNOWLEDGEMENTS

Special Thanks to Cultural Icon, Ben Vereen for his constant prayers and encouragement, my brilliant, compassionate co-editors Andrea Christofferson and Shannon Wong, and master graphic designer, Jeremy John Parker who have all been patient with me as my vision shifted when My Precious Mother, Betty J Tilman left this Earth Realm and this Legacy Project grew leaps and bounds with many delays.

I am grateful to All of the GOOD IS POWERFUL BEYOND MEASURE co-authors who trusted me with their Sacred ReMemberings and every name in the book who has offered their support to me and Ms. Betty J. Tilman. This is your legacy too!

To my Aunt Virginia McGant, Uncle Alexander "Butchie" McGant and all members of my birth and extended family including the AlNifays, the Blakeys, Dr. June Pickett Dowdy, Helena Hughes, Carrie McCray, Dr. Jerome McKinney & Family, Dr. Sandra Murray, Charlotte Onyundo, Dr. Carol A. Scott, Shirley Scott, Aunt Betty Wysong and Brandon Jennings who created a beautiful portrait of MOMBetty, Mayor Ed Gainey, Melvin Hubbard El, Denise Barton, Donna Baxter Porcher, Jason E. Fernandez Bernard, Donna Chernoff, Sage Crystal, Gayle Hodnett Dobbs, Naima Renee Dobbs, Sylvia Golbin Goodman, Joseph H. James, Jr., Carol Maillard, Rev. Dr. Sedrick Gardner, Elizabeth Anne Hin, Rev. Donald & Sheila Marbury, H. E. Mrs. Mmasekgoa Masire-Mwamba, Iman H. Daniel Mujahid, Lewis Nash, Judge Oscar & Sheila Petite, Olivia & Yamin Majdi-Panella, Tyrone & Barbara Rasheed, Louise Robinson, Muhammed "MO" Rum & Family, Scent Elate Gift Shop, Cory & Libra Sene, Delores Southers, William Tiga Tita, Larry Vickers, author Denise Woods (who was the very first person to SAY YES!), Andrew Zaeh and Eshe Zampaladus, your compassion, deep listening & kindness makes my heart sing!

To Linda Murray, dance curator at NYPL Performing Arts Lincoln Center & team for hosting our book launch, It was just my imagination but WOW! You made it happen. Thank You!

To My Life Supporting Compassionate, Global Tribe...

Kojo Ade, James Aloway, Jrome Andre, ChiChi Anyanwu, Deborah Ballard, Brian Scott Bagley, Suleika Jaoud Baptiste, Jon Batiste, Cherokee Black, Bruce & Patricia Blakey, A Gandhari Bouligny, Stephan Broadus, Pamela Buckner, Priscilla Burgess, John Butler, Marie Brown, Nitanju Casel, Norma Caquato, Esq., Donna & John Chernoff, Andrea Christofferson, Jane Collins, Martha Richards Conley, Esq., Rev. Cheryl Cotton, Verna Critchlow, Sage Crystal, Luna Diagne, Gayle Hodnett Dobbs, Naima Renee Dobbs, Dr. June Pickett Dowdy, Ger Duany, Marsha Ekunfeo, Kim El, Lawrence Evans, Kewe Faye & Family, Dale Fielder, Owen Gambill, Rev. Dr. Sedrick Gardner,

James Gillard, Sylvia Golbin Goodman, Donald Muldrow Griffith, Marian Hartsfield (aka Grandmother Dawn SkyWeaver), Dyane Harvey-Salaam, Jason Hee, our website designer, Elizabeth Anne Hin, Leslie Howard, Anthony Howell, Bro Melvin Hubbard El, Leona Hull, Joan Jai, Joseph H. James, Jr., Brian Anthony Johnson, Dr. James & Pamela Johnson, Mark Randelle King, Adam Khan, Dr. Martha Llanos-Zuloaga, Charisse Lillie, Esq, Dr. Marsha Lillie Blanton, Carol Maillard, Rev. Donald L. & Sheila Marbury, Stanley Wayne Mathis, Evelyn Nelson, Rev. Rhonda Mclean Nur, Angela McKee, Dr. Buba Misawa, Valerie & Saihou Njie, Olivia & Yamin Majdi-Panella, Regina Chow McPhie, Dale & Jean Miller, Lewis Nash, Evelyn Nelson, Theresa Nugent, Armando Ocando & Family, Herman Pike, David & Donna Baxter Porcher, Carl & Tawnya Redwood, Muhammed "MO" Rum & Family/Scent Elate, Jan Schmidt, Carlton Scott, Arthur Seabury, LCSW, Margaret E. Self, Lamine Sylla, Louise Robinson, Delored Southers, Joy Southers, Mark & Neicy Southers, Dr. Thupten Tendar, Dr. Bill & Bernice Tita, Rev. Charles E. Timbers, Jr., Michael Vann, Dr. Glory Van Scott, Denise Woods, Dr. Robert Woods, those whose names I have forgotten to mention, (please forgive me) twelve anonymous tribe members... & All of Our Readers...

I Am Forever Grateful. Through your compassion, generosity and sharing, we are building bridges of cooperation for future generations and showing the World that GOOD IS POWERFUL BEYOND MEASURE! This Is Our Collective Legacy!

With Loving Appreciation...
Melony McGant

AUTHOR BIOS

— A —

KOJO ADE was born on August 8, 1949 at Harlem Hospital to parents Eunice and Horace Booker. He attended school at Frederick Douglas Middle School and Taft High School. Kojo was an excellent student and graduated from high school near the top of his class. From an early age Kojo had a passion for the arts which he expressed through choral singing, and acting. His parents, extended family, and the Harlem community instilled in him a sense of purpose, spirituality, and pride in African and African-American history and culture. As a young adult, Kojo attended City College of New York majoring in Africana studies and Swahili. His studies at City College along with studies in Ghana and Nigeria, fueled his development as a global citizen interested in world culture, history and politics with a specific focus on the African continent. He also attended photography and arts marketing courses at AJASS and Third World Cinema.

Kojo is a people person who enjoys building bridges and fellowship among many people. He is known in New York City and beyond as a griot, communicator and Ambassador for the Arts. He is a linguist, and is able to greet people in Swahili, Yoruba, Spanish, French, Russian and Japanese.

Kojo has served many individual artists, writers, and arts organizations with professional services in audience development, group sales, public relations, and marketing. In this role, Kojo is a highly recognizable figure at Broadway and off-Broadway venues, festivals, and conferences throughout New York and nationally. Some of these organizations include: New York African Film Festival, The Dance Theater of Harlem, Alvin Ailey American Dance Theater, Dance Africa Brooklyn Academy of Music, Urban Bush Women, Ronald K. Brown Evidence, New Federal Theatre, World Music Institute, The National Black Theatre, The Apollo Theater, Paul Robeson Foundation, The National Black Arts Festival, and the Medgar Evers College-Center for Black Literature. Kojo served as a licensed, bonded group sales agent for Broadway and off-Broadway productions such as *Jelly's Last Jam, Fences, Jitney, Ma Rainey's Black Bottom, Joe Turner's Come and Gone, Sarafina, Gospel at Colonus, Fela, Death & the King's Horsemen*, and other productions.

———

JAMES E. ALOWAY retired from Zurich Insurance as Vice President & Director of Mining. He is a seeker of truth and hopes that "we remember the dreams we had as children and that we love each other more each day!"

———

JROME ANDRE is a recording artist/actor/writer who is also an Audelco award-winning performer who captivated the audience with a raw soul-stirring performance in Satan Never Sleeps. This fierce creative spirit has performed in theaters and clubs around the world.

He has performed in musicals and plays such as Exonerated as Robert, Dreamgirls as James Thunder Early, The Colored Museum as Miss Roj, Ain't Misbehavin as Ken & Andre, The Gospel of Colonus, Ugly Is A Hard Pill as Evilness, Hair as Hud, Ronnie, Steve, and The Exonerated as Robert. He has shared the stage with Dee Dee Bridgewater, Stephanie Mills, Tremaine Hawkins, Johnny Brown, Mable Lee, David Peaston, Emme Kemp, and others. He toured with the "Godfather of Urban Theatre" Shelley Garrett, performing in the hit play I'm Doing the Right Thing with the Wrong Man as Cookie.

When Jrome is not performing, he is writing and recording. He has recently joined the fight against gun violence with the organization Stand2Oppose--an organization dedicated to educating our young to learn to deal with issues before they escalate to violence. Soon he will be releasing a new single with a video package dealing with this issue. Jrome also continues to perform locally and internationally with his own band. All recordings and videos can be found on Amazon, YouTube, Trax Source, iTunes, Spotify and Pandora. Please visit: www.Jromeandre.com

———

A'MARIE B is an international Breath Doula who operates as a healer, teacher and friend. The Author of "The Reformation Of A Nation: The United State Of Remembrance" and helps others in facilitating their own remembrance through Breathwork and introspection. A certified Reiki Master and Crystal Healing practitioner who facilitates "Poetically Speaking: Many Voices, One Breath," a global and virtual open mic that highlights the poetic expressions of others and "Breathing With A'Marie," an online forum the offers quarterly breathing sessions to cultivate deeper connection with our core essence for healing, wholeness and guidance. Contact info: nrpiece@gmail.com

———

CHICHI ANYANWU founded CHI Talent Management after 10 + years working in talent representation in New York. Her experiences in casting made her discover that her true passion was nurturing and developing aspiring talent. CHI Talent Management aims to advise, guide, and empower a diverse array of talent in the entertainment industry. The clients she has represented have been seen on Broadway in MJ: The Musical, Ain't Too Proud, Clyde's, Chicago, and in national tours of Wicked, Charlie and the Chocolate Factory, and Jesus Christ Superstar. For more information about company and clients visit: www.chitalentmanagement.com

In her spare time, ChiChi also serves as a diversity audience consultant for Broadway and Off-Broadway theatres. ChiChi Anyanwu is a graduate of the University of Pittsburgh with a B.A. in Communication, Theater Studies minor & Certificate in African Studies. She was also the 2020 grant recipient of the American Express 100 for 100 program and on the Diverse Representation "The Ten to Watch in 2021" list.

BRIAN SCOTT BAGLEY former student of the Central Pennsylvania Youth Ballet and the Alvin Ailey American Theatre became choreographer of "In search of Joséphine" (A LA RECHER-CHE DE JOSÉPHINE BAKER) by Jérôme Savary at L'Opera Comique in 2006 in Paris, France during the centenary year of Joséphine Baker; choreographer for Dita Von Teese and Arielle Dombasle; and the first MC of African descent at the Crazy Horse de Paris cabaret. He was artistic director of the Parc de Joséphine Baker and the former Carrousel de Paris cabaret, which is the historic location of Josephine Baker's Chez Joséphine Baker. With the support of the City of Paris, he placed a plaque to honor Joséphine Baker at her site, the first cabaret, Chez Joséphine Baker in the 9th Arr. He is founder of the Musée de Josephine Baker and the Afro-Descendants of Paris.

JASON E. FERNANDEZ BERNARD is a native New Yorker from The Bronx, New York. He began experiencing theater at the age of four and began his Tap training at the age of six at The Ruth Williams Dance School and The Dance Theatre Of Harlem.

At the age of 17 Jason made his Broadway debut in the Tony Award-Winning musical Bring In Da' Noise, Bring In Da' Funk. In 2000, Jason made his feature film debut in The Spike Lee Film Bamboozled as J. Bunny.

Jason has had the honor of dancing alongside Gregory Hines in The Showtime Original Movie Bojangles. He also toured the world for ten years with the international dance show Riverdance in addition to briefly joining its Broadway cast.

Jason was featured in two productions for Cois Ceim Dance Theatre, Dodgems, and Boxes, both in Ireland. Most recently, he was featured in the Broadway production After Midnight (Cotton Club Parade).

Utilizing his extensive knowledge of the theater, Jason directed and was the wardrobe supervisor for Kris Johnson's Jim Crow's Tears. He has had the honor to learn from the masters of the art of Tap dance and is truly privileged to teach art all over the world!

BRUCE BLAKEY is a devoted husband, father and grandfather. Before retiring, he worked in many technical capacities at People Gas Company. A native of Pittsburgh, PA, Bruce Blakey enjoys sports, music and encouraging family.

DR. STEPHANIE CLINTONIA BODDIE is an Assistant Professor of Church and Community Ministries at Baylor University. She is affiliated with the Diana R. Garland School of Social Work, Truett Seminary, and the School of Education. Additionally, she works with Baylor's Institute for Studies of Religion, the Digital Humanities program, and Collaborative on Hunger and Poverty. Dr. Boddie also participates in initiatives at University of Pennsylvania, Washington University in St. Louis, the University of Michigan, Villanova, and the University of South Africa. Co-author of six books, 30 peer-reviewed publications, and the Unfinished Business musical documentary, her work drives research on faith-based initiatives that address community needs, including race relations.

———

I was born **JOHN CALVIN BROWN III**, January 28, 1967. Under the birth sign of Aquarius, son of John and Gloria Brown, brother to Ernie Davis Brown, born March 14, 1971. Aquarians are itinerant wanderers, always searching for knowledge. Honestly, I can remember coming out of the womb, and being held by the doctor, then put in the hands and arms of my mother. This began my life's quest for wisdom and knowledge. Fast forward this experience; I was educated at the University of Pittsburgh with a bachelor's degree in general studies, with a focus of translation in French and Spanish. Then I furthered my education at Robert Morris University with a MBA degree. I focused on several business sectors with a concentration in foreign currency speculation. Mrs. Tilman taught me how to be diplomatic, and make my life's quest for wisdom and knowledge, i.e., the quest for love and harmony in the universe. I have not stop searching due to her counsel.

SHEREE STATUM CAMEL is the Mother of Sydney and GrandMother of Kymmee. They are her greatest accomplishments and rewards. Sheree is an Herbal Enthusiast. She combined her early interest in plants, with years of instruction and training in the sciences, into over 50 years of research and practical experience using herbs to heal the body/mind. She believes herbs are "GOD's Medicines" and uses them daily in her own healing journey. Sheree's latest project is GGs Herbal Ministry, created to explore plant-based supports to healing anxiety, trauma, and grief. Her other interests include genealogy, formulating bath and body products, advocating for equity in public schools, and criminal justice reform.

———

DONNA C. CHERNOFF is an avid genealogist. She is a devoted mother, wife, and civil rights advocate for social justice, equality, and advancement. She is a retired Federal civil rights official for the U.S. Department of HUD. She previously worked with community-based organizations to advance housing and community development in struggling urban neighborhoods. She developed a non-profit advocacy organization to combat housing discrimination and advance fair housing in Western Pennsylvania. The advocacy organization still exists today.

———

REGINA CHOW MCPHIE. Born and raised in Washington, D. C., her parents came from southern China. Regina attended Washington, D. C. Public Schools. On Sundays, the Chow family went to the Chinese Community Church, and then D.C.'s Chinatown for socializing/networking.

Regina graduated from University of Pittsburgh with a Degree in Urban Studies. She is married to Neil McPhie, a Trinidadian American Attorney, and they have two grown children, Abby and a son, Sydney.

In the 1970's, Regina was a member of Eastern Wind, based in Wash., D.C.'s Chinatown. Eastern Wind promoted awareness of the social and economic needs of Chinatown residents. It sponsored the Chinatown Health and Community Fairs, published the Eastern Wind newsletter and created the Chinatown Wall Mural, displayed at 7th and H Streets for several years in the 1970's. Regina's career spanned almost four decades from the mid 1970's to 2019, most of them being various positions with the Equal Employment Opportunity Commission (EEOC). She also worked for the Social Security Administration and the Federal Emergency Management Agency (FEMA).

———

ANDREA CHRISTOFFERSON has worked in a cave, in a government bureaucracy, in a museum, and recently retired from her sales and marketing work for the University of Wisconsin Press. She loves exploring nature and learning about history. She currently volunteers as a Court Appointed Special Advocate for children under the legal protection of the court system.

———

MARY CHRISTOPHER grew up in a farming community in southwestern Oklahoma, learning to ride horses at an early age and working on the family farm while growing up. As a result of growing up with farmers and ranchers and school teachers, her classes, meditations, and spiritual practices usually include an awareness of Nature.

From 1969 thru 1980, Mary lived in a spiritual community. She was in charge of several training centers and served as a regional director. Mary taught meditation and spiritual practices. She organized the community's food and clothing programs and served as interim director for the center for homeless women and children in San Francisco. In the early 1970s, she studied with Murshid Samuel Lewis, who was teaching at the community, as well as several Buddhist teachers.

Mary has studied with Christian mystics, Native American, Hindu, and Buddhist teachers. Her classes are now online and she has a weekly podcast on Podbean. Her teaching and meditations are focused on embodying, developing, and sharing our gifts. She fiercely believes that the point of most spiritual effort and practice is to make Earth a better place for everyone, including plants, water, the soil, and all living creatures. Yes, Rocks do "talk"! We just have to slow waaaaay down in order to "hear" them. This Life is definitely a Wonderful Adventure and Good Beyond Measure.

———

MARTHA RICHARDS CONLEY, ESQ. a native Pittsburgher, was the first African American female graduate of the University of Pittsburgh School of Law and the first admitted to practice law in Allegheny County. She was employed by The United States Steel Corporation for 27 years and retired as Senior General Attorney.

She is a long-time opponent of the death penalty and Co-Chairs Pennsylvanians for Alternatives to the Death Penalty–Pittsburgh. She is an Official Visitor of the Pennsylvania Prison Society and was honored to escort the late **Archbishop Emeritus Desmond Tutu** to visit then death Row inmate **Mumia Abu Jamal** at SCI Greene in 2007.

Martha was inspired to study film by her experience visiting death row inmates. She began taking classes in filmmaking at Pittsburgh Filmmakers and Scribe Video in Philadelphia. She was an associate producer on the locally produced *Lost in the Hype*, written and directed by Aisha White, and served as assistant director on *Tango Macbeth*, directed by Nadine Patterson.

———

As a 17-year-old HS senior, **REV. CHERYL FANION COTTON**, joined the Civil Rights Movement in 1968, in support of the Memphis Sanitation Strike. She marched with Dr. King and Rev. James Lawson in support of the Sanitation Workers. She was at Mason Temple on April 3, 1968, when Dr. King gave his, "Mountaintop Speech."

Cheryl was appointed to serve on the Quadrennial Emphasis committee for the new merger of the United Methodist Church from 1968-1972. Cheryl appeared on a Sunday morning panel discussion dedicated to the "Sermon on the Mount" panel discussion broadcasted at NBC Studios in New York City.

Cheryl was selected to be a member of the North America Delegation to the 26th General Assembly of the World Student Christian Federation in Addis Ababa, Ethiopia in 1972. Students from 89 different countries were in attendance. She met Emperor Hailie Selassie at his Emperor Palace. Cheryl is also the mother of two beautiful daughters Indira Cotton-Williams and Norie Cotton. She is the wife of the late, former attorney, Clencie Cotton.

———

SAGE CRYSTAL is an American Writer, Holistic Doctor, Herbalist, Nutritionist, Fitness Expert, Spirituality Coach, and Sovereignty Mentor. Sage has a passion for writing. In 2010, she landed her first gig with National Geographic Wild TV as a staff writer. Sage has written countless articles and books on various subjects, which includes: Holistic Health & Nutrition, Cancer & Disease, Fitness, Meditation, Relationships & Communication, Spirituality, Nature, Animals, Self-evolution & Transformation. She has recently launched Sage Academy, a personal development and higher learning online school. Sage is an avid hiker and loves to play tennis and trivia games.

AJAK M. DAU is studying law at the University of Cairo. Before moving to Cairo, Ajak was born and raised in South Sudan. Currently he is Secretary for Planning & Research at SPLM Youth League- Egypt Chapter. He is studying diligently to obtain his degree. and dreams of being a widely published writer.

———

My name is **LUNA DIAGNE**. I was born and raised in Dakar, Senegal, October 19th, 1957. In 1982, I traveled to New York City. After 28 years working in restaurants and in an African art gallery, I returned home. I have 4 children. Luna Jr born in San Diego. Omar was born in San Diego and Khadija and Mohammed (8 and 7 years old) were born in Senegal. I am still doing catering.

———

Based in Brooklyn, **NAIMA RENEE DOBBS** is a practicing textile artist who received her B.A. in Africana Studies and Spanish from NYU in spring 2021. She currently works as an Young Adult Educator at the Brooklyn Museum. She loves to hike, make art, sing, and garden.

———

Born in Akobo, South Sudan in 1978, **GER DUANY** is a self-described "village boy". Ger remembers his early childhood as a herd boy tending to his family's cattle in the ways of his forefathers. Recollections of roaming vast grassy plains in search of pasture and of playing in the waters of the White Nile are etched in his memory.

He had his first experience of war at the tender age of seven. It marked the end of his idyllic childhood. His family and community uprooted. At age 13, war separated him from his mother and, like others, he resorted to becoming a child soldier as a means of survival during South Sudan's struggle for independence. Ger became a refugee in Ethiopia and then Kenya and was resettled to the United States from Ifo camp at age 16 on May 23,1994.

Ger struggled to assimilate in his new environment. He had to learn to adapt while dealing with post-traumatic stress disorder from life in the war zone. Ger went on to earn a Bachelor of Science in Human Services. He worked hard and built a successful career as an actor, model, and now an author of his memoir, Walk Toward the Rising Sun.

On 20 June 2015, World Refugee Day, UNHCR appointed Ger as the Goodwill Ambassador for the East and Horn of Africa region. Like many more refugees and former refugees throughout the world, Ger is driven by the urge to give back to the cause of forced displacement. Ger has not only survived a Civil War, he took great courage and dedication to turn his tragedies into success.

As an actor, advocate, and activist, Ger is working persistently to change the lives of refugees, not only in his home country of South Sudan, but all over the world.

Coupling his professional skills, advanced education, and obsession for transformative impact in the lives of broken communities such as refugees and conflict environments, Ger is positioned to help drive change.

Among other services, Ger is focused below following opportunities in Africa, and the World.
- Speaking Engagements
- Activist
- Acting/Filming

———

The hallmark of the career of **DR. LUCENIA WILLIAMS DUNN**, PhD has been innovation to improve the lives of people. She is a visionary administrator who seeks solutions to complex problems and challenges. Her award-winning professional career has been in rural and urban settings tackling challenges in community and economic development, health, education, and business. In the year 2000, she returned home to historic Tuskegee, Alabama and was elected the first woman as Mayor with 63% of the vote. Currently, she is the founder and President/CEO of the

Tuskegee Macon County Community Foundation, Inc. which focuses on the reduction of economic and health disparities and preservation of Black History. She is the proud mother of one daughter.

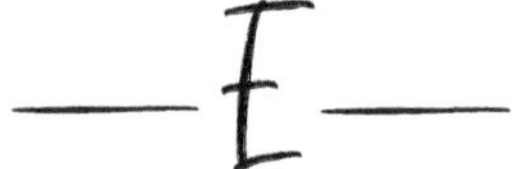

JARON EAMES was born in Baton Rouge, Louisiana, on December 21st in 1953. He is the youngest of six children. His late father, Louis L. Eames, started the first Black bank (along with six other men) in Baton Rouge in the 1950s and that bank eventually grew into the 7th largest Black Savings and Loan institution in the United States. JaRon attended Southern University in Baton Rouge for one year and then moved to NYC in 1972. He worked for Japan Air Lines for several years but quit to devote his time entirely to music. At one point he lived in Berlin, and then continued to perform in clubs in Germany thereafter. In 1998, he and Ms. Torrie McCartney hosted the first Billie Holiday Jazz Festival, held at the Billie Holiday Theater in Brooklyn, NY. JaRon has also performed several times in Japan, including Nagoya Japan's World Fair in 2005. Besides being a noted singer, archivist, and journalist, JaRon is equally renowned for the many interviews has conducted with countless jazz greats, such as Nancy Wilson and Joe Williams. He is also recognized for his many books and recordings–all of which are available on the Internet.

———

VINCENT ESOLDI has worked in many fields within the entertainment industry. He is a retired member of I.A.T.S.E. Local 764 Wardrobe and Local 798 Hairdressers. Within Broadway, he was a Costume & Properties Coordinator / Dresser/ Hairstylist. Some notable works he conceived, staged, and produced was the Annual "Night of a Thousand Gypsies Awards" Recipients. Vincent was also apart of coordinating events that occurred at the New Jersey Summer Festival, such West Side Story's 30th Anniversary Concert and the Centennial of the Statue of Liberty.

———

LAWRENCE EVANS is a New York based actor and casting consultant. He currently serves as Celebrity Coordinator for the National Black Theatre Festival. Regional theatre credits include: Triad Stage, Martha's Vineyard Playhouse, Florida Studio Theatre, Arkansas Repertory Theatre, freeFall Theatre, Caldwell Theatre Company, Charlotte Repertory Theatre, North Carolina Black Repertory Company, Short North Stage. New York theatre credits: *Black Stars of the Great White Way* (Carnegie Hall), *In a Clean House, Willie, Flat Street Sa'Day Nite, Monsieur Baptiste, the Con Man*. National tours: *And Still I Rise*, (written and directed by Maya Angelou), *The Sweet Spot* with Clifton Davis and Ja'Net DuBois, *Camp Logan*. Television: "New Amsterdam," "All My Children," "Another World," "Ryan's Hope," "As the World Turns," "One Life to Live," "The Good Wife," "Law & Order SVU." Film: "State Property II," "The Devil Wears Prada." He studied theatre at Jackson State University and the University of Michigan.

Casting credits: New Federal Theatre, National Black Touring Circuit, Billie Holiday Theatre, TheatreWorks Colorado Springs, Negro Ensemble Company, Black Spectrum Theatre Company, August Strindberg Repertory Theatre, Juneteenth Legacy Theatre.

Lawrence Evans is also affiliated with AUDELCO Nominating Committee, Actors' Equity Association, American Federation of Television and Radio Artists (AFTRA), Canaan Baptist Church of Christ, Harlem, NY, Metro New York Chapter/Jackson State University National Alumni Association, National Black Theatre Festival, Phi Beta Sigma Fraternity, Inc, and Screen Actors Guild (SAG).

DALE FIELDER is an American jazz saxophonist, composer and bandleader. He is a multi-instrumentalist who plays all four saxophones: soprano, alto, tenor and baritone. He is known for his original compositions and choice of performing rare, obscure jazz classics as well as his varied group concepts and variety of presentations. Fielder has recorded over 20 CDs as a leader. He grew up in Midland, Pennsylvania, a suburb of Pittsburgh where he studied oboe, bassoon and tuba in the school system. Fielder is also a product of the University of Pittsburgh Jazz Studies Program, where he studied as an ethnomusicology major under Dr. Nathan Davis. After relocating to NYC, he also performed with a host of current jazz stars such as pianist/composer Geri Allen and trombonist Robin Eubanks, among many others.

After eight years in NYC, Fielder moved to Los Angeles and studied with alto legend Charles McPherson as well as his Quartet, featuring legendary pianist Jane Getz. In 1996, Fielder recorded a national top-ten CD, "DEAR SIR: TRIBUTE TO WAYNE SHORTER". Fielder's recent recording projects include: "RESILIENCE!", DFQ~Dale Fielder Quartet 20th Anniversary 2-Disc CD released in 2016. In 2018, Fielder released a 35-year-old project featuring his late friend and jazz legend, Ms. Geri Allen; "SCENE FROM A DREAM–THE DALE FIELDER/GERI ALLEN SESSIONS, NYC 1986." And in 2019, Fielder recorded his 21st CD: "CONSENSUS" with his Quartet, now in its 27th year as of 2022, and that CD was considered for a Grammy nomination. As with all of his albums, they are currently available at Clarion Jazz.com, Apple Music, and Amazon.

———

SUNYA W, FOLAYAN is a Financial Wellness Professional in coaching practice. A certified Social Worker for 15 years, she had previously been a social work clinician for 40+ years. Currently, she enjoys her life in Mexico, where she works in her studio as an award-winning indigo textile artist and is building a global coaching practice. As the "Cashflow Coach", Sunya loves helping women 55+ who are feeling "sick and tired of working twice as hard and coming up with half as much" to create lives of freedom with more money, time for themselves, and renewed energy to go after their dreams.

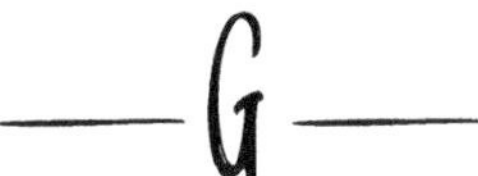

OWEN GAMBILL is a 2023 graduate of the University of Pittsburgh. Currently working as an editor and filmmaker in Pittsburgh, he aspires to move out to Los Angeles to pursue his dream of editing motion pictures. Owen is enthusiastic to work on all aspects of production and storytelling with a focus on documentary work. He is very appreciative of all the loved ones and family that he has in his life, and he would be nowhere without them. He hopes to continue working on films that tell important histories and stories that everyone can learn from.

———

REV. DR. SEDRICK GARDNER is a native Atlantan who has worked in public health, corporate marketing, and ministry. He is currently Associate Minister at Hillside International Truth Center and Dean of The Barbara King School of Ministry (BKSM). He has degrees from Duke University (Economics and Psychology), BKSM (Teaching and Ministerial Studies), Emory University School of Medicine (MPH), and The College of Metaphysical Studies (M.Div and D. Div). He is an initiated Shaman, President of Innovative Access Marketing, and travels the World on spiritual peace missions.

———

JAMES GILLARD is a native New Yorker—born and raised in the village of Harlem. James is concerned about the human condition and has a deep passion for documenting the social issues that face people of color in the African Diaspora. Metaphoric, poetic, and uncompromising is the way to best describe some of James' work.

James is an accomplished filmmaker, playwright, and author. His short films have been screened in film festivals across the United States. His film *Pendemonium* was part of the 2009 BET Film Festival. His short story "Jazz is Hip Hop" was featured in NYU's Renaissance noire magazine in 2005. That same short story was selected in 2007 as the best short film concept for the National Black consortium film festival.

In 2010, his short film Jazz is Hip Hop was awarded 2010 Harlem Arts Alliance Grant winner for best short film. James has since gone on to author 2 books–*If Harlem Could Talk it would Scream*, a collection of fictional short stories about the Harlem experience and *Can Anybody hear Me?*

———

SYLVIA GOLBIN was born to Jewish parents who escaped the Nazi Holocaust. She has served as a teacher, corporate communicator, and life coach. Together with her husband, David Goodman, she led the Andrew Goodman Foundation during its formative years, growing it into a successful non-profit that honors the legacy of Civil Rights Activist Andrew Goodman. Andrew Goodman, along with two other civil rights workers, James Chaney, and Michael Schwerner, was murdered by the Ku Klux Klan while registering African Americans to vote during the 1964 Mississippi Freedom Summer project. The Andrew Goodman Foundation today partners with universities and colleges to develop and nurture civic participation in American youth. Sylvia is a long-time member of the Executive Council of the Business Council for Peace. She is a wife, a mother, and a grandmother.

———

Music is the fulfillment of **RICHIE GOODS**' destiny – it's in his DNA. The youngest person ever inducted into the Pittsburgh Jazz Hall of Fame, bassist Richie Goods got an early start playing in church and clubs while still attending Pittsburgh Creative and Performing Arts High School. After graduating from the prestigious jazz program at Berklee College of Music, Richie moved to New York City, where he studied under jazz legends Ron Carter and Ray Brown. Richie credits jazz luminary Mulgrew Miller for helping him hone his jazz skills early in his career. Richie toured and recorded with Mulgrew for nine years. That opportunity brought Richie to the attention of many in the jazz community and afforded him the opportunity to record and tour with a variety of jazz and popular artists ranging from the Headhunters, Lenny White, Louis Hayes and the Cannonball Adderley Legacy Band, Milt Jackson, Russell Malone, Vincent Herring, the Manhattan Transfer and Walter Beasley to Brian McKnight, DJ Jazzy Jeff & the Fresh Prince, Whitney Houston and Christina Aguilera.

Richie's lengthy discography also includes Grammy award-winning and platinum albums of Alicia Keys and Common. Richie most recently toured with Grammy winning trumpeter, Chris Botti and Sting. When not on tour, he can be found in his Westchester, NY studio, producing records for his company, RichMan Music, Inc. His first three solo projects with his fusion/funk band, "Richie Goods and Nuclear Fusion, Live at the Zinc Bar," "Three Rivers" and "My Left Hand Man" all received critical acclaim. Richie is busier and more excited than ever, touring and promoting his new collaboration recording with Vibraphonist Chien Chien Lu "Connected."

———

DONALD MULDROW GRIFFITH, son of John and Edith Griffith. Born in Chicago, Illinois. Degree in Psychology from Loyola University. After therapeutic positions in mental institutions, hospitals, children's homes and with juvenile offenders, finally studied singing, acting, dancing, leading to performances in Chicago, New York City and by invitation, in Berlin, Germany. The journey continues into an interesting present and future, with the founding organizations Fountainhead Tanz Théâtre / Black International Cinema Berlin, The Collegium - Forum & Television Program Berlin, "Footprints in the Sand?" Exhibition Berlin and Cultural Zephyr e.V.

He played the starring roles in the Broadway Musicals "Pippin," "Stop The World, I Want To Get Off," "Lyrics Of Sunshine And Shadows," where he, under the direction of Oscar Brown Jr., portrayed the poet, Paul Lawrence Dunbar, and was also nominated "Most Promising New Off Broadway Actor," by the New York Drama Critics for his featured roles in "Contributions," a three act drama in which Donald Muldrow Griffith appeared in two of the three acts.

MARIETA HARPER is a specialist in African and African American history, now retired from the United States Library of Congress. By marriage she is the adopted mother of three wonderful sons from Malawi: Manford Chinkhota, Dalitso Chinkhota, and John Chinkhota, and a loving grandmother to eight grandchildren. Marieta Harper is an active member of Holy Comforter Episcopal Church in Washington, DC.

———

DYANE HARVEY-SALAAM is an award-winning performing artist, choreographer, founding member and assistant to the director of Forces of Nature Dance Theatre, dance educator at both Princeton and Hofstra Universities, and founder of Ma'at Pilates, (daughter, sister, wife, mother and grandmother. Aspects of her life have been recorded and preserved in the Lincoln Center Library Jerome Robbins Dance Division Oral History Project. A celebrated concert artist for 50+ years, she has also appeared on film, on and off Broadway, nationally and internationally. Her achievements represent the blessings of The Ancestors. Forever honored and humbled by their grace.

FEMI SARAH HEGGIE was resident stage manager at The Negro Ensemble Company for several years. She cherishes the lessons taught her by Douglas Turner Warner, Robert Hooks, and Carolyn Jones and is grateful to have worked with such a great company of actors. Femi has stage managed at such theatres as the Arena Stage, Folksbiene Yiddish Theatre, the Long Wharf Theatre, the Manhattan Theatre Club, The New Federal Theatre, the Public Theatre, The Lincoln Center Institute. Broadway credits include: *Once On This Island, Jelly's Last Jam, The Song of Jacob Zulu*, and *Rollin* on the T.O.B.A. First National Tours include: *Bubbling Brown Sugar, Chess, Home, Once on This Island*, and *Bring in Da Noise / Bring in Da Funk*. International Tours include: Houston Grand Opera's Production of Porgy and Bess, Home, Bubbling Brown Sugar and The Wiz. 'Femi received the first AUDELCO Award ever given to a stage manager. She is on the cover of the 8th edition of the book Stage Management by Lawrence Stern and is also featured in Mr. Stern's 9th & 11 Editions of Stage Management. She is a member of the Stage Manager's Association.

Femi was Production Manager for Aaron Davis Hall in New York City. She was Associate Technical Director for The Tribeca Performing Arts Center. As an Adjunct Professor she taught stage management at Pace University. In the entertainment industry, she was personal assistant to Ms. Aretha Franklin, Ms. Lena Horne , Ms. Nina Simone and to mezzo- soprano Ms. Hilda Harris. She is on the boards of Opera Ebony and The Duke Ellington Center for The Arts. Film credits include The Preacher's Wife, Malcolm X, and Crooklyn. Ms. Heggie is an alumna of Sarah Lawrence College.

DR. DONALD HENDERSON (February 1931 – June 2022) was most known for his work as the University of Pittsburgh's first Black provost. He made great contributions, pushing for changes that helped the University advance forward. Notable achievements Dr. Donald Henderson made was working with the Campus of the Future Initiative with AT&T and installing the first fiber network for the campus, combining several libraries to make the University Library System for easier access to resources, coordinating a visit from Nelson Mandela to Pitt, and served as the champion of the Pittsburgh Supercomputing Center. He was a mentor that was present when anyone needed him, which resulted in strong, lasting relationships with those he met. Dr. Donald Henderson passed away on June 8th, 2022 due to health conditions. Aside from his professional life, he had three children, Shelley, Mark, and Gerald, with his wife, Bebe, who also is deceased. Dr. Donald Henderson and his work will always be remembered.

GERALD HENDERSON, a former Lead Security & Police Officer with the University of Pittsburgh, served in security and police for 28 years. He is a graduate of the Allegheny Police Academy and attended Miami University, Oxford Ohio.

Born and raised in Harlem, New York, **VICTORIA HORNE** was exposed to music and the vocal styles of Billy Holiday, Sarah Vaughan, and Dinah Washington as a child, due to her Mother, Edith Dorothy Horne, a vocalist whose influence and passion for music had a direct impact on her daughter. Although a native New Yorker, Victoria's career and performances developed throughout Europe and Japan. Learning to sing in French, Italian, German, and Japanese was a necessary and difficult task, and planning to return to the USA was always the main goal. The work overseas kept her busy and, eventually, Victoria made her home in France.

Working as a primary and respected entertainer on European luxury cruise liners, allowed Victoria to explore many facets of her music, and travel extensively at the same time. A consummate collector of antiques, paintings, music, and all things beautiful, Victoria has a unique view of the world as a very small place where all people are connected through their cultures.

For more information, visit Victoria Horne's Website: www.victoriahorne.com

———

MELVIN HUBBARD EL serves as the Senior Community Adviser to the Honorable Ed Gainey, Mayor of the City of Pittsburgh. He last served as Chief of Staff to then-Representative Ed Gainey for the 24th District of the Pennsylvania State General Assembly for eight years. Mr. El earned his B.S. degree in Secondary Education in Social Studies from Clarion University. He serves on various non-profit boards, and has received numerous forms of recognition for his service. Melvin currently lives in Pittsburgh with his wife Kathy and attends the Moorish Science Temple of America.

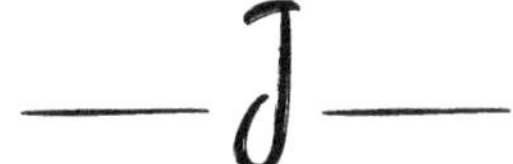

JOSEPH H JAMES, JR. - aka Joe James - is an Actor, Writer, Director, Producer and Author is a recipient of the Marquis Who's Who in America 2021-22. Currently the Head of Development at Shady Tree Films in New York and Executive Producer at DINK Entertainment. He's a veteran actor of television, film and stage. His work has taken him to Australia, Germany, London, Italy, Costa Rica, New Zealand, Canada and 48 states in the USA. Joe began his acting career as a child appearing on the Jimmy and Tammy Show and Sandy the Clown Show which lead to the starring role in CBN God's Trombones and a 2 year contract on the international televised soap opera Another Life. He continued to do featured roles on all of the New York soap operas until they went off the air. He had a recurring role on Sesame Street for 5 years as Gordon's father. He's worked extensively as an ADR looping actor in over 40 movies and television episodics. He's been the national Spokesperson for Manpower Temporary Services, Mercedes Benz and DIRECT-TV. Joe wrote, directed, produced and starred as the great Arthur Ashe in the award winning labor of love docudrama Arthur! A Celebration of Life. He also directed and styled over a dozen music videos. He's the author of the romance novel *Soul Baby* currently available on Amazon, Barnes & Noble and Lulu. He executive produced and costume designed the horror thriller feature film Soul To Keep available on Amazon Prime, Tubi and various streaming platforms. Joe's poetry "The Sky" is in the National Library of Poetry in Washington DC.

———

BRANDON JENNINGS is a devoted husband, father, brother and friend. Not only is he a much sought after fine artist whose work is collected by business owners and celebrities, he is also an award-winning graphic designer. Brandon is Creative Director and Founder of YOUR BRAND DESIGNS in Pittsburgh, PA. He has more than 30 years of experience in graphic design, marketing and illustration. He attended Point Park College. Brandon's career has shown him to be a highly effective leader who is successful in building brands and achieving high levels of client satisfaction. He also specializes in advertising, marketing, and public relations. He focuses on increasing one's brand awareness and visibility. In addition to developing and implementing client-based marketing campaigns.

BONNIE JOHNSON is an innovative design thinker, radio personality, and data engineer. She is producer and host of Colors of Jazz, a weekly program streaming live at the NPR affiliate station 90.5 WICN. Inspired by arts and culture, youth, and literacy, Bonnie is committed to engaging with people of all ages. Stealth in her track record of advancing the cultural exchange, she delivers STE(A)M leadership and seeks to find pathways for collaboration through the lens of music and social justice. Bonnie attended Howard University and holds a Masters in Communications and Information Management from Bay Path University.

JOYCE MORROW JONES, also known as Orisanmi Kehinde Odesanya, is a writer, storyteller, and multimedia fiber artist. Her works are influenced by the "art of story" to express spiritual transitions of life. Her themes are often culturally based in African and Diasporic traditions. Her work is widely exhibited and in permanent collections throughout the United States.

QUEEN ALENA D. JONES SMITH, aka Lana "LJ" Joseph, is the Co-founder of Look-Back R&Q InC and R'Empyre. These companies were founded by Queen and her husband, "Artist" Rodney Smith, to bring artists together for collaborative projects. Queen is a retired ELA and Theatre Arts teacher. She developed a deep passion for writing plays, short stories, and poetry while teaching middle school. Queen is the author of "God's Radiance," a collection of her poems and prose. Other literary writings of hers are included in multiple anthologies and magazines. Queen lives in San Joaquin County with her beloved husband.

My Name is **MARTHA K. JORDAN**, aka (Katie), born May 27, 1965, in Washington D.C, the niece of Betty Tilman. I come from a family of 8 children, Andre H. McGant, Chrystal William (deceased), William O. McGant (deceased), Carlyle McGant, Victor McGant, Patrick McGant, Zachariah McGant and my mother is Virginia G. McGant Jones. I hold a Bachelor's of Science in Information System from Penn State University and an MBA in Strategic Management from Amberton University. I am the wife of Dr. Charles Jordan and mother of 7 wonderful children (Tiffany

Hatcher, Obinna Asinugo, Ijeoma Asinugo, Iman Halim, Diannah Halim, Chadi Halim, and Yusuf Halim) which 4 of them have completed their undergraduate studies. I have had the opportunity to travel to Africa, Europe, and the Middle East. I had the fortunate opportunity to grow up in Washington D.C, Phoenix, AZ, and Lompoc, CA, and Washington, PA. I spent many of my adult years working as a Project Manager by profession in the Telecommunication industry and raising my kids in the Suburbs of Chicago, IL. I moved back to the East coast in 2015 to be closer to family. I now live in Wake Forest, NC with my husband and four kids.

———

ROSARIO JORGE DO AMARAL was born in Santiago de los Caballeros, Dominican Republic on November 13th, 1957. She studied Law at the Universidad Católica Madre y Maestra and did a Master in Commercial Law at Laval University in Quebec, Canada. She was a Dominican Diplomat since 1983 until 1988. She was Cultural Attaché at the Embassy of the Dominican Republic in Washington, DC and Delegate of the Dominican Republic Mission to the Organisation of American States. In 1986, she married a Brazilian Diplomat in Washington and when he was transferred to Brazil, she had to leave her Diplomat Carrear. She worked at the Inter-American Development Bank in Brasilia as a Public Relation Assistant. She moved to Geneva, Switzerland in 1990 and worked at the Political Refugee Center as a Social Collaborator. She was Advisor to the Chief of Ceremony of the President in Brasilia, Advisor to the Secretary of Strategic Affairs in Brasilia, International Advisor of the Ministry of Tourism and Sports in Brasilia, International Advisor of Sao Paulo Tourism in São Paulo Parlamentar Advisor at the Brazilian Congress in Brasilia, and Ambasarress of Brazil in the United Kingdom and France.

Originally from Southern California, and now residing in New York City, **ADAM KHAN** is a lighthearted and optimistic individual who is known for his remarkable ability to see the best in people and situations. Adam truly values the unique qualities each individual possesses, and enjoys drawing out their strengths to foster a sense of unity. He believes in the importance of doing good and finding joy in every aspect of life, and seeks to embody that through all of his actions and interactions.

———

MARK RANDELLE KING is an accessories, awards and jewelry designer who has been commissioned to do awards for Harry Belafonte, Dr. Selma Burke, Spike Lee, President Nelson Mandela, Gordon Parks, Grover Washington and George Wein, among many others.

For musical icon George Benson, Mark Randelle King has designed memorable guitars straps, and on various occasions, acted as his costume stylist. Mark has created one of a kind jewlery and other accessories for many celebrities including Cher, Phyllis Hyman, Marilyn McCoo, Joan Rivers, Naomi Sims and Mary Wilson.Mark Randelle King is a distinctive designer, and has acted also as a historical photojournalist.

Early in his career, he studied fashion design at F.I.T in NYC. One of his instructors was Donald Clafin, a well-known designer for Tiffany & Co., for fine jewelry design renderings and technique. He worked at Wideband Jewelry as a professional jewelry polisher, M+J Savitt as a jewelry bench worker.

Mark Randelle King continues to create unique designs and currently is focused on creating healing crystal bracelets.

DR. MARTHA LLANOS ZULOAGA is a Peruvian traveler with a passion to learn and share from diverse cultures. Her enthusiasm is reflected in her pioneering work devoted to human development with a focus on the rights of women and children.

A researcher in the field of resilience, she strongly believes in the power of the arts and play. She has been collaborating across the globe toward the development of policies for children's and women's health, education, and well-being. Trained as a psychologist at the Catholic University in Peru with postgraduate studies in Great Britain, the Netherlands, and USA, her specialization is in developmental and social psychology.

Martha loves music, dance, and theater and is a practitioner of theater of the oppressed, as well as a storyteller, and writer.

LYNNE LEE-BROWN's formal career of more than forty years was dedicated to the Human Resources profession. She utilized her people and analytical skills to counsel, nurture, and strategically guide employees and leadership toward creating positive organizational cultures in for-profit and non-profit industries including health care, banking, insurance, manufacturing, and utilities.

Lynne, a native Pittsburgher, and her husband, Albert, a Bronx New Yorker, chose to relocate to the Hilton Head, South Carolina area in the late 1980s. There, they enjoyed a quieter lifestyle where they excelled as business leaders while contributing to parenting four youngsters.

CAROLYN MAILLARD was born and raised in Philadelphia, Pennsylvania. In high school she began playing violin, and through her hard work and effort landed a scholarship and violin performance at Catholic University of America. She eventually changed her major to theater and joined the drama department. While studying at Catholic, she landed an audition for the newly formed DC Black Repertory Theater and began her training as a professional actress. It was there that the very beginnings of the internationally known and Grammy nominated vocal ensemble, Sweet Honey In The Rock began.

Carol eventually moved to New York to pursue her career as an actress and worked on and off Broadway, national and regional tours, commercials, TV, and film. She also used her vocal chops in cabaret performances and as a background singer.

Carol Maillard returned to SWEET HONEY IN THE ROCK® in 1992 and has been a member of the group since that time. She presently serves as a creative consultant for the group. She has produced several recordings and productions for the ensemble. She presently resides in New York City, and is the mother of amazing violinist and producer, Jordan Maillard Ware.

OLIVIA PANELLA MAJDI is originally from New York City but was born in the natural landscape of New Hampshire and now lives in France. She is the founder of UMA GAIA, a haven for inner and outer alignment. Olivia is a Reiki master, Quartz sound therapist, meditation leader, writer, painter and has a background in an array of other ancient healing modalities. Her garden and gift to this lifetime is to offer all walks of life, compassion, humility, gratitude, and unconditional love.

———

YAMIN MAJDI is a singer/songwriter/multi-instrumentalist, born and raised in France. He has always been a performer, since his parents placed him in the Music Conservatory at the age of three. In 2013, Yamin moved to London and produced his first album "Into the Blue" which is folk inspired. In 2018 he released his second album "Love Ascension" which is more rock/pop. Since then, he has had a slew of life-changing experiences which has inspired his third album to learn more pop rock and a fourth album of piano preludes which honors his roots as a pianist.

———

REVEREND DON MARBURY is an ordained African Methodist Episcopal Church elder and currently serves as the senior pastor of Ebenezer AME Church in Hagerstown, MD. He had been for 11 years the senior pastor of Ebenezer AME Church in Brunswick, Maryland, and from 2000 to 2005 he was the senior pastor of St. John AME Church in Benedict, Maryland. Marbury retired as an adjunct professor of reading, writing, and English at Montgomery College, Germantown in 2018 after 18 years, and he was also an adjunct professor, from 2001 until 2010, in the Radio, Television, Film and Video Department of the Howard University School of Communications, where he taught numerous, different courses in broadcasting. Marbury left a 27-year career in public broadcasting in 1997 to pursue his ministerial studies. He retired from the Corporation for Public Broadcasting (CPB), the parent company of the Public Broadcasting Service (PBS) as its Vice President of Domestic and International Programs. In that capacity, Marbury was responsible for the distribution and awarding of nearly $65 million a year in production funds to independent and station producers to create programs for the national PBS schedule. 2 His programming decisions brought scores of Emmys and Oscars to public television and gave starts to many then- fledgling producers who are now icons of the industry. In 1995, in a profile of his career, *Broadcasting Magazine* called him "one of the most powerful African- American men in television in America". A two-page profile of his decision to leave public broadcasting to enter the ministry, published in the "Style" section of the *Washington Post* in 1997, credited him with "setting the program direction of US Public Television over the last decade". A 1971 honors graduate of the University of Pittsburgh with a BA degree in English, Marbury also is a cum laude graduate of Wesley Theological Seminary, having earned a master's degree in Divinity. He is a well known performance art poet whose work has been published and featured in many television and radio broadcasts, and who has performed his work throughout the nation and internationally. His poetic autobiography, *My People, My People, My God* was published by Kharis Publishing House in October of 2018 and was the 2019 third-place competition winner of the Fischer Prize for Poetry.

———

ELLYN LONG MARSHALL was born and raised in Harlem, NY, to parents, Gretchen Cotton Long and Legendary Performer, Avon Long. Raised during the Harlem Renaissance (with older sisters, Janice and Gretchen), Ellyn made her Acting debut as a Cherub, at the age of 5, in the Broadway Production of "The Green Pastures" with her father, Avon; at 9, acted with Evelyn Ellis, Frederick O'Neal & Rosetta LeNoire in "Salvation On A String," at Off B'way's Theater De Lys; and performed on CBS Television's "Lamp Unto My Feet". Dance Training as a young child, included Tap with Henry LeTang and Ballet with Boston's Elma Lewis. As a teen, dance studies continued at the Martha Graham School, Luigi's Jazz Center & Arthur Mitchell's Dance Theater of Harlem.

Ellyn graduated with highest honors from Immaculata H.S. on NYC's lower East Side (where she met actor, Larry Marshall, with whom she was married for 25 years; and with whom she has two children, Stephanie Marshall Middleton and Avon Marshall; and grandson, Kofi Makai Middleton). Ellyn received a BA cum laude in Theater at Marywood University; followed by Graduate studies in Theater at Catholic University, and at CCNY.

Ellyn has taught Dance & Drama in Arts Programs within the NYC school system and Community-based groups. Professionally, she has acted and directed in several off-Broadway productions, and was Assistant to the Director of "Mourning Pictures" on Broadway. For seven years, Ellyn performed with and served as Artistic Director for "Nucleus", an inspirational Theater touring company, headed by Yolanda King & Attallah Shabazz (daughters of Dr. Martin Luther King Jr. & Malcolm X respectively).

Ellyn is currently in the process of compiling her colorful life experiences in her first book offering.

———

AMBASSADOR MMASEKGOA MASIRE-MWAMBA is currently Botswana's Ambassador based in Europe. She has served her country in different leadership positions over the past thirty years. In her previous roles in Botswana, she was responsible for promoting economic development, investment, and private sector participation. She served at an international level as the Deputy Secretary General for the Commonwealth Secretariat in London. There she held responsibility for the Political, Legal and Constitutional Divisions amongst the 54 member States. She holds a BSC in Electronics and Physics and an MBA in International Business and an LLB through the University of South Africa. She is well traveled, always seeking to engage young people at home and on her travels through mentoring and dialogue as part of building communities, maintaining a mindset to learn and grow from different sources always!

———

STANLEY W. MATHIS, born December 1st, 1996, is an American actor, singer, and dancer. In 1997, he was a part of the original Broadway cast of *The Lion King* and played as Banzai. In the 1999 revival of Clark Gesener's *You're a Good Man, Charlie Brown*, he played as Schroeder. In a 2009 Yale Repertory production of *Death of a Salesman* by Arthur Miller, he played as Stanely. Stanley also starred in a Broadway musical comedy *Nice Work if You Can Get It*, with co-stars Matthew Broderick and Kelli O'Hara and *The Book of Mormon* as Mafala Hatimbi, succeeding Michael Potts.

———

Now over 90 years of age, Mrs. **CARRIE MCCRAY**, her beloved husband, Leon and children were all members of the Community of Reconciliation (COR). Mrs. McCray was known as an entrepreneur and community activist. In this book, she has told her son Steven McCray her memories of Ms. Betty J. Tilman and highlights their more than 50 year friendship.

She and Ms. Betty J. Tilman acted as chaperones to members of the church's gospel choir when they traveled to Kenya and Tanzania on a trip that Ms. Tilman arranged. They were both friends with Mr. Fred Rogers from WQED television and were both involved in the creation of the University of Pittsburgh's African Heritage Classroom Committee. They have long been spiritual sisters and Mrs. Carrie McCray is one of Rev. Melony McGant's spiritual mothers.

———

ALLANTE MCGANT is the proud son of Lisa McGant and the grandson of Alexander "Butchie "McGant. Allante is also an electrician and a member of the US military. Like his grandfather and his Aunt Betty, he believes strongly in treating people with kindness!

———

REV. RHONDA AKANKE'. MCLEAN-NUR is an interfaith/ Interspiritual Minister who specializes in sacred ceremonies, weddings, baby blessings, folklore of the African Diaspora, funerals and healing circles! She is also a professional actress and griot who has performed around the globe! A Howard University graduate, she began acting at the age of 14 with Workshops for Careers in the Arts and the DC Black Repertory Theatre Company in Wash. DC has worked as an Arts Administrator with the NYC Dept of Cultural Affairs, HAi and YAI for over forty years! Receiving numerous awards for her work with homeless families, She is the founder and CEO of Mama Akanke Arts and Consulting LLC,President of the DC Black Alumni Association and serves on the board of Woody King Jr's New Federal Theatre!

———

NASSER SUNDIATA METCALFE is an American Actor, Writer and Producer born August 25, 1970, in Chicago, Illinois. Raised on Chicago's South Side, Nasser started acting at the tender age of 14, studying at the famed Goodman Theater. By age 18, he launched a career in stand-up comedy while simultaneously attending Morehouse College in Atlanta, Georgia. During his early days in stand up, Nasser was blessed to befriend and be directly mentored by the late great comic, Bernie Mac. Upon graduating from Morehouse, earning his BA in Theater with a concentration in performance, Nasser continued to perform stand up as well as in various theatrical productions and improv troupes around the country.

By the late 1990s he moved to New York City to focus on his acting. While electing to put stand up on the back burner at this stage of his career to concentrate on other creative interests, Nasser's comedy background continued to serve him well as he has frequently worked as host and on-camera personality for various film-related platforms. By the early to mid-2000s he was regularly contributing in these capacities as well as being a writer for blackfilm.com which led him to host and moderate a monthly series of independent film screenings from coast to coast at prestigious venues such as NYC's Lincoln Center and The Director's Guild of America in Los Angeles. Upon moving to New York, Nasser also sought out many of the luminary theatrical figures whose work he studied in college and made certain to enroll in their classes to learn directly from them. These instructors include Douglass Turner Ward and Lloyd Richards. Nasser has appeared on television opposite Dennis Leary and Bill Nunn in the ABC episodic, *The Job*. On the big screen Nasser appeared in the films *My Brother*, starring Vanessa Williams and Tatum O'Neal, and *Tennessee* starring Mariah Carey. His stage credits include *Macbeth*, *A Soldier's Play*, *Savage In Limbo*, and *The Mandela Architecture*, to name a few.

Nasser Metcalfe continues to reside in New York City where he works as an actor, writer, and producer. Some of his recent projects include the web TV series *Becoming Ricardo*, *Disciplinary Actions*, and *Money And Violence*. In 2012, Nasser was listed on IMDB's prestigious list of 40 "Up And Coming Actors To Look Out For!" He was also nominated for Best Actor at the prestigious International Television Festival in Los Angeles for his work in *Disciplinary Actions*.

———

DALE A. MILLER, SR. I was born April 1937, in Bridgeton, Pennsylvania, on my grandfather's farm to a young single mother. My father was unknown and we only speculated on his background. As a very young boy, I had to assume control of family functions in support of mother, younger brother, and sister. When I was twelve, my mother was hospitalized with mental illness. Me and my siblings were sent to live with relatives for a short while and subsequently settled with my grandfather on his farm.

After graduating from high school, I left the farm and began a quest for a professional baseball career. This led me to enter the famous black "Negro American Baseball League." Over the course of two years, I played portions of the time with Kansas City Monarchs, Detroit Stars, New York Black Yankees, and ended with the Indianapolis Clowns. I was drafted into the Army the same year with a promise of continuing baseball there, which did not happen.

After my discharge from the Army, I returned to New York City and entered a civil service job in the Postal Service where I served 33 years and ended my tenure as the manager of a very large station. While there I married my wife and our union produced five children, seven grandchildren and great grandchildren. I also began my pursuit for an education and received a bachelor's degree in business and was short of my master's degree in Humanities and Religion because of a dispute and disagreement with my thesis submission. I retired and began a new job with the New York State Insurance Fund as a senior safety officer with OSHA related responsibilities. I retired after 17 years of service at the age of 77 years old. After medical setbacks, I began a new healthy lifestyle and continue it today.

———

JEAN MILLER. I was born in Lowell, Massachusetts, in June of 1943. Growing up, I attended the local schools and graduated from Lowell high school in 1961. I remained at home for two years and worked locally at Honeywell and Raytheon electronic plants. I moved to NYC in 1963 and lived with my aunt in Harlem. While living with her, I attended CCNY (City College of NY) during the day and worked for the post office (inquiry window) in the evenings. This was my schedule for two years until I met my husband Dale Miller in 1965. I continued to work in the post office until we married in 1967. I then settled down and raised six children in Harlem.

During those early years while raising my children, I met Dr. Glory Van Scott who hired me as her administrative director of Dr. Glory's Youth Theater—a performing arts program she founded for young people interested in receiving training in theater arts. I am still involved as the administrative director in this amazing program. I returned to the workforce in 1988 when I was hired by the NYC Department of Education. I was the office manager for the Manhattan regional coordinator in the school food service division for 12 years. In 2000 I resigned from the NYC DOE and joined my daughter in running her security company (Jade to the Max) in Harlem. I managed the office for two years until I retired in 2002.

I am presently an active member of the Harlem Honeys & Bears Senior Synchronized Swim Team. I still compete and win medals on state and local levels and enjoy performing water ballets with the team.

—

DR. BUBA MISAWA is a Professor and Chair of the Political Science Department at Washington & Jefferson College located in Pennsylvania. He is also the Director of International Studies. Buba has Ph.D. and M.P.I.A. degree from the University of Pittsburgh and B.S degree from Bayero University, Kano.

"Rhythm Is My Business" is the title of **LEWIS NASH'**s 1989 debut recording as a bandleader, and legendary drummer Lewis Nash is all about the business of keeping rhythm. Universally recognized as one of the great drummers in jazz history, his illustrious career now spans over four decades.

Nash is one of jazz's most recorded musicians, appearing on over 500 recordings including 10 Grammy winners and numerous Grammy nominees. In fact, Nash has the distinction of being the only musician in jazz history featured on the winners in both the "Best Jazz Vocal" and "Best Jazz Instrumental" album categories in two separate years: the 2004 Grammys with Nancy Wilson and McCoy Tyner, and again in 2010 with Dee Dee Bridgewater and James Moody.

A native of Phoenix, Arizona, Lewis arrived in New York City in 1981 at the age of 22 and first gained international recognition as a member of vocalist Betty Carter's trio. This was a pivotal time in his development, as he traveled the world for nearly 4 years with Carter and had the opportunity to meet and engage with many of his musical peers and predecessors. In the years to follow, Nash toured, recorded and performed with many of jazz's most celebrated icons, and his resume reads like a "who's who" of jazz royalty. These jazz legends include: Oscar Peterson, Dizzy Gillespie, JJ Johnson, Sonny Rollins, Tommy Flanagan, Sonny Stitt, Clark Terry, Stan Getz, Benny Golson, Art Farmer, Gerry Mulligan, Hank Jones, Horace Silver, McCoy Tyner, Ray Brown, Milt Jackson, Jimmy Heath, Randy Weston, Cedar Walton, Ron Carter, Wynton and Branford Marsalis, and many, many more!

In 2012, The Nash, a jazz education center and performance venue named in Lewis's honor, was established in his hometown of Phoenix. It has been a focal point of the city's jazz activity since its inception, and has been named consistently by Downbeat magazine as a top jazz venue. Jazz masters Randy Weston, Jimmy Cobb, and Roy Hargrove played some of the final performances of their careers at The Nash. Lewis is in great demand for his educational expertise as well as his drumming skills and presents clinics, masterclasses, and workshops at institutions worldwide. He was a member of the very first jazz studies faculty at The Juilliard School in 2001 and has been a member of the faculty of the annual Vail Jazz Workshop for the past 20 years.

In 2017, Nash joined the jazz studies faculty at Arizona State University, where he was named the Bob and Gretchen Ravenscroft Professor of Practice in Jazz. In early 2021, the Lewis Nash Scholarship Endowment was created by the university to be awarded annually to a deserving ASU undergraduate or graduate jazz performance student.

———

Known as a "sculptor of clothing", **EVELYN NELSON** has shared her creative talents as a Fashion Designer, Theatrical Costume Designer, and Educator. She began her career after graduating from Fashion Institute of Technology where she received a degree in Fashion Design.

As a fashion design entrepreneur, she developed a couturier business creating "one of a kind" garments for a variety of clientele including: Diahann Carroll, Susan Taylor Taylor, Cicely Tyson, and Harry Belafonte. Her versatility afforded her the opportunity to use her craftsmanship in varied areas of movies, television, print publication and the entertainment industry.

Her theatre costuming career began over forty years ago when she designed costumes for the National Black Theatre's production of "Soul Journey Into Truth". She has also designed costumes for New Federal Theatre including: "Remembering We Selves" (Amari Baraka), "The Dance on Widow's Row," "Urban Transitions: Loose Blossoms," "In Dahomey," and "Conjure Man Dies."

Evelyn taught her skills to students at the High School of Fashion Industries, from 2001- 20017, and still teaches as a part time adjunct professor at Parson's School of Design (New School) where she has been since 1999.

———

RACHAEL NGETHE (MALKIAH) is a multifaceted individual making a positive impact both in the healthcare sector and online. As a certified nurse, she brings compassion and expertise to her profession. Beyond her role in healthcare, Rachael is a dedicated content creator, using her platform to inspire and uplift others. Residing and working in Europe, she is a proud mother to a son. Rachael's passions extend to travel, teaching, meditation, and spirituality, reflecting her commitment to personal growth and the well-being of those around her.

REV. DR. RONALD E. PETERS served as President of the Interdenominational Theological Center, Atlanta, GA and, prior to this, was Henry L. Hillman Professor of Urban Ministry and founding Director of the Metro-Urban Institute at Pittsburgh Theological Seminary, where he is currently on the Board of Directors. He held pastorates in Massachusetts and Florida and taught, lectured, and preached throughout sub-Saharan Africa, Asia, the Caribbean, and Europe. His writings include the now classic text, Urban Ministry: An Introduction (Abingdon, 2007), and Ministry Beyond the Walls (with R. Drew Smith and Stephanie Bodie; WJK, 2018) and several articles and chapters.

———

DONNA BAXTER PORCHER is a trailblazer in the media industry, using her platform, Soul Pitt Media, to uplift and celebrate the Black community in Western Pennsylvania and the surrounding region. This former rap artist turned Tech Diva has gone from "Rhymer to Digital Designer" and transformed her passion for Pittsburgh and technology into a thriving business. Donna is a sought-after speaker and digital consultant, empowering mature entrepreneurs and "technically challenged" individuals on the power of the internet and encouraging them to "Get Online or Get Left Behind!" Visit DonnaBaxterPorcher.com to learn more about her mission and work.

For many years at the request of Ebony Magazine founder Mr. John H. Johnson and then editor Lerone Bennett, Jr., **TYRONE RASHEED** was an Ebony/Jet photographer and shot a plethora of iconic figures. Before then, Tyrone Rasheed honed his photographic passion and understanding by working for Jim Hadley, K&L Color Lab, Joe Harris, and at TIME INC. in the photography lab, first as a photographer's assistant and assistant photographer (where he shot for the photographers) and through his extensive freelance portfolio.

Tyrone Rasheed has been inspired by renowned Harlem photographer Mr. James Van Der Zee, mentored by cultural icon, Mr. Gordon Parks; and currently has a prestigious studio portrait business located in his Harlem brownstone.

———

TAWNYA FARRIS-REDWOOD is a native Pittsburgher who has demonstrated her passion for art, health education and economic viability for those in need through her career and avocations.

A philanthropist, entrepreneur and volunteer, Tawnya is a seasoned board member of Primary Care Health Services, Inc. that helps underserved communities. Tawnya also serves on the board of the Pittsburgh Playwright's Theatre Company where she has supported the growth and development of one of the most creative and visionary community theater company's in the city. As a member of these boards, Tawnya gives guidance, advice and direction that fosters health and education, cultural opportunities and socio-economic advancement for thousands of Pittsburgh residents, with special emphasis of support to African American families.

During her stellar career in social services, Tawnya was clinical administrator and director for programs serving children and families with adoptions, foster parenting, parent education, and child abuse cases. She developed curriculums for providers and parents that were shared at conferences throughout the nation, including teaching incarcerated parents at the State Correctional Institute-Pittsburgh. In addition, Tawnya taught higher education courses at the University of Pittsburgh, Community College of Allegheny County and the former Duff's Business Institute. Tawnya earned professional certifications and master's degrees in social work and public health at the University of Pittsburgh. Tawnya is also a licensed realtor and is fortunate to serve the often complex needs of property owners.

Tawnya will tell you that her greatest passion is her family who is proud to live in the historic Hill District. The Redwood family includes nationally recognized community organizer and educator, Carl Redwood, and adult sons, Maurice and Carter. Tawnya's favorite avocation is serving as arts manager (Momager) for her sons who are professional actors, locally, nationally and internationally.

———

ANDREA PEARLMAN RICHARDS has been a pediatric Occupational Therapist for over 30 years, with the majority of her work with Deaf and Hard of Hearing children. Born and raised in Rockland County, NY in a culturally Jewish family. She received her Bachelor of Science degree in Occupational Therapy from Boston University in 1990, where she deepened her passion for civil rights and justice, became a vegetarian for animal rights purposes and was engulfed with the love for American Sign Language and Sweet Honey in the Rock. She received her Master's Degree in Deaf Education from Western Maryland College in 1999, and currently works in the School District of Philadelphia.

In 2003 she was blessed to become a mom to her son Michael. who now proudly serves his country in the military. Andrea remains committed to fostering the ongoing development of children, as well as herself, and believes life is truly enhanced with some Sweet Honey in the Rock in it!!

———

"I NEED to create," says **LOUISE ROBINSON**, actor, singer, producer, songwriter, creative-expression workshop master, author, and founding/current member of the internationally acclaimed vocal ensemble "Sweet Honey in the Rock".

Louise Robinson began nurturing her creative talents early in life when she started playing the concert bass. Her need and passion have been rewarded with experiences unimagined in her youth. Always cognizant of the intersection between talent and education, she landed entrance to the NY High School of Music and Art and then Howard University School of Fine Arts. As she attended Howard, her inner spirit pushed her to focus on the spoken word. She changed her major from music to theater and thus began her acting career. Excited to land her first job at the Arena Stage in Washington DC, subsequently she was noticed and then invited to be an inaugural member of the DC Black Repertory Theater's acting ensemble by the esteemed Robert Hooks. Included in "Lovely Lou's" list of acting credits are performances as "Ronnette" in the New York/L. A./National touring company productions of "Little Shop of Horrors", her Broadway debut in Michael Butler's production of "Reggae", and roles in "TinTypes", "Ain't Misbehavin'", and the Ruby Dee/Ossie Davis' production of "Take it from the Top."

Ironically, while an actor at the Black Repertory Theater, the seeds were planted in song for the start of "Sweet Honey in the Rock". Louise is a founding member of Sweet Honey and her work with them has placed her on stages around the globe from New York to Australia and Oman in the Middle East.

Demonstrating her grasp and understanding of leadership in the industry, and adding to her profile, Lou founded and directed the Bay area-based acapella ensemble "Street Sounds" which she led to national and international recognition. Recognizing her songwriting acumen, Nickelodeon features her composition, "I Like It That Way" on their "Jack's Big Music Show". She is also noted for her work as a producer having worked with Carol Maillard and Smokey Ronald Steven to present a series of variety shows featuring Gregory Hines, Andre DeShields, Sandra Reeves Phillips, Adolph Caesar, and other greats at New York's Village Gate. Currently, in between performances, Louise uses her decades of experience and insights as she facilitates experiential workshops in creative freedom and expression for executives, administrators, and staff at all levels for organizations that recognize the benefits of nurturing the seeds of creative thinking among those who work there. Louise approaches all she does with the mantra, *"We all have creative genius in us"*.

———

MUHAMMED (MO) RUM resides and works in Hell's Kitchen, NYC. He is the owner of Scent Elate, a mystical boutique referred to as a ministry, a womb and a safe place to express and break down walls to connection with others. A healing place, Scent Elate is a NYC destination that caters to spiritual seekers from every field the world over, from locals to transients, intellectuals to celebrities, it is a place where façade and guard are put aside and being your self is possible. The energy of Scent Elate is charged with love and sincerity.

When not at Scent Elate, Mo spends time with his family, a beautiful wife and three children. A creative in business, writing, painting and film, Mo enjoys long walks, philosophy and connecting with others. He is a graduate of Stony Brook University with a degree in political science. You can learn more about his shop at Scent Elate's website: http://www.scentelate.com/

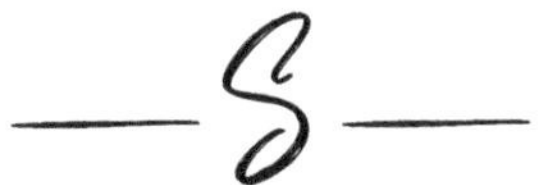

JAN SCHMIDT, an editor for literary magazine Cable Street, has published fiction in Anti-Heroin Chic, The Wall, Tupelo Quarterly, The Long Story, and New York Stories. Downtown published a series of her oral history interviews with hard-core, risky individuals' brushes with salvation. Her short story collection Everything I Need was a finalist for the Eludia Award, Hidden River Arts, 2019. Her unpublished novel Sunlight Underground was a finalist for the Novel Slices Award, 2021. In 2015, she retired from her position as Curator of the Jerome Robbins Dance Division, The New York Public Library for the Performing Arts, Lincoln Center.

———

CARLTON SCOTT is the current Chair of the African Heritage Classroom Committee at the University of Pittsburgh and has served as the Executive Director of the not-for-profit Intercultural House (ICH) since 2007. Carlton has played an integral role in the development of race-based programming that fosters student and community engagement and learning for the Intercultural House.

Carlton is also trustee of the Gertrude Stein Foundation (GSF). As a GSF trustee he works to financially support and promote programs and initiatives designed to heal the effects of systemic racism. Carlton has worked as an Academic Advisor at the University of Pittsburgh in the College of Business Administration and the Dietrich School of Arts and Sciences for the past 21 years. Mr. Scott earned his M.A.in Student Personnel and B.A. in Communication from Slippery Rock University. Both degrees helped to drive his interest both professionally and personally around the areas of race, culture, education, and diversity.

———

REV. DR. INGRID L. SCOTT is a an Interfaith/Interspiritual Minister who completed her

Doctorate at the age of 63, achieving the award for excellence for creating the Awaken App for the religiously unaffiliated! Free to download for iOS devices.

She believes that she is meant to be a beneficial change agent and to this end founded the Love is Kindness Ministry (Loveiskindness.org) which works towards social change globally; and the Sunday Soul Connection, a virtual eCommunity for weekly services held via conference call.

Having closed her manufacturing company after 38 years she's ready for the next chapter.

———

ARTHUR SEABURY. I was born in Sedalia Mo and I was a groundbreaking African American student in a very poor street economic environment. I attended CC Hubbard elementary school and was a member of Smith Cotton High in a very difficult and segregated climate.

The first African American AFS exchange student in Argentina in my Junior year. Was elected Student Body President my Senior year. Went to the Navy for six years and reserves for many more. Lived in San Diego, California, until 1985 and attended Mesa College majoring in African American studies.

Moved to Dallas and attended El Centro College and studied Psychology. Worked at Timberlawn Psychiatric Hospital as a substance abuse specialist. In 1992, I moved to Kansas City, Missouri and attended CMSU, and finished my degree in Psychology. Worked at the Scott Greening Center and commuted. Attended The University of Kansas School of Social Welfare where I received my Master's degree in 1999. Worked as a HUD servicer, substance abuse counselor, and school social worker all in urban settings. Was on the board of Directors for the National Council Against Drugs and Alcohol, Drug Court coordinator, and National Center for Fathering. I have a daughter at Yale finishing a PhD and who received a national science award. Her twin is an attorney who was awarded Top Black Attorneys under 40 in Missouri and a son who was recently married.

———

GRANDMOTHER MARIAN DAWN SKYWEAVER, AKA Marian Hartsfield. I am a member of Grandmothers Circle the Earth, a Storyteller, Ceremonialist, Teacher, Healer, Activist, and Artist. I value and respect my African American, Cherokee, and Southeastern Blackfoot heritage. I received my indigenous beliefs, values, philosophies from many grandfathers, grandmothers, sisters, and aunties along my more than 40-year pathway. I am passionate about reminding All that, "We are All Indigenous to Mother Earth". We have the responsibility to show respect, walk with wisdom, consider balance in all things, recognize peace as the right of all, know that we are an expansion of our ancestors and of the next 7 plus generations.

———

KAREN PORTER SORENSEN is a published author. Currently she is a Developemnt Officer at the University of Galway in Ireland. A creative fundraising leader with over 20 years of experience, Karen Porter Sorensen has a proven track record of global fundraising for major institutions in New York, Chicago, Galway, and Dublin. She employs an extensive philanthropic network to generate revenue from high-value funders and strategically designs unique mission-driven cultivation opportunities that advance meaningful donor engagement, and experienced at planning, leading and participating in direct solicitations.

———

MRS. DELORES SOUTHERS is a resident of the historic Hill District's 'Sugartop" in Pittsburgh, PA and a United States Veteran.

Mrs. Southers is a daughter, sister, cousin, wife, mother, grandmother, aunt, devout Christian and Loving friend to many. She considers Ms. Betty J. Tilman her "Sister in Christ." Now in her 80's Mrs. Southers is involved in and supports a host of organizations.

Mrs. Delores Southers is a guiding light and mentor to many. She is a board member of Pittsburgh Playwrights Theatre Company, a church elder, a spiritual mother to many including Rev. Melony McGant, an after-school tutor and a community leader.

———

JOY SOUTHERS is the founder of B-Listed Media Inc., a global company based in Washington, D.C., that focuses on facilitating the distribution of BIPOC independent films. They are a 2021 fellow of the Halcyon incubator for social entrepreneurs in Georgetown. B-Listed Media Inc. was recently appointed to The George Washington University's School of Business Advisory Council's Digital Marketing Program.

She has worked on many high-profile events for actors, politicians and world leaders—from inaugural events and political tv ads and conferences to prominent film festivals like Tribeca and Hamptons International Film Festival. On occasion, she has helped cast Netflix series and feature films like MINDHUNTER and RUSTIN, produced by the Obamas' Higher Ground Productions. In 2021, she was a contributor in a published anthology, Dear Kamala: Women Write to the New Vice President. As of 2022, she serves as the production coordinator for the USO's Global Entertainment.

Originally from Pittsburgh, she received her B.A. in Media Communications from the University of Pittsburgh and Master's in Organizational Management from Point Park University.

———

YORO SOW is a language teacher and a cross-cultural facilitator who originated from the northern region of Senegal Saint Louis. After a Master Certificate in English from University Cheikh Anta Diop, he joined Ecole Normale Supérieure (Teacher Training College) to become an English Teacher before travelling to the USA as an Amity Institute Intern.With a rich experience at Peace Corps Senegal as a Language and Cross-cultural Facilitator (LCF), Mister Sow still works as an English Language Teacher in Senegal where he also provides language and cultural services; including translation, local language classes and cultural advice to many foreigners visiting or working in his country. Married and father of 4, Yoro likes writing and exploring new cultural experiences and environments.

———

MARIO E. SPROUSE is a native New Yorker whose parents were born in the Dominican

Republic. A product of NYC public schools, Mario attended DeWitt Clinton High School and has a BA in Music from The City College of New York. Mario has been active in the arena of music, theater and film for over 50 years. He's been musical director for a number of theatrical events, including "Black Nativity--a Gospel Song Play" by Langston Hughes, directed by Jesse Wooden Jr. Most recently (2019) Mr. Sprouse was the composer and AUDELCO Award winner for Outstanding Musical Direction for "The Dark Star from Harlem"--a tribute to Josephine Baker at La Mama Theater in New York City. Carmen McRae, Grover Washington jr. Gregory Hines, Phylicia Rashad, Hubert Laws and Buster Williams are among the many who have performed his original music and arrangements.

For 20 years Mario was the music assistant of the late, legendary, modern Renaissance man Gordon Parks and is a member of the Board of Directors of the Gordon Parks Foundation.

Mario is also the Arts Ministry Coordinator at Marble Collegiate Church in NYC and author of "Precious & Honored – a Spiritual Handbook for Artists." Available at www.preciousandhonored.net

— T —

DR. THUPTEN TENDHAR was born to Tibetan parents. He holds a Ph.D. in Education from the University of Rhode Island (URI) and a Geshe (doctorate) in Buddhist Studies from Drepung Monastic University. He is a certified Level 3 Trainer in Kingian Nonviolence from the URI Center for Nonviolence and Peace Studies. He coordinates the inner peace project and directs the International Nonviolence Summer Institute, teaching nonviolence globally. Tendhar authored two poetry books, Peace: Rhythm of My Heart and Love: Beating My Heart. He teaches courses at URI and the Rhode Island School of Design.

———

GEORGE TEROY grew up in San Diego, California and resides in Los Angeles with his son, Sebastian. From an early age, he realized having a natural ability to see auras while healing others with his hands, visualizing their energy flow. With a diverse background in the healing and performing arts, his travels stem across the global from Australia, Chicago, New York, to Europe including City Moves in Sydney, San Diego Civic and Chicago Lyric Opera, "FAME" --the Musical European Tour debuting in Germany and France, pre-Broadway production of "Flower Drum Song" and the Broadway cast of "Miss Saigon" in New York City Equity Benefits. Working parallel in the corporate and metaphysics world, he graduated from the University of California, San Diego, in Economics and earned his Master of Business in Management. A Reiki practitioner certified as a Usui Reiki Master and Karuna Ki Reiki Master/Teacher, he performs bio-field sound attunements and crystal healing both in-person and distant healing. He connects with spiritual guides as a channeler through meditation and dowsing.

———

SEBASTION TEROY is a high school student in Southern California who excels in wrestling and other martial arts. He enjoys preparing meals of many cultures and like his father, George Teroy, he embraces compassion and kindness as an important part of his life journey.

———

DR. WILLIAM TIGA TITA is a devoted husband, father and Grandfather. Dr. Tita is a business professor at Northeastern University (Retired, has been Chief Technical Advisor in the Private Sector Development Program of the UNDP, and is the founder of several computer services companies. He has served on several high-tech company boards. Dr. Tita has been recognized by the International Development Agencies, notably the World Bank, as a pioneer and expert in distance learning as well as in keeping developing countries within reach of the emerging information society and networked economy.

———

CHARLES (CHUCK) TIMBERS has been a performer for more than 30 years, appearing in over 30+ plays in Pittsburgh, and he is an active member of SAG/AFTRA and Actors Equity Association (A.E.A). He is currently the producer and director of his own show on PCTV, a local cable access channel, a program called *Health Focus with Chuck* which discusses current healthcare issues. When he is not acting, Mr. Timbers is a full time, certified, and registered Nurse Practitioner. Chuck is a collective member and board member of the Demaskus Theater Collective, and part of the Community Empowerment Associations (C.E.A) Arts Renaissance Collective.

Mr. Timbers has been seen with Pittsburgh Playwrights Theater Co. as Cutler in *Ma Rainey's Black Bottom* and at the Short North Stage Theater in Columbus, Ohio, where he received the Excellence in Acting Award 2016 from the Theater Roundtable of Columbus, as well as in LOTTO with New Horizons Theater, and The Summer King with the Pittsburgh Opera. He has appeared with the Mendelssohn Choir in the production of *Let my People Go: A Spiritual Journey Along the Underground Railroad* as the narrator. Charles was executive producer and narrator for the short film documentary *Black Mary*.

His film credits include several local and national TV commercials, industrial and student films: *Black Mary, Rehabilitation of the Hill, Dead and Alive,* and he played the role of Dr. Hayes in the ABC T.V movie *The Jacksons: An American Dream*. He also participated in the program *Spirit Everlasting: A Tribute to Reverend Martin Luther King Jr.* hosted by the August Wilson Center in Pittsburgh. Recently performed in *The Bold and the Sanctified, One Monkey Don't Stop No Show,* and appeared in *Jitney* by August Wilson with Pittsburgh Playwrights Theatre Company.

For over 20 years, UrbanAcres founder **MICHAEL VANN** has been on a personal mission to build a national integrated foodservic e company. The Company's multi brand retail development in Newark's Gateway Center will lay the foundation for the company's national model and mandate .."Building Brands that Build Communities". Mr. Vann's entrepreneurial career and expertise is rooted in the development, ownership, and management of several New York landmark restaurants.

As co-founder and developer of the world-renowned Shark Bar restaurant, his vision and expertise secured the Shark Bar as one of the premiere restaurants serving upscale soul food in America during the 1990s. His additional restaurateur credits include co-founder of national restaurant company, Soulfood Concepts, developer and co-founder of New York's Soul Café, lead consultant for Sean "Puffy" Comb's Justin's in New York and one of the key managers of the landmark restaurant B. Smith's, from February 1987 to August 1990. As a consultant, Mr. Vann was instrumental the IHOP restaurant on 135th & ACP in Harlem.in helping Carl Redding, founder of Amy Ruth's, transform his restaurant into a nationally recognized brand and one of the best restaurants in its niche category.

In 2004, he successfully spearheaded and negotiated a license agreement between Amy Ruth's and Foxwoods Resort Casino. In 2007, he was hired by Abyssinian Development Corporation to assess the feasibility and operational efficiency of In addition to his career as an entrepreneur, Vann has successfully navigated the retail industry as well. In 1979, he served as an executive with New York retail giant Lord & Taylor. Over the span of 7 years, Vann advanced within the company to hold several executive merchandising positions in their Menswear and Boy's divisions. In 1986, he joined Northwear Fashions of Canada as Vice-President of Sales & Merchandising of Boy's Outerwear.

DINO VIPER, AKA ROBERT SHOCKEY. Spiritually-guided producer, author, and Thought Leader. From the concrete jungles to remote places on the planet, the search for answers was never outside, they were from within. As a vocal artist by craft, guided meditations began with stories for children to sleep and to release the pain from daily life. Shared with audiences worldwide. There have exceeded 2 million plays. With reviews from people all over the globe.

"I have been involved in the entertainment industry for over 10 years, working with artists and writers to help them reach new heights. Along this journey, I experienced many successes but also some failures that left their mark on me as well. It was only through meditation -which helped heal my own pain-that led back to finding light at end of the tunnel; helping others do exactly what you just did!

I combine hypnotherapy sessions seamlessly blended by frequencies tailored specifically towards each individual's needs so they can experience rapid transformation without worry or frustration My stories will resonate deeply within your subconscious mind while guided meditations guide both body & spirit forward."

Few entertainers today are as accomplished or versatile as **BEN VEREEN**. His legendary performances transcend time and have been woven into the fabric of this country's artistic legacy. His first love and passion is and always will be the stage. "The theater was my first training ground. It taught me discipline, dedication, and appreciation of hard work and values that will stay with me for a lifetime. The stage sharpens the creative instrument and encourages you to go deeper inside and try new things," states Ben.

Ben wrapped the Chuck Lorre series B POSITIVE on CBS, and last season, completed multiple episodes of THE GOOD FIGHT, playing FREDERICK DOUGLAS, also on CBS. He performed his concert act for the Star Trek Convention in Las Vegas in August, and has upcoming dates in Chicago, Las Vegas, and the Carolinas in 2022. Before Broadway reopened, Ben appeared on CBS Watch Here, performed in Times Square for the Juneteenth celebration and was featured in Town and Country. He recently appeared in the national commercial to bring back NYC and Broadway "It's Showtime in NYC."

Ben performed an abundance of virtual events during Covid in 2020 and most of all his deep passion for the Homeless, led him into producing, directing, and starring in a benefit for 'Care for the Homeless.' His passion for the arts and education is ongoing and each year teaches classes online and in person.

Ben appeared in MAGNUM P.I. and BULL for CBS, multiple episodes of STAR for Fox, and the BET Series TALES. Ben also co-starred with RICHARD GERE in TIME OUT OF MIND, CHRIS ROCK in TOP FIVE, and was featured as Dr. Scott in the re-imagined THE ROCKY HORROR PICTURE SHOW for 20th Century Fox. Bryan Cranston picked Ben to co-star in SNEAKY PETE for Amazon. Ben continues to tour the country with his concert act, motivational lectures, and master classes. He performed sold out runs at Jazz at Lincoln Center, as well as in Toronto, Los Angeles, San Diego, Las Vegas, Pittsburgh, as well as a lecture at Tuskegee University for Black History Month. As you know, he won a Tony Award/Drama Desk for Pippin, starred in such musicals as Jesus Christ Superstar, Fosse, Hair, Jelly's Last Jam, Chicago, Wicked, I'm Not Rappaport, to name a few and is remembered for films like 'Sweet Charity', 'All That Jazz,' and the Emmy winning role of Chicken George in the iconic 'Roots.'

Ben is an active member of Americans for the Arts, the largest advocacy group of the Arts in America. He went to Washington DC and spoke before Congress defending the National Endowment for the Arts against the proposed budget cuts. He also attended the Democratic National Convention where he spoke to various senators, congressmen, governors on the arts and education and later sang "WHAT THE WORLD NEEDS NOW" on television in front of the approximately 50,000 delegates. Ben was inducted as an honorary member into Phi Beta Sigma and continues to be an active member.

Ben has received a number of awards including Israel's Cultural and Humanitarian Awards, three NAACP Image Awards, an Eleanor Roosevelt Humanitarian Award and a Victory Award. He has received honorary doctorates from the University of Arizona, Emerson College, and Columbia College in Chicago. He received an Achievement in Excellence Award from his alma mater, the High School of the Performing Arts. Ben has also been inducted into The Theatre Hall of Fame, the Dance Hall of Fame, and has received various Emmy and Golden globe nominations. In, New York City he received the Broadway World Cabaret Award for BEST CELEBRITY MALE VOCALIST and the Career Achievement Award (Le Prix International Film Star Awards Organization). He is most proud of his ongoing work involving the Arts and Education, and providing the youth with arts programs across America. Ben received the Lifetime Achievement Award from The Gold Coast International Film Festival, and this past year he was honored as a living legend by THE AMERICAN BLACK FILM INSTITUTE. This coming week, he will be awarded the inaugural JUNETEENTH LEGACY AWARD from the Broadway League.

Recently, Ben recorded a new song/video for Ukraine: "We Sing for Ukraine" which will benefit both UNICEF and ABUNDANCE INTERNATIONAL, raising money for the children of Ukraine. He already raised thousands of dollars. He is now doing publicity to promote this and continue to help Ukraine on a larger scale. Ben produced an event for CARE FOR THE HOMELESS, served on Ballet Florida's Board of Directors, worked with the AMERICAN RED CROSS and SUDDEN INFANT DEATH SYNDROME ASSOCIATION, and THE ACTORS FUND. Ben spearheaded his own organization, CELEBRITIES FOR A DRUG FREE AMERICA which raised money for drug rehabilitation centers, educational programs and inner city community-based projects. The Community Mental Health Council awarded Ben with their 2004 Lifeline Celebration Achievement Award Scholarship for the Performing Arts, and in 2004, he received an Achievement in Excellence Award from his alma mater, the High School of the Performing Arts.

"It's always pleasant to spend time in the company of a survivor, a pro, and a performing prince. Ben Vereen is all three." – New York Times

DARYL WALKER is retired executive from Xerox Corporation. As a Vice President over many years, he was responsible for the customer satisfaction, strategy development, services innovation and deployment, and delivering business results through the sales and marketing of Xerox's complete portfolio of offerings, including office systems, production printing systems, and global services throughout the United States and internationally. He was the recipient of 19 President Club awards throughout his career.

Walker is a Past Chairman of the Board for the Irving Chamber of Commerce and has served on the board of Directors for the Texas Association of Businesses (TAB) as well as for the Boys and Girls Club of Greater Fort Worth. He currently serves as a Board Director for the Children's Medical Center of Dallas.

Walker retired from Corporate America in 2018 so he could better tend to the needs of his beloved cousin, Micki Grant, during the final years of her life. Retiring afforded him the opportunity to be in New York more often to ensure she was doing well, that all her needs were taken care of. He is so thankful to God for giving him that opportunity, responsibility, and privilege, and considers these past years with Micki as PRICELESS.

Walker resides in Southlake, Texas with his wife and their three children.

———

BONNIE WEAVER is an experienced and dedicated individual with exceptional public relations skills and an ability to communicate effectively and quickly establish positive rapport with people of all ages, cultures, and personalities.

She's a community activist with a passion towards youth empowerment, community organizing, and developing prevention programs targeting young women.

She enjoys listening to smooth jazz, leisure walks around her neighborhood, gardening, and being called "grandma."

———

A Paris-based author, TV commentator, and journalism lecturer, **NITA WIGGINS** is called "a brave woman who changed her life" and "the female James Baldwin" by readers of her Civil Rights Baby: My Story of Race, Sports, and Breaking Barriers in American Journalism memoir.

She helps others write to bring out empathy through her Listen to Others as you would have them listen to you® training.

The graduate of ESJ Paris and Augusta University appears on France 24 TV, and has been interviewed on Cameroon and Senegal television and in The Washington Post and Le Figaro. She is on the Black Women in Europe® Power List for 2018.

During her U.S. career, she received the RTNDF's national Michele Clark Fellowship and a regional Emmy.

———

SHANNON WONG was born in Brooklyn, New York and has lived there all her life. She comes from a Chinese background. In January of 2023, she graduated from Brooklyn College with a BFA degree in Creative Writing. Currently, she works at The New York Public Library. Her hobbies include reading, writing, binge watching T.V, and daydreaming. She hopes to write for young adults in the genre of fiction, sci-fi, or fantasy and create stories that other Chinese-Americans who grew up in the USA can find comfort in.

———

DENISE WOODS is an Internationally Renowned Vocal Coach and author of the book, *The Power Of Voice*. In the insightful book, Denise shares the secrets, tips, lessons, and stories that have helped the biggest film stars, including Will Smith, Halle Berry, Kirsten Dunst, Idris Alba, Rachel Weisz, and Jessica Chastain, to become confident, effective communicators. Academy Award winner Mahershala Ali wrote the Foreword.

Woods has been the "voice behind the voice" of a stellar array of actors for the last twenty years. She was the creative consultant for Halle Berry's directorial debut of the film Bruised, contributing to the authenticity of Berry's performance in the starring role. Denise was also the vocal coach for Mahershala Ali's Academy Award and Golden Globe winning performances in Green Book and the 3rd Season of HBO's True Detective. She is currently coaching the Sony Pictures, Whitney Houston biopic, "I Wanna Dance With Somebody," and she also just completed work on the Tyler Perry feature film, A Jazzman's Blues. Last season, Denise was the dialect coach for the Netflix film, The Harder They Fall, starring Idris Elba and Regina King, and she coached Don Cheadle in the critically acclaimed Showtime series, Black Monday. Her other clients include Academy Award winning actor Common, Golden Globe winner David Oyelewo, Academy Award nominated actor Will Smith for the title role in the film Ali and Ken Watanabe for his work in the film The Last Samurai.

Denise worked with Audra McDonald on her fourth Tony Award winning performance for Gershwin's Porgy and Bess on Broadway, and was Zoe Saldana's Dialect Coach in the feature film based on the life of Nina Simone. Her dialect coaching talents can also be heard in the 20th Century Fox film, Hidden Figures, starring Taraji P. Henson, Octavia Spencer and Janelle Monae, and the Focus Features film, Harriet, starring Cynthia Erivo in the title role. Denise coached Tyler Perry for his role as Colin Powell in the 2018 Annapurna Pictures film, Vice; and she is featured in Perry's 2018 film, Acrimony, starring Taraji P. Henson, as the 'only-heard' Therapist.

Denise has trained executives for public speaking at corporations such as US Borax, UPS, and Bear Stearns. She has coached broadcast news anchors at NBC Nightly News, CNBC, Bloomberg News, The Today Show, CNN, Inside Edition, KTLA News, and the TV Guide Channel; and she has prepared NBA and NFL athletes for on-camera commentary.

For over two decades, Denise's clients have included Queen Latifah, Will Smith, Halle Berry, Jessica Chastain, Amber Heard, Anthony Mackie, Phylicia Rashad, Ellen Burstyn, Jeanne Tripplehorn, Soledad O'Brien, Morris Chestnut, Taye Diggs, Paul Rodriguez, David Alan Grier, Victoria Rowell, Kellan Lutz, Ray Liotta, Portia De Rossi, Rachel Weisz, Mekhi Phifer, Maggie Gyllenhaal, Jeffrey Wright and Mike Myers.

She is a graduate and former faculty member of The Juilliard School, and a long time faculty member of California Institute of the Arts. Denise is committed to giving disenfranchised voices the courage and tools to use their words, their thoughts and their stories in ways they never thought possible by dismantling fear, shame and insecurity. Her first book, The Power of Voice, published by HarperCollins Publishers, is out now.

Denise worked with Audra McDonald on her fourth Tony Award winning performance for Gershwin's Porgy and Bess on Broadway, and was Zoe Saldana's Dialect Coach in the feature film based on the life of Nina Simone. Her dialect coaching talents can also be heard in the 20th Century Fox film, Hidden Figures, starring Taraji P. Henson, Octavia Spencer and Janelle Monae, and the Focus Features film, Harriet, starring Cynthia Erivo in the title role. Denise coached Tyler Perry for his role as Colin Powell in the 2018 Annapurna Pictures film, Vice; and she is featured in Perry's 2018 film, Acrimony, starring Taraji P. Henson, as the 'only-heard' Therapist.

Denise has trained executives for public speaking at corporations such as US Borax, UPS, and Bear Stearns. She has coached broadcast news anchors at NBC Nightly News, CNBC, Bloomberg News, The Today Show, CNN, Inside Edition, KTLA News, and the TV Guide Channel; and she has prepared NBA and NFL athletes for on-camera commentary.

For over two decades, Denise's clients have included Queen Latifah, Will Smith, Halle Berry, Jessica Chastain, Amber Heard, Anthony Mackie, Phylicia Rashad, Ellen Burstyn, Jeanne Tripplehorn, Soledad O'Brien, Morris Chestnut, Taye Diggs, Paul Rodriguez, David Alan Grier, Victoria Rowell, Kellan Lutz, Ray Liotta, Portia De Rossi, Rachel Weisz, Mekhi Phifer, Maggie Gyllenhaal, Jeffrey Wright and Mike Myers.

She is a graduate and former faculty member of The Juilliard School, and a long time faculty member of California Institute of the Arts. Denise is committed to giving disenfranchised voices the courage and tools to use their words, their thoughts and their stories in ways they never thought possible by dismantling fear, shame and insecurity. Her first book, The Power of Voice, published by HarperCollins Publishers, is out now in hardcover since January 2021. The softcover will be out in the first quarter of 2022. www.speakitclearly.com

———

DR. ROBERT WOODS, PHD., is an educator, author, consultant, and advocate for learning equality with an extensive background in developing and implementing special programs for non-traditional and at-risk students. He teaches within the Business Department at the City University of New York and has chaired academic programs at Berkeley College and Kentucky State University. His corporate experience includes apparel designing for the Gucci enterprise in Florence, Italy, where he executed men's wear for studios in Italy, London, and New York. Dr. Woods is co-author of *No Mother, No Mirror: A Guide to Gaining A Personal Edge with Business Dress For Women and Men* (Houghton Mifflin). His latest book, *The Brown Boy Crisis: Educators Must Step Up to Meet the Challenges of Educating Non-White Males* (Luminare Press), explores the hidden agendas of school culture and misinformation(s) that fuel the higher retention and dropout rates of Native, African, and Hispanic American males in our schools and colleges.

Before hitting his stride as a celebrity/advertising photographer and VMA-Nominated director, **ANDREW ZAEH** held creative positions at major record labels where he helmed the visual

branding for some of today's top recording artists. When an opportunity to photograph the SXSW festival presented itself, Andrew's focus shifted to shooting. Since then, Andrew has had the pleasure of photographing celebrities such as Jon Batiste, MJ Rodriguez, Jay-Z, and Janelle Monáe, lensing campaigns for American Express, AT&T, Pfizer, WW, and Johnson & Johnson, and directing music videos featuring Fall Out Boy, 2 Chainz, Elton John, and Courtney Love. Andrew is a proud member of the LGBTQIA community and happiest spending a day on location getting to know a subject while making authentic imagery in the process. You can view his portfolio at www.andrewzaeh.com.

———

ESSHE ZAMPALDUS is a social media content creator, spoken word & creative artist, and an intuitive writer. She is a lover of love, an affirming Queen that promotes positive thinking, feeling & speaking things into existence. She says "positive words are like honey--affirmational healing for our soul, heart & mind." She loves using African cultural fashion, intuitive arts, textiles & crafts as muses to encourage, inspire & connect with people of all ages. She has two beautiful children, and adores being a mother, as it continues to teach & surround her in an abundance of love, laughter, & happiness

ABOUT THE AUTHOR

Rev. Melony McGant, aka Miss Mellie Rainbow, loves to travel, explore cultures, connect with people, and dreams of a compassionate World with safe, loving communities, equal opportunity with justice and peace for the next seven generations (and beyond) of All the Earth's children.

She truly believes that "peace is possible through compassion, cooperation, courage, creativity, deep listening, faith, forgiveness, good purpose, healing, hope, humility, integrity, joy, kindness, mercy, patience, respect, understanding and the gift of Love!", and uses social media platforms to inspire others.

She is a storyteller, thought-leader, poet, & compassionate communications professional with more than 30 years' experience in assisting both people and organizations discover and promote their professional or personal life missions. From business and not for profit CEO's to job seekers, elders, parents and children; through deep listening, Melony has quietly impacted, coached or supported thousands of people on their life journeys.

Currently a resident of New York City, Melony has worked as a marketing professional, owned her own full-service marketing firm and was assistant to cultural icon, choreographer and Oprah Legend, Miss Katherine Dunham. Through her she met Dr. Glory Van Scott who became an important mentor. For several years Melony assisted Dr. Van Scott with marketing Dr. Glory's Youth Theatre and her book GLORY: A Life Among Legends.

She also worked for more than 8 years as a Labor Services Representative for New York State Department of Labor where she was able to hone her skills as a career/life coach and personal empowerment workshop facilitator; has a BA in Communications from Marshall University, is a Certified Level One Trainer in Kingian Nonviolence (University of Rhode Island Summer Institute), and is a Vietnam era war veteran (United States Navy).

An avid reader, in 2018 she appeared in two episodes of the Great American Read, an eight-episode national television show on PBS that "explored the many ways in which novels affect, reflect and connect us all."

An ordained Interfaith Minister, and author of the coming of age novel "Sunshine & Olivier: A Parable of Love" (IUniverse), which was reissued for the 20th anniversary of its publication, Melony is also the primary author of "The Healing Adagio: A Love Symphony In Five Parts" and the journal, empowerment workbook "Seeker Dreamer: Amazing, Brilliant, Compassionate YOU!" (both published by Authorhouse). Her books are available on Amazon.

Rev. Melony McGant's writing is also featured in several other books, magazines and newspapers including the first edition of The Poetry Cafe (Art for Awareness), W & Art (an international women's premium art talk magazine), African Voices Magazine, MBE/WBE Magazine, Our Time Press, and the Chicago Citizen. Early in her career she was a columnist for The New Pittsburgh Courier.

Her writing also appears in GLORY: A Life Among Legends by Dr. Glory Van Scott (Water Street Press), "Passing It On: Moving Stories of Activists 1960 to 2000" by Bev Jenai-Myers (Archway Publishing), "Go Tell Michelle: African American Women Write to Michelle Obama" (SUNY Press), "The Book of Hope" and "The World Book of Healing" (both by Beyond Borders Press).

While living in Pittsburgh, PA, Melony served on the boards of Big Brothers and Sisters and the Pittsburgh Branch NAACP. She has been an avid supporter of the Andrew Goodman Foundation VOTE EVERYWHERE program and strongly believes in embracing the values of good citizenship.

Rev. Melony McGant has received the New Mexico Not Even One Service Award, the 911 Red Cross Volunteer Award in NYC, the Pittsburgh City Council Women's Recognition Award, and the Minority Business Enterprise Legal Defense and Education Fund Award for Service (MBELDEF)

To contact Rev. Melony McGant, email: melonymcgant@yahoo.com

WEBSITE & CONTACT INFORMATION

Looking for more details on this book? Check out our website https://goodispowerfulbeyondmeasure.com, created and maintained by Jason Hee.

For any questions relating to the content and contributors, please feel free to email us at info@goodispowerfulbeyondmeasure.com

In Honor of Ms. Betty Tilman, donations to the African Heritage Room Committee Scholarship can be made online by visiting www.nationalityrooms.pitt.edu

Select the About button at the top left and then select Donate to the Nationality Rooms!

To donate by check, make the check payable to the University of Pittsburgh and mail to: University of Pittsburgh, PO Box 640093, Pittsburgh, PA 15264-0093.

Donations online and in the check memo line can be noted as: African Heritage Room Committee Scholarship in memory of Ms. Betty J. Tilman.